China's Impact on the African Renaissance

Kobus Jonker • Bryan Robinson

# China's Impact on the African Renaissance

The Baobab Grows

Kobus Jonker
Nelson Mandela University
Port Elizabeth, Eastern Cape
South Africa

Bryan Robinson
Nelson Mandela University
Port Elizabeth, Eastern Cape
South Africa

ISBN 978-981-13-0178-0     ISBN 978-981-13-0179-7  (eBook)
https://doi.org/10.1007/978-981-13-0179-7

Library of Congress Control Number: 2018942560

© The Editor(s) (if applicable) and The Author(s) 2018
This work is subject to copyright. All rights are solely and exclusively licensed by the Publisher, whether the whole or part of the material is concerned, specifically the rights of translation, reprinting, reuse of illustrations, recitation, broadcasting, reproduction on microfilms or in any other physical way, and transmission or information storage and retrieval, electronic adaptation, computer software, or by similar or dissimilar methodology now known or hereafter developed.
The use of general descriptive names, registered names, trademarks, service marks, etc. in this publication does not imply, even in the absence of a specific statement, that such names are exempt from the relevant protective laws and regulations and therefore free for general use.
The publisher, the authors and the editors are safe to assume that the advice and information in this book are believed to be true and accurate at the date of publication. Neither the publisher nor the authors or the editors give a warranty, express or implied, with respect to the material contained herein or for any errors or omissions that may have been made. The publisher remains neutral with regard to jurisdictional claims in published maps and institutional affiliations.

Cover image by the authors
Cover design by Tom Howey

Printed on acid-free paper

This Palgrave Macmillan imprint is published by the registered company Springer Nature Singapore Pte Ltd.
The registered company address is: 152 Beach Road, #21-01/04 Gateway East, Singapore 189721, Singapore

*Friends and Family*
*Ejtleen, Jacques and Nadia*
*Johan*

# ACKNOWLEDGEMENTS

The successful publication of this book, *China's Impact on the African Renaissance—The Baobab Grows*, is thanks to an array of people and institutions that have facilitated making our aspiring desire of delivering a thought-provoking and important contribution to the conversation on Africa's ascendency a reality.

The Nelson Mandela University Business School with a proud history of developing responsible business leaders needed to tackle the development priorities of Africa has provided support for this project from inception to completion and therefore deserves acknowledgement.

The paradigm proposed in the book of the African Tree of Organic Growth is grounded upon theoretical constructs and models proposed by visionary leaders and academic thought leaders. From the vision of former South Africa President Nelson Mandela to former South African President Thabo Mbeki's conceptualisation and popularisation of the African Renaissance, many have paved the path for this book. Dr Alexis Habiyaremye, Senior Research Specialist in the Economic Performance and Development Department of the Human Sciences Research Council (HSRC); Elling Tjønneland, Political Scientist and Senior Researcher at the Chr. Michelsen Institute (CMI) in Norway; and Professor Xiaoyang Tang, Deputy Director, Carnegie-Tsinghua Center for Global Policy in Beijing, have answered the critical questions we needed answering.

The Forum on China–Africa Cooperation, the World Bank, the Pew Research Center, the United Nations, McKinsey & Company, Transparency International, The World Wildlife Fund, and an array of researchers and academic writers are credited for providing the facts and insights which we were fortunate enough to build upon as we developed this book. And then there were many individuals who provided greater understanding on the issues that were affecting Africans on a day-to-day basis: taxi drivers, community members, entrepreneurs and business owners, people on the street—those who contributed to the business and human elements of our research in the countries we visited.

Palgrave, our publisher, with special mention of Jacob Dreyer the Commissioning Editor for Politics and Economics in Shanghai, who was immediately positive about our planned publication and who has guided us through the intricacies of publishing.

# Contents

1 **China in Africa: New Colonists or Facilitators of Development and Growth**   1
   1.1   *Perceptions in the African Media*   3
   1.2   *The 'Complementary Development' Approach of China in Africa*   5
       1.2.1   *A Historical Overview on Relations Between Africa and China*   6
       1.2.2   *The Facilitating Role of the FOCAC in China's Policy Towards Africa*   7
   1.3   *Synergies Between Chinese Policy and the African Union and United Nations Development Goals*   10
   1.4   *Chinese Aid and Investment Approach*   13
   1.5   *The Potential Outcomes of China's Engagement in Africa*   15
   1.6   *Conclusion: The African Agenda*   15
   *References*   18

2 **Renewal of Africa: The African Tree of Organic Growth Paradigm**   19
   2.1   *The African Renaissance and Organic Growth*   21
       2.1.1   *The African Tree of Organic Growth*   22
   2.2   *The Core Resources, Assets and Structures Necessary for Growth (Roots of the Tree)*   22
       2.2.1   *Natural and People Resources*   23

|   |   | 2.2.2 | Location, Geopolitical Importance and Critical Assets | 24 |
|---|---|---|---|---|
|   |   | 2.2.3 | Political and Economic Structures | 25 |
|   |   | 2.2.4 | Cultural and Social Structure | 27 |
|   | 2.3 | \multicolumn{2}{l}{The Creation of Growth Channels to Produce Wealth (Trunk of the Tree)} | 29 |
|   | 2.4 | \multicolumn{2}{l}{Creating Prosperity and Wealth for African Nations (Leaves and Fruit)} | 33 |
|   | References |  |  | 34 |

3  **Economic Growth and Diversification Fuelling Development in Africa**  35
   3.1  The Challenge and Potential of Economic Growth in Africa  36
       3.1.1  Prominent Growth Sectors  36
       3.1.2  Economic Transformation and Growth Drivers  41
   3.2  Alternative Paths to Growth and Development in Africa  46
   3.3  Organic Growth in Africa: Impact of China on Growth and Diversification  48
   3.4  The Case of Kenya  49
       3.4.1  Economic Growth and Diversification  50
       3.4.2  Impact of China on the Organic Growth of Kenya  53
   3.5  The Case of Nigeria  60
       3.5.1  Economic Growth and Diversification in Nigeria  62
       3.5.2  Impact of China on the Organic Growth of Nigeria  65
   3.6  Lessons Learned from the Kenyan and Nigerian Case Studies  70
   References  75

4  **Infrastructure: The Most Important Enabler of Organic Growth in Africa**  77
   4.1  The Impact of Infrastructural Utilities on Organic Growth  77
   4.2  Infrastructure Shortcomings in Africa  79
       4.2.1  Power  80
       4.2.2  Water and Sanitation  81
       4.2.3  Information and Communication Technology (ICT)  81
       4.2.4  Transport Infrastructure  82
   4.3  China: The World Leader in Infrastructure Investment  84

| | | |
|---|---|---|
| 4.4 | China's Impact on Infrastructure Development in Africa | 86 |
| 4.5 | Providing Africa with Integrated Transport Infrastructure | 90 |
| | 4.5.1 China's First Major Investment in Africa's Infrastructure: The Case of the Tan–Zam Railway Line | 90 |
| | 4.5.2 Integrated Transport Infrastructure Development in Ethiopia | 92 |
| | 4.5.3 Can a Road Change the Lives of Poor Rural People in Africa? The Case of Lesotho | 97 |
| 4.6 | The Contribution and Consequences of China's Infrastructural Investments | 108 |
| References | | 109 |

## 5 The Role of Effective Governments and Institutions — 111

| | | |
|---|---|---|
| 5.1 | Democracy and Dictatorships | 113 |
| | 5.1.1 Losing Hope in Zimbabwe, Finding Hope in The Gambia and Savouring the Success of Ghana | 114 |
| | 5.1.2 Chinese Peacekeeping Efforts in Africa | 120 |
| | 5.1.3 China's Non-interference Policy | 122 |
| 5.2 | Core Institutions | 123 |
| 5.3 | Policies for Development | 125 |
| | 5.3.1 Poverty Alleviation | 125 |
| | 5.3.2 Adopting a Workfare Approach in Job Creation | 125 |
| | 5.3.3 Infrastructure | 126 |
| | 5.3.4 Agricultural Policies | 126 |
| | 5.3.5 Industrial Policies | 127 |
| | 5.3.6 Education | 127 |
| | 5.3.7 Health and Healthcare Finance | 127 |
| | 5.3.8 Fiscal and Monetary Policies | 128 |
| | 5.3.9 Allowing the Market to Function | 129 |
| 5.4 | Why Policies Fail: Poor Planning and Service Delivery Inefficiencies in Public Administration | 130 |
| | 5.4.1 Why Government Policies Fail: Corruption | 132 |
| 5.5 | Concluding Remarks | 134 |
| 5.6 | China's Impact | 135 |
| References | | 135 |

## 6  A Skilled and Educated Workforce for Africa — 137
- 6.1  A Well-Educated and Skilled Workforce: The Key to Sustainable Growth and Prosperity in Africa? — 138
  - 6.1.1  Quality and Relevant Education — 138
  - 6.1.2  Preparing the Growing Youth Population of Africa for Growth and Employment — 142
- 6.2  China in African Education — 144
  - 6.2.1  Higher Education and Academic Partnerships — 144
  - 6.2.2  The Effectiveness and Role of Chinese Confucius Institutes and Cultural Centres — 145
- 6.3  A Case Study on the Impact of China on Employment Creation and Technology Transfer in North Africa — 147
  - 6.3.1  The Case of Algeria — 147
  - 6.3.2  The Case of Egypt — 150
- 6.4  A Case Study on the Impact of China on Local Employment in Angola and the Democratic Republic of the Congo (DRC) — 152
  - 6.4.1  The Case of Angola — 153
  - 6.4.2  The Case of the Democratic Republic of the Congo (DRC) — 156
- 6.5  China and the Development of a Productive Work Force for Africa: Closing Remarks — 158
- References — 164

## 7  Developing a Sustainable Africa through Green Growth — 167
- 7.1  Interpreting Sustainability — 167
  - 7.1.1  The World at Risk in the Face of Global Climate Change — 169
- 7.2  Environmental Concerns in Africa — 171
  - 7.2.1  Deforestation and Desertification in Africa — 171
  - 7.2.2  Pollution and Waste: Africa's Beautiful Sunsets and Toxic Air — 172
- 7.3  China's Environmental Impact on Africa — 176
  - 7.3.1  China Takes Cognisance of Environmental Issues while Africa Lags Behind — 176
  - 7.3.2  Concerns Regarding the Negative Environmental Impact of China's Investments in Africa — 179

|   |   |   |   |
|---|---|---|---|
| 7.4 | Examples of China's Impact on Sustainability in Africa | | 180 |
|   | 7.4.1 | Learning from China's Switch from Fossil Fuel to Clean Energy | 180 |
|   | 7.4.2 | Water: The Essence of Life | 183 |
|   | 7.4.3 | Food Insecurity in the Fertile Lands of Africa | 185 |
| 7.5 | China's Impact | | 187 |
| References | | | 188 |

**8 Improving the Human Well-Being of All Africans** — 191
- 8.1 Towards Improved Well-Being for Africa — 193
  - 8.1.1 Poverty Alleviation — 196
  - 8.1.2 Food Security — 197
  - 8.1.3 Health and Education Disparities — 197
  - 8.1.4 War, Law and Order — 198
  - 8.1.5 Living Standards — 198
  - 8.1.6 Economic Inequality — 199
  - 8.1.7 Inequality in Human Rights and Human Capability — 199
- 8.2 Analysis of China's Contribution to Improving the Well-Being of African People — 201
- 8.3 Case Study: China Makes a Decided Impact in Its Response to the Ebola Epidemic in Liberia, Guinea and Sierra Leone — 201
- 8.4 Case Study: Caring for Displaced Somalians — 207
- 8.5 Case Study: A Critique of the Impact of Chinese Mining Operations on Social Wealth and Capital in Africa — 209
- 8.6 China's Impact — 213
- References — 214

**9 Integrated Organic Growth: The Cases of Cameroon and Mauritius** — 217
- 9.1 The Case of Cameroon — 218
  - 9.1.1 Historical Overview of Cameroon's and China's Relationship — 220
  - 9.1.2 The Impact of China on the Integrated Growth and Development of Cameroon — 222
- 9.2 The Case of Mauritius — 235
  - 9.2.1 The Historical Relationship Between Mauritius and China — 238

    9.2.2   The Impact of China on the Integrated Growth
            and Development of Mauritius    239
9.3  Closing Remarks on the Integration of Organic Growth
      in Both Countries and the Impact of China on This Process  259
References   260

## 10 The Impact of China on the African Renaissance: Let the Baobab Grow…    263

10.1  Growth in Africa: The Evolving Paradigm   263
    10.1.1  Moving from 'Economic Growth' to 'Inclusive
             Growth' in Africa   264
    10.1.2  Moving Towards the Paradigm of 'Organic
             Growth'   265
10.2  Engagement and the Impact of China on the Organic
      Growth in Africa   270
    10.2.1  Does China's Own Experience
             as a Developmental State Offer Lessons
             for the Growth of Africa?   271
    10.2.2  The Fallacies and Facts About the Impact
             of China in Africa   274
10.3  Responsibility for the Future of Africa   278
    10.3.1  The 'African Responsibility'   278
    10.3.2  Responsibility of China in the Future
             Development of Africa   280
10.4  Concluding Remarks   281
References   282

**Index**   285

# List of Figures and Maps

| | | |
|---|---|---|
| Fig. 1.1 | The United Nations 17 Sustainable Development Goals (2015) | 12 |
| Fig. 2.1 | The beautiful and stark Baobab in rural Tanzania | 20 |
| Fig. 2.2 | The African Tree of Organic Growth | 22 |
| Fig. 3.1 | The African Tree of Organic Growth | 35 |
| Fig. 3.2 | Primary resource transformation. (Authors' own) | 43 |
| Fig. 3.3 | Strategic process for the industrial transformation of a country | 47 |
| Fig. 3.4 | Kenya Vision 2030. (Authors' depiction) | 51 |
| Fig. 3.5 | The impact of China on the economic growth and diversification of Kenya | 56 |
| Map 3.1 | Rail and road network linking the Port of Mombasa to the interior. (Google Maps) | 58 |
| Map 3.2 | Nigeria highlighting Lagos and the Niger Delta. (Google Maps) | 61 |
| Fig. 3.6 | The effect of China on the economic growth and diversification of Nigeria | 70 |
| Fig. 4.1 | The African Tree of Organic Growth | 78 |
| Fig. 4.2 | China's investment: percentage of GDP from 1952 to 2016. (CEIC 2016) | 84 |
| Map 4.1 | The Tan–Zam railway line connecting Zambia to the Port of Dar es Salaam. (Google Maps) | 91 |
| Fig. 4.3 | The sleek new Chinese-built trams in Addis Ababa | 94 |
| Fig. 4.4 | Elevated tram system | 95 |
| Fig. 4.5 | The blue container ticket sales office on a busy Addis Ababa street. (The staff requested they not be photographed) | 95 |
| Map 4.2 | The railway line linking Addis Ababa and the Port of Djibouti. (Google Maps) | 98 |
| Map 4.3 | Lesotho landlocked by South Africa. (Google Maps) | 99 |

| | | |
|---|---|---|
| Fig. 4.6 | Road construction in Lesotho | 101 |
| Fig. 4.7 | Chinese contractors weaving the new road en route to Sani Pass | 101 |
| Fig. 4.8 | Unpaved road on the South African side of Qacha's Nek border post | 102 |
| Fig. 4.9 | A bridge on the new Roma to Ramabanta road | 103 |
| Fig. 4.10 | One of the twisting road passes on the Roma to Ramabanta road | 103 |
| Fig. 4.11 | One of many of the new schools built near smaller communities | 105 |
| Fig. 4.12 | A regular sight of schools and clinics alongside the road | 106 |
| Fig. 4.13 | Every home in this village has its own new toilet | 106 |
| Fig. 4.14 | A view only now accessible due to the new Roma to Ramabanta road | 107 |
| Fig. 4.15 | One of the many landslides along the older A4 road | 107 |
| Fig. 4.16 | Contribution of China's infrastructural investments to the African Tree of Organic Growth | 109 |
| Fig. 5.1 | The African Tree of Organic Growth | 112 |
| Fig. 5.2 | Organogram of effective governance. (Authors' own) | 113 |
| Fig. 5.3 | China's impact | 135 |
| Fig. 6.1 | The African Tree of Organic Growth | 138 |
| Fig. 6.2 | The education and skills development dimension in Africa | 159 |
| Fig. 7.1 | The African Tree of Organic Growth | 168 |
| Fig. 7.2 | The integrated nature of sustainability. (Adapted from the United Nations' 17 Sustainable Development Goals per sustainable development themes (Sustainable Development Goals 2015)) | 169 |
| Fig. 7.3 | Invitation for sundowners on Lake Malawi | 173 |
| Fig. 7.4 | Fishing boats on a serene Lake Malawi | 174 |
| Fig. 7.5 | Fires on Lake Malawi's shore | 175 |
| Fig. 7.6 | View from Moshi of the mighty Mount Kilimanjaro in Tanzania is totally obscured by smog | 175 |
| Fig. 7.7 | Vendors selling charcoal alongside the road in Zambia | 176 |
| Fig. 7.8 | The 2000 metre Three Gorges Dam | 181 |
| Fig. 7.9 | Environmental sustainability and the African Tree of Organic Growth | 188 |
| Fig. 8.1 | The African Tree of Organic Growth | 191 |
| Map 8.1 | The geography of happiness. (Helliwell et al. 2015: 20) | 194 |
| Map 8.2 | Geographical distribution of new and total confirmed cases of Ebola: 30 December 2015. (World Health Organisation 2015) | 206 |
| Map 8.3 | Somalia on the Horn of Africa. (Google 2017) | 208 |
| Map 8.4 | Katanga in the Democratic Republic of the Congo | 212 |

| | | |
|---|---|---|
| Fig. 8.2 | China's contribution to the well-being and cultural wealth in Africa | 213 |
| Fig. 9.1 | The African Tree of Organic Growth | 218 |
| Map 9.1 | Cameroon and neighbouring countries. (Google Maps) | 219 |
| Map 9.2 | Mauritius. (Google Maps) | 236 |
| Map 9.3 | Geographic location of Mauritius in the Indian Ocean off the African coast. (Google Maps) | 237 |

# LIST OF TABLES

| | | |
|---|---|---|
| Table 1.1 | Media perceptions towards China's engagement in Africa | 3 |
| Table 1.2 | Characterisation of Sino–African relations, 1949–present | 6 |
| Table 1.3 | Commitments made at the first FOCAC | 8 |
| Table 1.4 | FOCAC Johannesburg Action Plan (2016–2018) (2015) | 9 |
| Table 1.5 | Agenda 2063 | 11 |
| Table 1.6 | Authors' comparative analysis of the alignment of the African Union's Agenda 2063 and the UN's 17 Sustainable Development Goals and the FOCAC Action Plan 2016–2018 | 12 |
| Table 1.7 | Positive contribution by China in Africa | 16 |
| Table 1.8 | The negative consequences of China's engagement in Africa | 17 |
| Table 3.1 | Africa's GDP growth across sectors 2002–2007 | 37 |
| Table 3.2 | Background to Kenya | 49 |
| Table 3.3 | Summary of historical relations between Kenya and China | 54 |
| Table 3.4 | Background information on Nigeria | 62 |
| Table 3.5 | Summary of the relationship between Nigeria and China | 66 |
| Table 4.1 | Infrastructure in Africa | 80 |
| Table 4.2 | Chinese proposed, financed and built infrastructural facilities: Media releases by FOCAC during 2016 and 2017 | 87 |
| Table 5.1 | Examples of Zimbabwe's failure to provide free and fair elections | 116 |
| Table 5.2 | Comparative analysis between elections in Zimbabwe, The Gambia and Ghana | 119 |
| Table 5.3 | Comparative analysis between Zimbabwe, The Gambia and Ghana's leadership and internal and international influence | 120 |
| Table 5.4 | Critique against China's non-interference policy in Africa | 123 |

| | | |
|---|---|---|
| Table 5.5 | Major themes and subthemes related to perceived barriers to the delivery of quality emergency obstetric and neonatal care services in Burundi and Northern Uganda | 131 |
| Table 7.1 | Climate change observations | 170 |
| Table 7.2 | Examples of climate change effects in Africa | 171 |
| Table 7.3 | Grand Inga Dam concerns | 183 |
| Table 8.1 | Causes of the happiness deficit in Africa | 195 |
| Table 8.2 | Summary of the FOCAC Action Plan points related to improved well-being in Africa | 202 |
| Table 8.3 | Selected FOCAC news releases in 2017 detailing interventions aimed at improving the well-being of Africans | 204 |
| Table 8.4 | Chinese humanitarian support of Somalia | 210 |
| Table 9.1 | Overview of historical relations between China and Cameroon | 220 |
| Table 9.2 | The 'Root System' of the African Tree of Organic Growth in Cameroon | 223 |
| Table 9.3 | Current strengths and weaknesses of the Cameroonian economy | 225 |
| Table 9.4 | The 'Trunk' of the African Tree of Organic Growth in Cameroon | 226 |
| Table 9.5 | The 'Leaves and Fruit' of the African Tree of Organic Growth | 231 |
| Table 9.6 | Cameroon's Vision 2035 | 236 |
| Table 9.7 | Historical overview of the relationship between China and Mauritius | 240 |
| Table 9.8 | The 'Root System' of the African Tree of Organic Growth in Mauritius | 243 |
| Table 9.9 | The 'Trunk' of the African Tree of Organic Growth in Mauritius | 246 |
| Table 9.10 | Pragmatic political approach to development taken by the Mauritian government | 247 |
| Table 9.11 | The economic diversification trajectory of Mauritius | 250 |
| Table 9.12 | The 'Leaves and Fruit' of the African Tree of Organic Growth for Mauritius | 255 |
| Table 10.1 | Definition of inclusive growth | 264 |
| Table 10.2 | A comparison of economic growth, inclusive growth and organic growth paradigms | 269 |
| Table 10.3 | The four elements of Chinese engagement and impact in Africa | 270 |
| Table 10.4 | Lessons that China offered for the organic growth of African countries | 273 |
| Table 10.5 | Fallacies and facts about the impact of China on Africa | 277 |

CHAPTER 1

# China in Africa: New Colonists or Facilitators of Development and Growth

China's presence in Africa has led to a heated debate by various authors over the last decade or two. The debate centred on the reason for the involvement of China and the implications of this involvement for the development and growth on the African continent. Chinese investment in Africa has skyrocketed in the last couple of years, outpacing every other nation. China finances more infrastructure projects in Africa than the World Bank and has become a key provider of aid. The Chinese model, with no colonial past in Africa, is considered a legitimate challenger to the Western aid status quo. Most of the research and analysis on China in Africa tends to focus on generalisations about Africa, without necessarily considering the unique growth trajectories of each country. The main purpose of this book is to evaluate the impact of China on Africa by evaluating case studies in African countries in terms of the influence on their specific growth and development phases and in terms of 'The African Tree of Organic Growth' presented in Chap. 2.

The success of China's own 'renaissance' has proved that a transformational agenda directed at the conditions of a specific country can succeed and abet a large segment of the population out of poverty. While China's poverty reduction is often associated with economic growth and diversification, much of it actually occurred in the early phase of China's reform. In 1978, China embarked on a national restructuring process that facilitated more than 30 years of rapid economic growth and social development starting with agricultural reforms to jumpstart poverty reduction.

China also has an impressive organic development history, where the rents on resources were used to fuel economic and infrastructure development, while industry partnerships with developed countries secured the technology transfer for important new industries. China can therefore serve in more than one way as a benchmark for Africa. A number of countries, such as Ethiopia and Senegal, confirm that they have a lot to learn from China's successes. Others are not so pleased with China's increasing presence. The recently successful election of the new president of Zambia, Michael Sata, who threatened to throw all Chinese investors out of Zambia, is a good example of this reaction.

The involvement of China in Africa offers some clear advantages for the growth and development of African counties. One of the key advantages is speed. Chinese firms are able to deliver quickly and provide a package of financial and implementation partners and support, which makes execution of projects fast and effective. Timing and speed are a big comparative advantage of the Chinese in Africa, especially because of existing bottlenecks in Africa, especially in infrastructure development and energy provision. Chinese construction companies are globally very competitive and are able to effectively deliver on big projects at an affordable cost. Africa's information and communications technology (ICT) needs remain high, and telecommunications infrastructure has become very reliant on Chinese technology, which tends to be competitively priced, durable and enjoys strong back-up service. The rising African middle class is also providing opportunities for affordable consumer goods to be exported from China to Africa, facilitated by the World Trade Organization (WTO) having decreased tariffs and opened up the African marketplace—an attractive opportunity for China.

As a growing economy, China needs Africa's energy, resources and access to African markets. As a rising power, China needs the political support of African leaders as a bulwark against the West. During his visit to the African Union in 2014, Chinese Premier Li Keqiang announced that China expects to achieve US$400 billion in trade volumes with Africa in 2020 and raise its direct investment in the continent to US$100 billion. Most African countries are in a transformative developmental state and therefore need the investment and support of world powers like China.

Africans do have reciprocal power in their relationship with China, and should therefore make sure that these investments and support contribute to their own internal renewal and growth process. African governments are learning that China's growing needs and aspirations mean that they need Africa as much as Africa needs them. A good example is that of Angola, who in 2011 walked away from an oil deal after having struck many similar deals before; months later the Chinese came back with a better offer. Similarly, local protests in Mozambique forced China to rethink land settlement plans.

It is clear that the response to potential Chinese exploitation has been growing and that Africa will continue to play a more prominent role in setting the rules of engagement to ensure that its citizens directly benefit from these interventions and investments.

## 1.1 Perceptions in the African Media

Before detailing China's historical and current engagement in Africa, it is worthwhile evaluating what the perceptions are towards the Chinese in Africa. One way of doing this is to investigate media reporting on the matter.

A 'snapshot' was taken of 155 media articles for the period 1 January 2016 to 31 December 2016 in two North African nations, two West African nations, two South African Nations and two East African nations. The results are reflected in Table 1.1.

Table 1.1 Media perceptions towards China's engagement in Africa

|    | Country of publication | Total | Positive | Neutral | Negative |
|----|------------------------|-------|----------|---------|----------|
| 1  | Algeria                | 34    | 32 (94%) | 2 (6%)  | 0        |
| 2  | Egypt                  | 10    | 10 (100%)| 0       | 0        |
| 3  | Egypt                  | 7     | 6 (86%)  | 1 (14%) | 0        |
| 4  | Cameroon               | 3     | 0        | 1 (33%) | 2 (66%)  |
| 5  | Cameroon               | 2     | 2 (100%) | 0       | 0        |
| 6  | Nigeria                | 11    | 7 (64%)  | 3 (27%) | 1 (9%)   |
| 7  | Nigeria                | 19    | 14 (74%) | 2 (10%) | 3 (16%)  |
| 8  | South Africa           | 12    | 11 (92%) | 0       | 1 (8%)   |
| 9  | Zambia                 | 18    | 17 (94%) | 1 (6%)  | 0        |
| 10 | Malawi                 | 17    | 14 (82%) | 1 (6%)  | 2 (12%)  |
| 11 | Kenya                  | 18    | 7 (39%)  | 7 (39%) | 4 (22%)  |

It is noted that the analysis was limited in terms of Internet access and search options on the respective websites. Media websites were limited to English medium reporting. The evaluation did not consider media bias or independence of the publications

It is immediately clear that there is an overwhelmingly positive regard by the press for China in Africa: 94% of press releases of Algerian publications, 100% of Egyptian, 64% and 74% of Nigerian, 92% of South African, 94% of Zambian and 82% of Malawian publications were positive news reports. Some exceptions include the Kenyan newspaper, where only 39% were positive, but then a further 39% were neutral, with only 22% being negative; and in Cameroon, one publication was mostly negative in reporting while the other was positive.

A survey in 2013 by the Pew Global Attitude Survey drew similar conclusions, finding 72% of Africans surveyed viewed China favourably. This was in stark contrast to the rest of the world: only 37% of US citizens, 43% of Europeans, 45% of Middle Eastern citizens, 58% of the Asia Pacific population and 58% of Latin Americans have a favourable disposition towards China (Pew Research Center 2013).

Further analysis of media reports was conducted on common word usage within the reports, and similar themes became immediately apparent.

The positive news articles describe the intense political, economic and cultural cooperation; strategic consultation on a number of levels; the positive benefits of the close relationship ('win-win'/'side-by-side'/'hand-in-hand'); the trust and respect; and the growing strength of the affiliation of China and the respective African nation.

The media coverage included themes that were both particular to each country analysed and general themes involving both countries. The general themes described the political interaction between the countries, such as state visits, agreements and memorandums of understanding entered into between the countries, donations, humanitarian aid, peace and security efforts, cultural and sports events, infrastructural and mining projects, investments in manufacturing, loans and financing, training and education, technological transfer and job creation.

The neutral or negative articles described concerns of high levels of bilateral trade resulting in trade deficit problems for African countries, quality of imported Chinese-manufactured goods, illegal activities by Chinese nationals, lack of investment by the Chinese, the damage of imports to local industries, high and unsustainable debt levels, the One-China Policy, the threat of Chinese language institutes compromising African languages and culture, transparency (for instance, a 'sweetheart deal' in favour of a Chinese firm without public bidding process), concerns in relation to loans and projects provided by the Chinese and poor working conditions in Chinese businesses.

The unique approach of China and the impact it has on Africa's renewal will be a constant 'thread' throughout this book. In order to understand China's approach, it is necessary to scrutinise China's historical development and the evolution of its foreign policy in Africa.

## 1.2 The 'Complementary Development' Approach of China in Africa

Similarities between Africa and China, and the need for them to support each other, were highlighted during the 'Chinese Dream, African Dream' seminar held in Tanzania in 2013 (FOCAC 2015a). Lu Shaye, the Director General of the African Department of China's Ministry of Foreign Affairs, spoke of the alignment of China's and Africa's four dreams of achieving peace, development, rejuvenation and greater strength through independent efforts (a policy of self-reliance and non-interference).

From a development perspective, resolving inequality was a key issue in his address. He mentioned that although China is the second largest economy in the world, its per capita gross domestic product (GDP) ranks 90th in the world with over 100 million people living below the poverty line. For China he states that "it is our goal to accelerate economic transformation to make our development more sustainable, to strengthen social development to ensure that people live a better secured and happier life, and to uphold social equity and justice so that the fruits of development can benefit the entire population more fairly". Similarly, for Africa "to reduce poverty, improve livelihood and achieve sustainable development remains urgent tasks for the African continent". And therefore "the same task for development gives us more common ground and greater scope for cooperation. China and Africa are highly complementary in economy, presenting important development opportunities to us."

From a global perspective, The Five Principles of Mutual Coexistence formulated in 1954 heralded a shift towards greater interaction by China with the world—these principles were 'mutual respect for each other's territorial integrity; non-aggression; non-interference in each other's internal affairs; equality and mutual benefit; and peaceful coexistence'.

This synopsis provides a useful introduction to China's foreign policy towards Africa. In the following sections, China's historical engagement with Africa will be detailed, and China's foreign policy towards Africa will be discussed with reference to the Forum on China–Africa Cooperation (FOCAC).

### 1.2.1 A Historical Overview on Relations Between Africa and China

Apart from archaeological findings dating between 960 and 1279 AD, and Chinese exploration of the continent in the 1400s, there was little interaction between China and Africa due to the adoption of a 'closed-door' policy by the Chinese Qing dynasty lasting from 1644 until 1911 (Taylor 2011).

This changed during the revolutionary China under the leadership of Mao Zedong as foreign policy evolved internationally including the Five Principles of Mutual Coexistence discussed earlier.

The relationship China had with Africa was decidedly influenced by global foreign relations and internal changes. Taylor (2011) details how these influenced African exchanges in Table 1.2.

The Bandung Conference held in Bandung, Indonesia, in 1955 was the first compelling effort by China to develop ties with Africa (Taylor 2011). The conference was between Asian and African leaders and led to the first

**Table 1.2** Characterisation of Sino–African relations, 1949–present

| Period | Remarks |
|---|---|
| 1949–1955 | Foreign policy dominated by ties to Moscow. Focus on rebuilding post-war China and the Korean War imbroglio. Minimal links to Africa |
| 1955–mid-1960s | Bandung Era—greatly enhanced relations with newly independent Africa, but also growing tensions with Moscow |
| Mid-1960s–mid-1970s | Cultural Revolution—diplomacy characterised by strident ideology, fierce denunciation of both Moscow and Washington amid accusations that China was damaging the liberation struggles. While the period saw China finally enter the United Nations (UN) with Africa support, it also saw the nadir of China's role in Angola, being caught out on the side of the United States and Apartheid South Africa |
| Mid-1970s–1989 | With the death of Mao in 1976 and the ascendency of Deng Xiaoping in 1978, the Chinese progressively lost interest in Africa as investment was sought from the West and Africa went through its 'lost decade' of debt and economic collapse |
| 1989–2000 | Re-evaluation of the developing world post–Tiananmen Square saw a return of Africa to Beijing's foreign policy as a useful support constituency |
| 2000–present | Exponential explosion of Chinese economic interest in Africa |

Taylor (2011: 21)

official diplomatic ties in Africa, namely with Egypt, followed by Morocco, Algeria and Sudan. Chinese delegations to Africa and African delegations to China increased rapidly during this period, within the context of a number of newly independent African nations. This trend continued with many more African nations assuming diplomatic ties with China and diplomatic visits occurring.

The early 1960s saw further evidence of China's active participation in African affairs with increased trade and the support of liberation movements in countries such as Angola, Mozambique, Namibia, South Africa and Zimbabwe (Taylor 2011: 13). This was short-lived with the Cultural Revolution of China resulting in the withdrawal of most Chinese ambassadors from African states and the souring of political relations between China and Africa. The early 1970s saw a rekindling of African relations by China including a significant aid programme for many African states. These new-found relationships were to prove valuable to China as they resulted in the admittance by the UN of China as a member nation. China self-proclaimed itself as the leader of the 'Third World' of developing nations of Asia, Latin America and Africa. Mao Zedong's passing in 1976 heralded a new focus by China towards economic modernisation, and with the anticipated growth, there was acknowledgement by China of its requirement for resources that Africa could provide—a further stimulant for improved relations with Africa.

Post–Tiananmen Square saw a revitalised foreign policy towards the developing world after the damaging effect the Tiananmen Square event of 1989 (when the Chinese army killed several hundred demonstrators) had on relations with the Western World. Trade links with African nations were bolstered, diplomatic ties strengthened and China encouraged organisations to enter joint ventures and participate in economic activities with Africa. Chinese organisations also saw the huge potential of the African market for their manufactured goods.

The relationship between China and Africa continued and still continues to grow strong. The establishment of the FOCAC was one of the significant steps taken to further this relationship in a structured manner and provides useful guidelines on China's policy towards Africa.

### 1.2.2 The Facilitating Role of the FOCAC in China's Policy Towards Africa

The FOCAC was heralded as a new approach by China in Africa that aimed to strengthen the relationship and further cooperation. The first forum was held in Beijing in 2000, and a further five forums every three years thereafter, with the sixth forum having taken place in South Africa in 2015.

The commitments made at the first FOCAC in Beijing are summarised in Table 1.3 (FOCAC 2000).

The first FOCAC had a strong Chinese-focused commitment to Africa. As illustrated in Table 1.3, the commitment was primarily economic in nature, describing the establishment of a joint business council; the promotion of bilateral trade and investment by Chinese corporations in Africa; the support of Chinese corporations in order for them to develop infrastructure in Africa including tourism infrastructure; funding of socio-economic development through grants and favourable loans; and the establishment of a fund to promote training within Africa.

China has committed increasingly larger amounts to investment, trade and aid at subsequent forums: US$5 billion financing at the 2006 Forum, US$10 billion in 2009 and US$20 billion in 2012. The forums have

**Table 1.3** Commitments made at the first FOCAC

Increased intergovernmental cooperation with high-level visits, development assistance, grants and loans

Developing a strategy that provides an enabling legal and business environment which facilitates trade and capacity-building; encourages, protects and guarantees investments; avoids double taxation; and includes some levels of preferential treatment

A move towards a more balanced trade relationship and a reduction of Africa's dependence on primary commodities. It also committed to the establishment of a China–Africa Joint Business Council and a China–Africa Products Exhibition Centre in China to promote African products in China

Greater levels of investments in Africa; joint equity and cooperation projects; and the assistance in development of special economic zones

Cooperation in engineering and other infrastructural projects

Financial cooperation between financial institutions, including between China and the African Development Bank Group

A commitment to debt relief and debt cancellation for heavily indebted poor African countries

A range of other cooperation efforts were covered: cooperation in tourism; migration and facilitating work permits and visas; increased beneficiation by Africa of its natural resources; scientific, technological and cultural cooperation; medical care and public health; education; human resource development; environmental management and biodiversity; arms control; and multilateral cooperation

FOCAC (2000)

evolved considerably since the initial commitments of 2000, as evidenced with the 6th Ministerial Conference and Johannesburg Summit of the Forum on China–Africa Cooperation, which further cemented ties between China and the continent of Africa. The resulting FOCAC Johannesburg Action Plan (2016–2018) (2015) reiterated the perceived complementary nature of the development goals encapsulated in China's Two Centenary Goals and the African Union's Agenda 2063.

The themes and commitments have changed significantly since the first FOCAC commitments detailed earlier. There has been greater involvement by African nations in the determination of China's engagement in Africa, and the forums have moved towards a mutually beneficial approach which is much wider in scale. The action plan theme of FOCAC 2015 was detailed as 'China–Africa Progressing Together: Win-Win Cooperation for Common Development'. The action plan includes the following intentions (the intentions are numbered by the authors for later comparative purposes) (Table 1.4).

**Table 1.4** FOCAC Johannesburg Action Plan (2016–2018) (2015)

**Intention 1: Political cooperation** through high-level visits; consultations and cooperation mechanisms; and interaction between African Nations, regional bodies and the African Union with China

**Intention 2: Economic cooperation** focusing on the following areas:
　　1. Agriculture and food security by supporting the Comprehensive African Agriculture Development Programme
　　2. Industry partnering and industrial capacity cooperation to "ensure Africa's independent and sustainable development"
　　3. Infrastructure development to remove "bottlenecks hindering independent and sustainable development of Africa"
　　4. Energy and natural resources exploitation for mutual benefit including beneficiation of resources in Africa
　　5. The ocean economy
　　6. Tourism
　　7. Investment and economic cooperation, increasing direct investment from US$32.4 billion in 2014 to US$100 billion in 2020
　　8. Trade cooperation including increasing trade volume from US$220 billion in 2014 to US$400 billion in 2020
　　9. Financial aid including US$35 billion in favourable loans and increasing the China–Africa Development fund from US$5 billion to US$10 billion

**Intention 3: Social development cooperation** such as developing medical care and public health provision; and education and human resources development

(*continued*)

**Table 1.4** (continued)

**Intention 4: Poverty reduction exchanges** to better develop poverty eradication policies and practices
**Intention 5: Science and technology cooperation and knowledge sharing**
**Intention 6: Environmental protection and tackling climate change**
**Intention 7: Cultural cooperation and people-to-people exchanges** such as press and media exchanges including technology transfer; exchanges between academia and think tanks through the China–Africa Joint Research and Exchange Plan and the holding of FOCAC Think Tank Forums; and people-to-people exchanges
**Intention 8: Security cooperation** that continues to support and advocate for African solutions to African challenges without interference from outside the continent while pledging support to the UN's efforts in resolving regional conflicts
**Intention 9: Consular, immigration, judiciary and law enforcement cooperation**
**Intention 10: International cooperation** to "establish a new model of global development that is based on equality, accountability, mutual respect and that is more balanced, stable, inclusive and harmonious … while maintaining the sovereignty to choose their development paths"

This action plan, in contrast to the commitments made in Beijing in 2000, has a greater focus on social development and cooperative engagement, such as security, political, legal, international and scientific cooperation. In addition, humanitarian and green growth considerations were also included, such as poverty alleviation and protection of the environment.

It is worthwhile considering the context of these intentions, especially in view of the aspirations of the African Union and the UN sustainable development goals.

## 1.3 Synergies Between Chinese Policy and the African Union and United Nations Development Goals

The African Union has embarked on the ambitious 50-year socio-economic transformation strategy named Agenda 2063. The strategy highlights seven aspirations the agenda hopes to achieve, detailed in Table 1.5.

The aspirations detailed in Agenda 2063 aim to eradicate many of the concerns and long-term gripes African countries have in the age of globalisation, such as the attainment of self-reliance and self-determination, maintenance of a strong cultural identity, and the goal of the continent to

Table 1.5   Agenda 2063

**Aspiration 1**: "A prosperous Africa based on **inclusive growth** and sustainable development" which would see the eradication of poverty and build prosperity through socio-economic transformation
**Aspiration 2**: "An integrated continent, politically united, based on the ideals of Pan-Africanism and the vision of **Africa's Renaissance**"—a journey towards **African unity** with development founded on self-reliance and self-determination
**Aspiration 3**: "An Africa of **good governance**, democracy, respect for human rights, justice and the rule of law"
**Aspiration 4**: "**A peaceful and secure Africa**" with the African Union stating that by 2020 "all guns will be silent" and a culture of peace and tolerance will be engendered
**Aspiration 5**: "An Africa with a **strong cultural identity**, common heritage, values and ethics"
**Aspiration 6**: "An Africa whose development is **people-driven**, relying on the potential of African people, especially its women and youth, and caring for children"
**Aspiration 7**: "Africa as a strong, united, resilient and influential **global player and partner**" in the face of "continued external interference including, attempts to divide the continent and undue pressures and sanctions on some countries"

be influential in the world without the "continued external interference". While the aspirations of prosperity, good governance, respect for human rights and peace are all commendable, the test will be whether these can be achieved.

In September 2015, the UN replaced the previous Millennium Development Goals with the 17 Sustainable Development Goals (2015) aimed at ending poverty, protecting the planet and that ensures prosperity for all. These are illustrated in Fig. 1.1.

The question arises as to how Chinese foreign policy, reflected in FOCAC's development plan, is aligned with the UN's 17 Sustainable Development Goals and the African Union's Agenda 2016. A comparative analysis was conducted and is reflected in Table 1.6.

While acknowledging that the aspirations, goals and intentions are generalised and can be widely interpreted, the comparative analysis does yield some significant insights. First, it would appear that there is some discord between the UN's 17 Sustainable Development Goals and the African Union's Agenda 2063 aspirations. There is little emphasis in the aspirations on sustainability issues such as clean energy, climate action, life on land and below water, sustainable cities and communities and responsible consumption, all of which are encapsulated in the sustainable development goals.

**Fig. 1.1** The United Nations 17 Sustainable Development Goals (2015)

**Table 1.6** Authors' comparative analysis of the alignment of the African Union's Agenda 2063 and the UN's 17 Sustainable Development Goals and the FOCAC Action Plan 2016–2018

| African Union 2063 | United Nations 17 Sustainable Development Goals | FOCAC Johannesburg Action Plan 2016–2018 |
|---|---|---|
| Aspiration 1: Growth and sustainable development | Most goals reflect a determination for socio-economic improvements | Intention 2: Economic cooperation; Intention 3: Social development cooperation; Intention 4: Poverty reduction exchanges |
| Aspiration 2: Integrated continent with vision of Africa's renaissance | Not strongly reflected in goals | Somewhat reflected in Intention 1: Political cooperation; Intention 10: International cooperation |
| Aspiration 3: Governance, democracy, human rights, justice | Goal 16: Peace, justice and strong institutions | Limited synergy, justice is reflected in Intention 9: Consular, immigration, judiciary and law enforcement cooperation |
| Aspiration 4: Peaceful and secure Africa | Goal 16: Peace, justice and strong institutions | Intention 8: Security cooperation |

(*continued*)

**Table 1.6** (continued)

| African Union 2063 | United Nations 17 Sustainable Development Goals | FOCAC Johannesburg Action Plan 2016–2018 |
| --- | --- | --- |
| Aspiration 5: Cultural identity, values and ethics Aspiration 6: People-driven development, relying on African people, care for youth and children | Not strongly reflected in goals Goal 3: Good health and well-being; Goal 5: Gender equality | Intention 7: Cultural cooperation and people-to-people exchanges Intention 3: Social development cooperation |
| Aspiration 7: Global player in face of external interference | Not strongly reflected in goals | Intention 1: Political cooperation; Intention 8: Security cooperation; Intention 10: International cooperation |

There seems instead to be more harmony between the African Union's aspirations and the intentions of China in Africa. For instance, FOCAC's intentions support aspirations of self-determination without outside interference, global development that is more balanced and cultural interaction that supports cultural identity. FOCAC's intentions also include a sustainability focus that incorporates environmental protection and tackling climate change—aspects not strongly reflected in Agenda 2063.

## 1.4 Chinese Aid and Investment Approach

The two contrasting approaches of China and of the West to Africa mirror long-held debates in the international community on the merits of each. The West is well known for its focus on direct financial support, conditional on aspects such as promoting democracy and reducing corruption. China, however, provides large and cheap finance to African governments in exchange for securing access to natural resources, with few or no conditions attached.

The financial and other assistance can sometimes contribute to the country's development and improve their governance systems. The conditional approach practised by the West rightly recognises the importance of good governance for the effectiveness of aid, but sometimes fails to recognise that African countries are in different phases of growth and development, and that often inadequate governance is a consequence of the country's development phase.

Mutual economic benefits, on the other hand, are the driving force of China's approach to aid in Africa, even if it means offering support when the government is still corrupt and ineffective. Instead of providing finance with conditions, China tries to avoid this by addressing direct growth constraints, such as focussing on infrastructural development in bilateral agreements, and places little emphasis on political development.

China's non-interference policy is a major pillar of China's foreign policy, and has been so since the Five Principles of Peaceful Coexistence were formulated. Investment in countries with poor human rights records and high levels of corruption is therefore not a paramount consideration for the Chinese. This is not a surprising fact given that China has often been criticised for its own human rights record, and lack of transparency, which makes it rather difficult for them to impose political conditions on other countries. Some of Chinese companies involved in infrastructural projects have been found guilty of human rights violations. In reaction to critique, Chinese authorities have asserted that civil and political rights (CPR) should not be given primacy over economic, social and cultural rights (ESCR) (Zakaria 1994). China has also expressed a strong conviction of the non-universality of human rights.

China's involvement with corrupt governments in Africa has received criticism, especially from the West. They argue that China should use its economic leverage as a political tool to enforce ethical conduct from these governments. Although this argument has its merits, it ignores empirical data which show that the conditional approach practised by the Western countries has failed to actually bring the anticipated change envisaged by those countries. Condon (2012) refers to the growing body of literature which argues that the Western development approach is demanding too much, too soon, from governments on their progress in terms of human rights, transparency and democracy. In actual fact, these demands are getting in the way of growth, and sometimes also in the way of improving governance, thus limiting institutional development.

Although corruption and unethical conduct can never be defended, eliminating these should be a goal rather than a condition. Empirical evidence shows that in cases of good growth in most countries, the elimination of corruption, empowerment of civil society and good governance practice were long and ongoing developmental processes starting at grass-roots level. This observation is also applicable to China because it had substantial growth without making major progress towards the rule of law or respect for human rights. The communist party has in fact done a good job of increasing the average income of its people, broadening economic participation, and generating producing and financial capital for reinvestment.

Future conflict between China and other Western powers, to ensure investment opportunities and access to resources, could have negative implications for the growth and development of Africa. It seems clear that the solution will have to be an African one. African nations are more and more empowered to stand up for themselves and also more adamant in creating 'rules of engagement' for their dealings with foreign investors (Condon 2012). The approach of African nations should be to set social and sustainable growth requirements that will suit their country the best. The best approach for the West will therefore be to avoid an aggressive bilateral stand-off with China over investment standards, and rather encourage the African agenda and capacity-building, through the setting of engagement rules that will contribute to the internal renewal and growth process of Africa.

## 1.5 The Potential Outcomes of China's Engagement in Africa

The arguments in favour of and against China's impact on Africa are complex and wide-ranging. While the book will go to lengths to evaluate the outcomes of China's engagement in Africa, it is worthwhile summarising some of the potential outcomes of this engagement.

There is no doubt that China's involvement in Africa has, and continues to have, a positive impact on Africa. Some of the positive influences are given in Table 1.7.

While the positive impact of China on Africa is significant, a number of criticisms have been levelled at China. These are included in Table 1.8.

## 1.6 Conclusion: The African Agenda

While this chapter has helped shed light on the perceptions of Africans towards the Chinese, the context of China's political and economic dispensations, China's foreign policy towards Africa, the competitive rivalry between the West and East on the African continent and the potential impact China can have, it has yet to consider the African agenda.

**Table 1.7  Positive contribution by China in Africa**

**Political support for the interests of the developing world**
Fundamentally, China is still a developing nation experiencing many of the challenges of the developing world. It has aligned itself with the developing world and takes a leadership role in the G20, and attempts to address imbalances in global governance and trade in the International Monetary Fund (IMF), World Bank, WTO and the United Nations Security Council

**Peace and security**
Peacekeeping activities by China in Africa have taken place for over 20 years, with thousands of armed forces and civilians been deployed in Southern Sudan, Liberia and the Democratic Republic of Congo

**Health and welfare**
By 2010, China had sent 17,000 medical workers to 48 African countries treating 200 million patients. Through contributions to the Global Fund, China assisted in the building of hospitals and medical facilities, trained local health workers and helped prevent and treat HIV. This is in addition to far-ranging welfare interventions on the continent such as the provision of low-cost housing and poverty reduction efforts

**Economic growth**
Much of the growth seen in sub-Saharan nations over the last decade has been the result of China's increased demand for oil and precious minerals. In addition, policies of FOCAC and the establishment of the China Africa Development Fund has enabled Chinese investment by Chinese firms in Africa

**Debt financing and debt cancellation**
China provides low-interest loans, interest-free loans and the waiving of loans in many sub-Saharan countries

**Land acquisition**
India, South Korea and some Middle Eastern countries, as well as large multinational organisations, have bought much land in Africa, which is mostly perceived in a negative light. China, on the other hand, has refrained from purchasing much land

**Bilateral trade**
Bilateral trade has increased phenomenally in recent years and China is now Africa's largest trading partner. Chinese exports comprise mostly manufactured goods, machinery and transport equipment, while African exports to China are raw materials, minerals, oil, chemicals and agricultural products

**Infrastructural development**
Many African nations and their people are benefiting from China's provisions of basic infrastructure such as electricity, road, rail, health and other services

**Renewable energy provision**
China has played a significant role in investing in solar and wind power in Africa, contributing towards the electrification of rural areas through the production of renewable energy technologies

**Skills development and skills transfer**
With the assistance of China, over 100 schools had been built by 2009; 5000 scholarships offered per year; by 2010, 30,000 Africans undertook training programmes; and 100 senior agricultural technical experts and youth volunteers from China have been sent to Africa to provide guidance and services

Adapted from Mai and Wilhelm (2012: 143–144), Ciochetto (2014: 38), and the authors' observations

**Table 1.8** The negative consequences of China's engagement in Africa

**China's non-interference policy**
The influx of money into sub-Saharan countries resulting from the sale of resources is helping to fund certain conflicts and civil wars. China has been criticised for its non-interference policy and lack of transparency requirements in countries such as Sudan and the Democratic Republic of Congo and Sudan, which the West has blacklisted, and in Zimbabwe, where funds from resources maintain the power of corrupt leadership and fuel internal conflict

**Human rights**
Supporting countries with poor human rights records justified in terms of China's non-interference policy and their prioritisation of poverty alleviation and economic development

**Resource acquisition**
Resource acquisition is considered a contributing factor to the 'resource curse' experienced by many African nations due to the inability to diversify these economies

**Chinese goods and services**
Reiterating Rossouw's (2014) view, the importation of Chinese goods tends to be a double-edged sword—poor people are better able to afford cheaper goods, although sometimes these goods are of poor quality and undermine the business of local businesses

**Poor labour practices**
China has been criticised for unsatisfactory labour practices, including low wages, poor working conditions and poor treatment of workers by Chinese managers

**Importation of labour**
Instead of utilising local labour in African nations, China is often criticised for importing its own labour force resulting in little provision of knowledge, skills transfer and training

**Resource deprivation**
One example of environmental deprivation is provided by Ciochetto (2014: 37)—that of the timber industry. He cites the fact that China is the largest consumer of tropical timber, and is responsible for much of the illegal logging taking place in sub-Saharan Africa, leading to the damage and destruction of forest ecosystems, depriving developing governments of much needed tax revenues and economic loss

**Environmental concerns**
China has a poor environmental record both in China and in Africa

Adapted from Ciochetto (2014: 35–37), Rossouw's (2014), and the authors' observations

The African agenda encompasses the perspective of what individual African nations require for their growth and development trajectory, and the responsibility these countries have in channelling Chinese engagement for maximum prosperity. The New Partnership for Africa's Development (NEPAD) is a programme of the African Union which reflects the obligation of Africa to take responsibility for its own destiny.

This book makes an important contribution to this vision by providing a uniquely African approach in leveraging China's engagement in Africa, for its own renaissance. Chapter 2 will introduce the reader to a growth model founded in the potential of African nations to self-determine their future.

## REFERENCES

Agenda 2063. 2013. African Union. [Online]. Available from: http://au.int/en/agenda2063 (accessed: 19 October 2016).

Ciochetto, L. 2014. 'The Impact of China on Sub-Saharan Africa's Ability to Work Towards a Sustainable Future', *The Global Studies Journal*, 6: 33–43.

Condon, M. 2012. 'China in Africa: What the Policy of Non-intervention Adds to the Western Development Dilemma', *The Fletcher Journal of Human Security*, xxvii: 5–25.

FOCAC. 2000. Programme for China-Africa Cooperation in Economic and Social Development. Accessed from: http://www.focac.org/eng/ltda/dyjbzjhy/DOC12009/t606797.htm (accessed: 13 September 2017).

FOCAC. 2015a. Chinese Dream, African Dream Speech by Mr. Lu Shaye. [Online]. Available from: http://www.focac.org/eng/xsjl/zflhyjjljh/t1059481.htm (accessed: 20 February 2015).

FOCAC Johannesburg Action Plan (2016–2018). 25 December 2015. Forum on China-Africa Cooperation. [Online]. Available from: http://www.focac.org/eng/ltda/dwjbzjjhys_1/t1327961.htm (accessed: 19 October 2016).

Mai, X. and Wilhelm, P. 2012. 'Evidence of China's Aid to Africa and the Outlook on Sino-African Development', *Competition Forum*, 10 (2): 141–146.

Pew Research Center. 18 July 2013. Who Is Up, Who Is Down: Global Views of China & the U.S. [Online]. Accessed from: http://www.pewglobal.org/2013/07/18/who-is-up-who-is-down-global-views-of-china-the-u-s/ (accessed: 3 February 2017).

Rossouw, D. 2014. *African's Perceptions of Chinese Business in Africa*. Paper presented at the 2014 Ben-Africa conference, Stellenbosch.

Sustainable Development Goals. 25 September 2015. United Nations. [Online]. Available from: http://www.un.org/sustainabledevelopment/sustainable-development-goals/#prettyPhoto (accessed: 19 October 2016).

Taylor, I. 2011. *Global Institutions: The Forum on China-Africa Cooperation (FOCAC)*. New York: Routledge.

Zakaria, F. 1994. 'Culture Is Destiny: A Conversation with Lee Kuan Yew', *Foreign Affairs*, 73: 109–126.

CHAPTER 2

# Renewal of Africa: The African Tree of Organic Growth Paradigm

The mighty baobab (Fig. 2.1) tree epitomises much of the strength and potential that Africa holds. Resembling an upside down tree (according to Bushmen legend, the tree offended god who retaliated by planting the tree upside down) these trees thrive in harsh African climatic conditions they find themselves in. Some of these trees can grow to gigantic proportions, such as the Sunland Baobab, touching the skies at 22 metres in height, with a circumference of 47 metres, and is estimated to be between 1000 and 6000 years old.

The baobab plays an important role in the ecosystem of Africa. Its fruit is generous in nutrients with high protein, calcium, oil and phosphates, and elephants, monkeys and baboons sometime depend on the fruit for their survival. The leaves are high in protein and are similar to spinach in texture, the trunk can be used to weave mats or make paper, while beer and tea can be produced from the bark.

The baobab is a useful analogy for Africa's growth, development and the well-being of its people. Prahalad and Hamel (1990: 81) also used a tree as a metaphor, in their case, to describe the internal growth of a business. They describe an organisation as a tree whose roots represent specific core resources and competencies. Out of these roots grow the organisation's trunk representing the core products, which in turn flourish into branched business lines with particular end products (leaves and fruit). This book will also use the tree analogy, but this time to develop an integrated framework of organic growth that can be applied to all African countries.

Fig. 2.1 The beautiful and stark Baobab in rural Tanzania

It is important to note that Africa is a complex continent, and that the discussion contained in this book needs to be contextualised when applying the concepts to individual African countries. Africa comprises 54 recognised countries, with an additional two nations of Somaliland and Western Sahara with limited recognition.

These countries differ on so many levels. Environmentally, climatic differences result in desert conditions in the north and south, with equatorial rain forests in Central and East Africa. Countries such as Mali, Egypt and Ethiopia have a rich history in mathematics, art, architecture, religion, astronomy and literature, while Southern Africa was inhabited by pastoral tribes such as the Khoisan. Africa has been fundamentally influenced by colonisation, with language, economic policies, legal precedents and culture often remaining long after colonial powers relinquished their governing role: Mozambique and Angola are Portuguese-influenced; Namibia has a strong German character; South Africa has its own language of Afrikaans derived from the Dutch; much of East Africa a British flavour; and Nigeria and much of West Africa a strong French connection.

Many African nations are blessed with an abundance of natural resources, but these differ and have an impact on the development opportunities that accrue from such resources. Oil in Nigeria and Angola, Diamonds of Botswana, Gold in South Africa, Emeralds in Zimbabwe, Copper in Zambia—the list goes on. There is also, of course, water with its potential to drive hydroelectric power and the rich fertile land with agricultural potential. Its natural beauty and culture are also key components to economic diversification in the tourism sector.

Countries in Africa vary significantly in their level of economic development. South Africa has a strong industrial sector and prosperous stock market, while many countries lag behind and are mostly dependent on foreign aid, such as the case of Rwanda. Infrastructure ranges from first-world, to non-existent, often a result of years of war. The stability of these nations and their potential for development are influenced by the level of democracy versus autocracy or dictatorship, peace versus conflict, and the scourge of corruption.

Many of these countries are in themselves very complex. For example, Ethiopia, which has been experiencing an increasing level of social unrest since 2016, comprises over 100 million people making up varied principal religious groups, and numerous ethnic groups reflected in the approximately 90 languages spoken.

## 2.1 The African Renaissance and Organic Growth

The 'African Renaissance' is the concept that African people and nations shall overcome the current challenges confronting them on the continent and achieve cultural, scientific and economic renewal. The African Renaissance concept was first articulated by Senegalese politician, historian and anthropologist Cheikh Anta Diop, and further popularised by former South African President Thabo Mbeki during his term in office.

Pending the interpretation of the term, an African Renaissance may therefore imply the initiating of internal growth processes in African countries, as well as across countries, ultimately resulting in a better life and dispensation for all Africans living in these countries. This renewal process implies that growth will be organic in nature, driven from within the countries itself and by Africa's own people.

Organic growth can therefore in this context be defined as pursuing a path of national well-being for all citizens through the effective development of core resources and critical assets of the country. This process of organic growth can also be metaphorically presented by the image of a tree which grows outward and higher from the bottom up. It is a growth

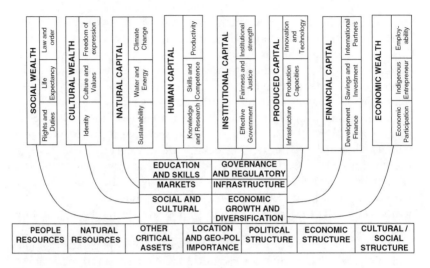

**Fig. 2.2** The African Tree of Organic Growth

that will be exponential and not linear: One cell divides into two, which divides into four, which divides into eight and so on. A tree branch on the other hand will produce multiple new twigs, each of which can sprout out into multiple leaves and fruits. The tree, if nourished, will grow bigger year after year with corresponding new growth appearing at the end of existing branches.

### 2.1.1 The African Tree of Organic Growth

The African Tree of Organic Growth that was developed for this book is depicted in Fig. 2.2.

The African Tree of Organic Growth is divided into three sections: the root, the trunk, and the leaves and fruit.

## 2.2 The Core Resources, Assets and Structures Necessary for Growth (Roots of the Tree)

The root system at the bottom provides nourishment, sustenance and stability. These are the core resources, assets and structures that the country will have in place at any point in time. Some countries might only have natural resources and people, with very little to offer in terms of governance and socio-economic structures, and, as a result, no capital or initiatives to stimulate the needed growth in the trunk of the tree. This negatively impacts fruit production of social and national goods for the citizens of the country. The root system will therefore, like the balance sheet of a business, give a true reflection of the assets and liabilities of a country at any point in time.

This process of organic growth, as alluded to before, is not a linear process. For instance, the development of some or all of trunk processes, like education and economic diversification, will not only stimulate the tree upwards, but will also increase the core assets and structures and therefore the root system downwards.

### 2.2.1 Natural and People Resources

Africa is a continent endowed with immense natural as well as people resources. About 70% of sub-Saharan Africa's export revenues are still predominantly derived from the sale of natural resources like minerals and oil. Half of the world's future population growth will be driven by Africa (not because of higher fertility, which is declining, but due to higher life expectancy). This trend could lead to an estimated adult population of 800 million by 2030 compared to 460 million in 2010, thus offering huge opportunities in terms of consumer growth, as well as enormous potential in terms of people development.

The capacity of a country in Africa to develop and grow is dependent on how the country manages these resources while developing capabilities that are critical for the future. This observation also supports the African Renaissance argument that the renewal of the country should come from within. Natural resources can therefore be an important element of the root system for the growth of a country. This can happen through growth diversification, capabilities and the generation of revenues for reinvestment. Capabilities represent the things a country can do—its know-how and competencies as well as its capability to deliver on public goods and services like infrastructure, education and health. Countries with a strong natural resource base can through the development of this industry also develop related industries and capabilities. South Africa, for example, based on its experience in the mining industry, developed capabilities in the manufacturing of mine equipment and is now an important supplier of such equipment in the world. The revenues of natural resource utilisation can also be reinvested in potential industries or other national goods. Proceeds from mining and or oil production can be used to fund crucial inputs in structural growth support such as education and health, as well as infrastructure or the generation of energy.

The wealth of a country also depends on the development and effective utilisation of people resources. Natural resources are passive factors of production; people are the active agents that accumulate capital, utilise natural resources and build economic, political and social institutions that facilitate growth and development. A country which is unable to educate and develop the knowledge, competencies and capabilities of its people, and employ them effectively in the economic transformation of the country, will not be able to develop and grow. People are therefore an essential part of the root system in the organic growth of a country.

### 2.2.2 Location, Geopolitical Importance and Critical Assets

The location and geopolitical importance of a country will directly influence its ability to grow as well as influence its attractiveness for foreign direct investment (FDI). Being landlocked, hence far from ports or navigable rivers, resulting in long overland transport distances, will reduce a country's potential for growth and development. Distance and being landlocked will directly influence a country's access to international markets and hinder its ability to exploit economies of scale and lower its production efficiency.

Economic isolation is more acute in sub-Saharan Africa where 31% of the countries are landlocked. Nearly 40% of sub-Saharan African population live in these landlocked countries with high transportation costs and poor trade facilitation (Ndulu (World Bank) 2007). Therefore, a favourable location with good transport linkages and access to ports will facilitate access to markets and reduce transport costs.

The location or geography of an African country, as well as its attractiveness for business investors from foreign powers such as China, the United States and European countries, will also play an important role in their growth and development. Attractiveness factors such as abundant resources, good infrastructure and critical assets will increase the geopolitical appeal of a country. Africa has overall become the centre of geopolitical competition because of its abundance in natural resources such as oil and minerals. Where the United States and the European Union (EU) have long been attempting to dominate and revive the old colonial pattern of relationships, China has now emerged as a major competitor in this process. What has made Africa geopolitically attractive is its growth potential as well as the vast reserves of natural resources, especially oil. Africa is becoming the fastest-growing oil-producing region in the world and experts believe that there are still large undiscovered oil fields with immense potential.

Critical assets of a country are those infrastructure and assets that provide an enabling environment for a country to grow and develop. Examples of these are transport, telecommunications, information technology, energy, water and finance.

Evidence and research has shown that good basic infrastructure, such as quality roads and water and electricity provision, are not adequate in most African countries. During the 1990s, African governments and their development partners sharply reduced further the share of resources allocated to infrastructure in favour of scaling spending on social priorities. Decades of neglect currently manifest itself in the form of huge infrastructure gaps with some serious implications for the growth potential of most African countries. A prime example is energy shortages which negatively affect growth because business, especially manufacturing, is dependent on secure energy supplies. Gaps in other infrastructure assets, such as water and transport, have similar effects on the growth potential of a country.

### 2.2.3 Political and Economic Structures

The success in moving beyond structural adjustments into long-term sustainable growth will be determined by the ability of African leaders to reduce barriers to economic growth and development, through creating an enabling environment that supports investment, business and service delivery.

Africa's growth in the last two decades has been dominated by multi-level transitions which in some countries have often run concurrently; from war to peace, from one-party rule to multiparty governance, from apartheid to non-racial democracy, and from communal economies dominated by government to privatisation, FDI and international trade. In a few African countries, the transition was unfortunately in the wrong direction and proved counterproductive; from relative peace and stability to intensified civil wars and in certain cases genocide.

Many scholars who examined the causes or roots of poverty and poor growth in Africa have identified political opportunism, political violence and non-sustainable economic structures as some of the main contributors to this negative trend. Some researchers have also argued that the critical determinant of poor macroeconomic performance in Africa, and hence continued poverty and underdevelopment, was caused by policy mistakes by political leaders. Many governments in Africa have either been unwilling or been unable to perform their traditional duties of providing public goods and maintaining law and order. The failure to do so has resulted in the emergence of a significant sector of non-governmental organisations (NGOs), which have met the dire needs of many communities in the provision of basic services, such as health and education. In order for the state to perform its protective functions it must put structures in place that will be effective in maintaining law and order, and protecting the rights of people, which enhances entrepreneurial activity and maximises the welfare of its citizens. Included among these structures are an independent judiciary, press and central bank.

The economic structure of a country on the other hand will determine how much wealth is created, distributed and consumed. The economic structure consists of primary, secondary and tertiary sectors. The primary sector includes activities directly related to the extraction of natural resources, for example, the agricultural, mining and oil industries. The secondary sector covers goods of production such as manufacturing and construction. The tertiary sector covers all services such as banking, insurance and tourism.

Agriculture is Africa's largest economic sector representing 15% of the continent's GDP. It is highly concentrated, with Egypt and Nigeria producing 35% of the total output. Africa's agricultural potential is massively larger than its current output, and so are its food production requirements to feed the African populace. With more than 25% of the arable land in the world, it only generates about 10% of the global output. The literature supports the fact that productivity-led agricultural transformation can still play an important role in many African countries and can make agriculture an important driver of specifically early economic growth. While agricultural growth has been the precursor to the acceleration of industrial growth in a number of emerging economies such as China, Brazil and India, in Africa, current agricultural productivity seems to be very low.

Other sectors that experienced positive growth in the last decade are mining, oil, gas, consumer goods production, and the provision of services like banking, information technology and telecommunications. Despite early signs that economic growth is broadening across sectors, the global financial and economic crisis exposed one of the major weaknesses of a number of African economies: their dependence on too few export commodities to generate economic income. In this structure of economic production, it is not only important to consider what a country produces, but also who produces it. The main players here are the public versus the private sectors, and the formal versus the informal sectors. After economic independence most African governments pursued state-led economic development strategies based on import substitution, which was considered to be the answer to industrialisation. Governments created large state-owned enterprises in strategic sectors, and introduced trade barriers to protect domestic production.

In the 1980s several African countries put structural reforms in place that began unprecedented growth from the 1990s onward. Tanzania, Kenya and Zambia, for instance, dismantled state-led institutions in favour of privatisation. Their approach was to change the role of the state into a regulator and facilitator with the private sector driving economic growth. Entrepreneurship, and more specifically micro and small enterprises, constitutes the largest numbers of businesses in Africa and are also the main source of employment and income for the poor. The majority of these businesses are located in the informal sector. The informal sector is large and plays a critical role in Africa's economy. It is estimated that it represents 40% of GDP in sub-Saharan Africa ranging from under 30% in South Africa to 60% in Nigeria, Tanzania and Zimbabwe. It is also estimated that the informal sector represents about 75% of non-agricultural employment and is the biggest creator of new jobs.

Most of Africa's largest corporations are based in a handful of middle-income countries and are primarily in the extracting industry. One of the exceptions is that of South Africa whose big corporations account for the majority of market capitalisation of Africa's top 250 corporations. The private sector, including both big and small industries, dominates Africa's production and accounts for most of its total production. It seems, however, that Africa's growth is not inclusive as poverty and inequality remain high. The distribution and consumption of economic wealth remains a sensitive issue in Africa.

### 2.2.4   *Cultural and Social Structure*

Why do some countries do very well, while others fail to develop even if all the political and economic factors seem to be in place? A number of recent authors, proponents of the cultural dimension of growth, are suggesting that that it is the cultivation of values and attitudes that will in certain cases provide the stimulus for growth or alternatively restrain growth. Growth in a country will therefore first be embedded in the cultural and historical context of that country.

Although this cultural dimension will have strong historical roots, it can also change over time based on the development of thinking and beliefs influencing the main philosophies in a country. China was, for example, the world's most developed country in the Middle Ages and then stagnated, even went backwards partly because of nurturing a culture of self-sufficiency and control that led to the closing of its borders. In the 1980s, China decided to change this philosophy and deliberately decided to adopt a more 'open culture' that interacts more freely with the rest of the world. External or foreign influences can also have an effect on culture over time. The effect that globalisation had on culture, especially national cultures, is immense and diverse. In Africa, the loud echoing advertisement rhythms of Coca Cola soft drinks can be heard across boundaries in towns, cities and even in the most remote rural areas where drinking water and even bread are a problem to get hold of. It is well known that the introduction of cell phone technology in Africa changed information flow to people, and therefore had a direct influence on their beliefs and value systems. Other international trends also had permanent influences. Most of the African youth, for example, prefer international music to their local musical roots, and their hairstyles, shoes and clothing keep to the trends of the Western fashion scene.

A major advocate of the cultural paradigm in development, the renowned Kenyan scholar Professor Ali Mazrui (1991), has observed that cultural forces drive national behaviours, politics and affairs. In his book *Cultural Engineering in East Africa* he outlined four challenges facing the Africans: How to indigenise what was foreign; nationalise what was indigenous and sectional; and emphasise what was African?

Africa does not have a single universal culture but a bank of rich cultural heritages and value systems that on a daily basis influence the behaviour and attitudes of people. Many African counties are also characterised by diverse ethnical groups and cultures. Intuitively it makes sense that this diversity can complicate interaction amongst a smorgasbord of ethnic cultures, races, languages and values, sometimes resulting in discrimination and conflict situations, which can and have in some circumstances stunted African countries in their ability to develop.

## 2.3 The Creation of Growth Channels to Produce Wealth (Trunk of the Tree)

The creation of growth channels to produce wealth is reflected in The African Tree of Organic Growth's trunk. If one considers again the mighty Baobab, its roots are the conduit for water and nutrients to enter the tree, provide the foundation for the tree, and store nutrients and sugar. The massive trunk provides the strength to support the branches, leaves and fruit, and is a channel for transporting water and nutrients from the roots to these branches, leaves and fruit. Not only is there an upward flow, but the trunk also transports sugar down to the roots. The trunk, rather aptly, is often referred to as the plumbing system of the tree. Applying the analogy to the natural growth of a country means that the trunk of the tree will provide the growth channels for the creation of wealth upwards as well as the distribution of capital (sugar) downwards, stimulating a new cycle of growth for the tree.

The tree analogy also fits well into Alfred Marshall's concept of organic growth theory developed from his earlier works from 1873, an economic construct Marshall hoped would provide insight into alleviating poverty, hence a concept especially useful for African countries.

Kenichi Yamamoto and Susumu Egashira (2012) provide a useful interpretation of Marshall's organic growth theory, based on Marshall's and others' interpretation of the theory, in the following discussion.

Pivotal to organic growth theory is 'economic biology', where society, or in this instance a country, is treated as an organism. It articulates the relationship between humanity and the economy, and stresses the importance not only of economic growth, but also improvement in the quality of life—the well-being of mankind. Marshall emphasised that economic growth does not necessarily solve the problem of poverty; it does not result in the acquiring of skills by unskilled workers who don't make an effort to improve themselves due to harsh working conditions; and confirms that poverty is a hindrance to progress itself.

Organic growth is fundamentally different from other static economic theories of cause and effect (which Marshall regarded as imperfect)—rather organic growth 'evolves' and 'progresses' due to a multitude of factors with different influences. One critical aspect of progress is the progress of humanity which shifts the production function of economic growth.

The following are some important consequences of this theory and further insights from Marshall's organic growth theory:

1. "The progress of human nature accelerates economic growth and the resulting rise in the standard of life drives the progress of human nature … on the one hand, humans are labour resources that are important factors of production and other variables, and on the other hand, a human is a variable organism that is influenced by environmental changes" (Yamamoto and Egashira 2012: 237).
2. The development of the domestic market and international trade are essential to long-term growth prospects of any country.
3. Acquiring knowledge and education is fundamental to human progress and development.
4. The connection between time periods was termed the 'thread' of continuity and emphasised the evolutionary nature of progress.
5. The Business Sector played the role of a social leader, which Marshall termed 'chivalry', in utilising its wealth for society's benefit. "Economic progress would be achieved by businessman who acquired economic chivalry because a labour environment managed by such businessmen is much better and influences labour positively" (Yamamoto and Egashira 2012: 241).

In essence, Marshall's organic growth theory hypothesises that the development of humans and the 'chivalry' of business managers over generations is a necessary factor of economic growth which can contribute to the betterment of humanity's well-being.

A World Bank study entitled 'Can Africa Claim the 21st Century' (World Bank 2000) provides some pointers of what is necessary to achieve growth that is sustainable—the four pillars for sustainable growth in Africa:

1. Improving governance and resolving conflict
2. Investing in people
3. Increasing competitiveness and diversifying economies
4. Reducing aid dependency and strengthening partnerships

Governance and regulatory structures have had some of the biggest economic and historical impacts on the growth path of African countries. While ineffective and unethical governance can reverse good growth, good and supportive governance and policies will have an exponential effect on growth. Emerging economists also showed that countries in Africa have a key role to play in economic diversification and structural transformation. The success of the State will be determined not only by its involvement in the economic transformation process, but also by its capability to lead the country's growth process through a proper institutional and regulatory process. Africa also generally lags behind the rest of the world in terms of improving education and skills, infrastructure, and market development and diversification. No single country in Africa is in the exact same position and every African country will organically develop and grow into its own future state based on its available resources, structural sophistication, as well as level of economic diversification.

Leke et al. (2010) (excerpted from "What's driving Africa's growth", June 2010, McKinsey & Company, www.mckinsey.com Copyright © 2017 McKinsey & Company. All rights reserved. Reprinted by permission), in their useful analysis of the growth factors in Africa published by McKinsey & Company, identified four main development paths for different groups of countries in Africa based on their sophistication as follows:

1. **Diversified economies: Africa's growth engines**
   The continent's four most advanced economies: Egypt, Morocco, South Africa and Tunisia are already broadly diversified, especially into manufacturing and services. Domestic consumption is the largest contributor to growth in these countries. Africa's diversified economies, however, need to improve their education systems. Although they already have relatively high literacy rates, they need to build their competency and skills base, especially in technology and innovation, to ensure future growth.

2. **Oil exporters: enhancing growth through diversification**
   Africa's oil and gas exporters have the continent's highest GDP per capita but are also the least diversified economies. This group consists of Algeria, Angola, Chad, Congo, Equatorial Guinea, Gabon, Libya and Nigeria. Economic growth in these countries remains closely linked to oil and gas prices. The oil exporters generally have strong growth prospects if they are able to use their resource wealth to finance the broader development and diversification of their economies. The experience of other developing countries shows it will be essential to make continued investments in infrastructure and education and to undertake further economic reforms that would spur market and business growth. But like oil-rich countries in general, those in Africa face challenges in maintain-

ing political momentum for reforms, resisting the temptation to overinvest (particularly in the resource sector), and maintaining political stability—in short, they need to avoid the 'resource curse' that has impacted many other oil exporters of the world.

3. **Transition economies: building on current gains**

    Africa's transition economies—Cameroon, Ghana, Kenya, Mozambique, Senegal, Tanzania, Uganda and Zambia—have lower GDP per capita than the countries in the first two groups but have started with a process of diversification. These countries are diverse: some depend heavily on one commodity, such as copper in Zambia or aluminium in Mozambique, while others are slightly more diversified. The agriculture and resource sectors together account for as much as one-third of GDP in the transition countries and for two-thirds of their exports. These countries increasingly export manufactured goods, particularly to other African countries. Successful beneficiation attempts include processed fuels, processed food, chemicals, apparel and cosmetics. Expanding intra-African trade will be important for the future growth of these countries, because they are individually small but have the potential to grow this sector when regional integration creates larger markets. If these countries improve their infrastructure and regulatory systems they could also become globally more competitive. Local service sectors such as telecommunications, banking and retailing can also be attractive for diversification and investment.

4. **Pre-transition economies: strengthening the basics**

    The economies in the pre-transition segment—The Democratic Republic of the Congo, Ethiopia, Mali and Sierra Leone—are still very poor, with GDP per capita at about one-tenth of the diversified countries. Some, such as Ethiopia and Mali, have meagre commodity endowments and large rural populations. Others, devastated by wars in the 1990s, started growing after the conflicts ended. Some of the pre-transition economies are now growing very fast. The three largest (The Democratic Republic of the Congo, Ethiopia and Mali) grew, on average, by 7% per year between 2000 and 2010, after not expanding at all in the 1990s. Although the individual circumstances differ greatly, their common problem is lack of the basics such as strong stable governments and other public institutions, good macroeconomic conditions and sustainable agricultural development.

The key challenges for this group will include maintaining the peace, upholding the rule of law, getting the economic fundamentals right and creating a more predictable business environment. Poverty and social issues can also be addressed through agencies or philanthropic organisations. Some of these countries could also utilise their natural resources to finance economic growth. The Democratic Republic of the Congo, for example, controls half of the world's cobalt reserves and a quarter of the world's diamond reserves.

## 2.4 Creating Prosperity and Wealth for African Nations (Leaves and Fruit)

Economists traditionally measure prosperity in a country by using GDP per capita, which captures the values of all goods produced by the economy. Problems, however, exist when this statistical indicator is the only measure in developing countries like those in Africa. Prices do not exist for the public goods provided like health and family care and the informal sector is normally ignored. The Prosperity Index generated by the Legatum Institute (2016) provide a more comprehensive measurement of prosperity using a combination of variables based on economic wealth and quality of life including Economic Fundamentals, Entrepreneurship and Innovation, Education, Democratic Institutions, Governance, Health, Personal Freedom, Security and Social Capital. The World Bank in its publication 'Where is the Wealth of Nations' (2006) identified the capital generated by the country as the wealth of the nation and divided it into tangible and intangible capital with tangible capital representing the natural capital and produced capital and intangible capital representing the human capital and institutional capital.

Working towards a paradigm of organic growth in Africa means that communities must enjoy the fruits of this process and experience how the combined wealth generated improves their lives year after year. For the growth to be sustainable and for the tree to grow bigger it will be essential that the stock of capital be increased so that it can be reinvested in the next growth cycle to produce even better results. The framework developed in this book therefore clearly distinguishes between the wealth elements and the capital that must be generated by the growth process.

## References

Legatum Institute. 2016. The African Prosperity Index. [Online]. Available from: http://www.prosperity.com/rankings (accessed: 23 Jan 2017).

Leke, A., Lund, S., Roxbourg, C. and Van Wamelen, A. June 2010. Excerpted from "What's Driving Africa's Growth". McKinsey & Company. www.mckinsey.com. Copyright © 2017 McKinsey & Company. All rights reserved. Reprinted with permission. Accessed from: http://www.mckinsey.com/global-themes/middle-east-and-africa/whats-driving-africas-growth (accessed: 3 March 2017).

Mazrui, A. 1991. 'Cultural Engineering in East Africa In Edigin, L.U. Role of Culture in African Development'. *Pakistan Journal of Social Sciences 2010*, 7 (4): 295.

Ndulu, B. 2007. *Challenges of African Growth: Opportunities, Constraints, and Strategic Directions*. Washington, DC: World Bank. © World Bank. https://openknowledge.worldbank.org/handle/10986/6656 License: CC By 3.0 IGO.

Prahalad, C. and Hamel, G. May–June 1990. 'The Core Competence of the Corporation', *Harvard Business Review*, 68: 79–91.

World Bank. 2000. *Can Africa Claim the 21st Century*. Washington, DC. © World Bank. https://openknowledge.worldbank.org/handle/10986/22962 License: CC By 3.0 IGO.

World Bank. 2006. *Where Is the Wealth of Nations? Measuring Capital for the 21st Century*. Washington, DC. © World Bank. https://openknowledge.worldbank.org/handle/10986/7505 License: CC by 3.0 IGO.

Yamamoto, K. and Egashira, S. 2012. 'Marshall's Organic Growth Theory', *The European Journal of the History of Economic Thought*, 19 (2): 227–248. 1981.

CHAPTER 3

# Economic Growth and Diversification Fuelling Development in Africa

The question as to whether economic growth is reducing poverty and inequality is a highly debatable and controversial topic in Africa. The number of people living below the poverty threshold has decreased; however, due to population growth, there were more poor people in Africa in 2012 than in 1990. According to Zamfir's analysis published by the European Parliament Research Service, many dimensions of social well-being like literacy rates, life expectancy, malnutrition as well as the number of deaths from political violence have improved.

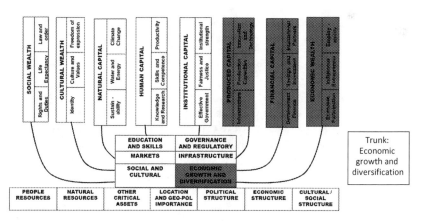

**Fig. 3.1** The African Tree of Organic Growth

© The Author(s) 2018
K. Jonker, B. Robinson, *China's Impact on the African Renaissance*,
https://doi.org/10.1007/978-981-13-0179-7_3

Economic growth and diversification is considered to be an important generator of country well-being (economic and social wealth) as well as country capital (financial, human, produced and institutional capital) needed for future growth (Fig. 3.1). The capability to produce this wealth and capital will be based on the resources, assets and structures available for growth as well as the integration, coordination and governance of the other support functions in the trunk, such as infrastructure, education and skills, and stimulation of the domestic market to get the maximum output. Economic growth and diversification were identified as part of the trunk of our African Tree of Organic Growth described in Chap. 2 and are described in the following text.

Despite the economic growth in the last two decades, Africa is the continent that has achieved the least progress on the United Nations Millennium Development Goals (now replaced by the 17 Sustainable Development Goals). This can be directly attributed to the way in which African countries were successful or not in transforming themselves on their growth path. Most Africans continue to earn their living in the primary sectors and the traditional economy. Oil and mineral extraction, and agriculture, play an important role in development, and employ more poor people than any other sector in Africa. Improvements in productivity, as well as diversification into more growth sectors, are needed to increase income and employment and reduce poverty.

## 3.1 THE CHALLENGE AND POTENTIAL OF ECONOMIC GROWTH IN AFRICA

### 3.1.1 Prominent Growth Sectors

The global financial and economic crises 2007 onwards and the oil crisis of 2014–2016 exposed the weaknesses of a number of African economies due to their dependence on a few export commodities, and only one or two economic sectors. Countries dependent on a few commodities are exposed to the boom and bust cycles of these commodities and need to progress to the next step in their development by diversifying into the beneficiation and effective utilisation of these commodities, or utilise the rents on those commodities to diversify into other products and industries. Countries that are in the early stages of economic development can therefore leverage their natural endowments to boost economic gains in niche sectors, which is the next logical step. While Africa's increased

**Table 3.1** Africa's GDP growth across sectors 2002–2007

| Economic sector | Percentage 100% = US$235 billion |
|---|---|
| Resources | 24 |
| Wholesale and retail | 13 |
| Agriculture | 12 |
| Transport and telecommunications | 10 |
| Manufacturing | 9 |
| Financial services | 6 |
| Public administration | 6 |
| Construction | 5 |
| Real estate and business services | 5 |
| Tourism | 2 |
| Utilities | 2 |
| Other Services (education, health, household services and social services) | 6 |
| Total | 100 |

Leke et al. (2010)

economic growth and momentum is widely recognised, its sources and differentiation in growth for different countries are less understood. Although a third of the economic growth since 2000 was still from basic commodities, the rest of the growth can be attributed to elements of diversification that have spurred the domestic economies in those countries. The sectorial share of Africa's GDP growth between 2002 and 2007 is given in Table 3.1.

*Resources*
A country that has abundant resources does not need to import certain raw materials and can fuel its growth through income gained from exporting these resources. These commodities are the primary factors of production and the availability of a specific and sometimes scarce resource can give that country a comparative advantage in trade. Those who have few, little or no resources will need to import everything for their industries. Africa has a large quantity of natural resources and much of its resources are still inaccessible or undiscovered. Despite this abundance of natural resources, some authors suggest that Western nations like the United States and Europe as well as emerging nations like China and India often exploit Africa's natural resources, causing the benefits and value to go to the West and Asia rather than to Africa, thus causing poverty in Africa.

It is well known that natural resources do not necessarily change the growth prospects of resource-rich countries. Academic researchers in fact discovered in certain countries a direct linkage between resource wealth and economic, political and social misfortunes. This is termed 'The Resource Curse'. Recent contributions challenge the conventional wisdom of 'the resource curse' and provide evidence that natural resources are not a curse per se, but that their impact on growth is constrained when the resource becomes the source of conflict, or corruption and inefficiency. Nigeria was traditionally considered a leading example of 'the resource curse', struggling to grow its economy based on its resource wealth. Nigeria has, however, made considerable progress in investing the rents of its oil resources in diversification and growth for the economy. Nigeria is one of the cases that we will discuss further in the chapter.

Resources that are managed and utilised well can have a positive effect on growth. Resource-rich countries in sub-Saharan Africa have generally recorded higher rates of economic growth than other countries since 2000. It unfortunately also shows that the population as a whole has not necessarily benefited from this increased economic growth.

Exploitation of the resource base is still the most likely route to prosperity for African countries with an abundance of natural resources. Botswana has already transformed itself from an impoverished desert country to a middle-income country status via this route. Other resource-rich countries can therefore, with the correct guidance and support, use these rents to support diversification of their export bases, thereby reducing their dependence on natural resources. A first step could be to create appropriate value chains both upstream and downstream of commodities extraction, to maximise local employment and skills. A good example that took place in Botswana, a country rich in diamonds, is the development of a local industry for the processing of rough diamonds. Focusing on high-value, low-weight product proved to be suitable for Botswana, a landlocked country with high transportation costs. A country which is resource-rich should therefore exploit these resources to increase the range of exports and goods the country produces, especially through beneficiation.

*Agriculture*
There are different views on the role of agriculture in Africa's growth and development. There is a view that advocates a rapid move from agriculture into manufacturing while others argue that productivity-led

agricultural transformation can play an active role in economic transformation and growth. Evidence from other developing countries strongly suggests that agriculture can be an engine of growth, especially in the early stages of development of a country, and, therefore, also an important force for employment creation and poverty reduction. Most food products in Africa are imported, and weigh heavily on the balance of payments of a country.

Africa possesses the basic elements for successful agriculture: uncultivated arable land (about half of what is available in the world) and good water resources. Despite this, agricultural transformation in Africa has been slow, and productivity is still way below yield potentials. Landownership and capital for investment are also obstacles for growth in this sector. Because of the importance of the sector to provide employment and reduce poverty, the World Bank suggested in its 2008 World Development Report that the sector must be placed at the centre of the development agenda if the Millennium Development Goals of halving extreme poverty and hunger are to be met. The literature is replete with examples of productivity-led agricultural transformation playing a central role in the economic growth and development of countries, especially through the creation of upstream and downstream activities, as the sector starts growing. Madagascar has, for instance, through this process, started to turn their raw cocoa production into expensively wrapped milky and nutty bars.

*Infrastructure*
Inadequate infrastructure in Africa is considered to be one of the biggest factors preventing economic growth, trade integration and poverty reduction. Transport costs are among the highest in the world, and insufficient and unreliable electricity hinders diversification and industrialisation. There is therefore a strong drive to provide needed infrastructure, and the construction of this infrastructure constitutes in itself a boost to economic growth. Some countries have made building of infrastructure one of their main drivers of growth, following China's model.

According to the Africa Infrastructure Development Index (2013) produced by the African Development Bank (AfDB), improvements in infrastructure in the last decade were driven mostly by the provision of information and communications technology (ICT), and to a lesser extent, access to water and sanitation. It shows further that energy provision stagnated and transportation development was limited. Overall, African transportation infrastructure development has been inadequate, with the share of paved roads remaining low and few new rail developments. This has contributed to high export costs, especially in landlocked countries.

*Services*
Services have been the fastest-growing sector in most African countries. As indicated in Table 3.1 the growth in services was mainly in the areas of transport and telecommunications, financial services like banking, business services and tourism. The growth in the telecommunications sector, including its influence on other sectors, has had a big impact on the economy. The use of cell phones and cellular phone technology has exploded directly because of the absence in most African countries of a landline infrastructure. These new technologies are penetrating remote areas, bringing not only effective communication services, but also giving them access to the world of information, knowledge and markets. Financial services have also grown quickly, often founded on innovative business models based on technology platforms, giving a better and more effective service to the 'bottom of the pyramid' in Africa.

*Tourism*
Tourism has only shown moderate growth in the twentieth century with a small proportion of these being international tourists. Whilst Africa has a smorgasbord of tourism products, crime, conflict and terrorism severely compromise the potential of this industry.

*Wholesale and Retail*
The wholesale and retail sectors are also growing quickly due to growth of the middle-class consumer group in Africa. For instance, Shoprite/Checkers, Carrefour and Walmart respectively from South Africa, France and the United States have all expanded their operations to Africa. This can directly be attributed to the increase in consumer spending in Africa, which is having a significant impact on the growth of domestic markets in African countries. Africa's long-term growth will increasingly reflect inter-related economic and social changes creating new domestic engines of growth. Key among these will be urbanisation, an expanding labour force and the rise of the middle-class African consumer (Leke et al. 2010).

*Manufacturing*
Industrial production is low in Africa and is concentrated mainly in northern African countries such as Algeria, Egypt, Morocco and Tunisia, and in

South Africa in the south (Zamfir 2016). According to Zamfir, chemical and petroleum industries, coal, rubber and metal manufacturing are the leading heavy industries. Agro-processing and manufacturing of textiles, leather products and building materials, like cement, is also taking place. The automotive industry is very strong in South Africa and is established in other countries like Egypt, Kenya, Nigeria, Algeria and Morocco.

Africa has the opportunity to grow its manufacturing base in a broad range of industries. Beneficiation of resources seems to be a very logical first step, while the growing middle-class population can provide growth for consumer industries like food processing, furniture and lifestyle goods, as well as personal care products. Secondary industries such as construction and infrastructure should also have good future potential. Africa needs to develop a strong value-added manufacturing base. About one-third of China's GDP came from manufacturing while countries like Nigeria, Kenya and Zambia are still on levels of about 10%. The main constraints for manufacturing in Africa are factors of low productivity, lack of efficiencies of scale, insufficient skills and an under-capacitated infrastructure base.

*Trade*
The export of commodities has contributed greatly to the economic growth of Africa, especially in the last 15 years but has decreased since the global economic crisis in 2008. Intra-African trade also increased significantly, much of which is intra-regional, with a growing proportion being manufactured goods, indicating that diversification is starting to hold (Zamfir 2016). The African Union also recently launched a project to create a pan-continental free trade area by 2017 that will further boost intra-African trade. Economic and trade integration across Africa will help foreign investors to access larger markets and reduce transaction costs.

Trade patterns in Africa are changing with new products, new trading partners and new technologies, all influencing the way African countries trade with each other and with the world. China has now become Africa's top trading partner, and Africa is now China's major import source and fourth largest investment destination.

### 3.1.2 Economic Transformation and Growth Drivers

Economic transformation entails the evolutionary process of developing new growth sectors and activities out of the traditional sectors. Economic transformation is therefore a process (normally led by the government) to promote diversified production and export competitiveness, resulting in progress over time from low-output activities to high-productivity activities. It should facilitate social well-being through more equal income distribution, skills development and employment. Most African countries have traditionally suffered from a lack of economic diversification and sophistication. Countries with more diversified production and exports tend to have higher per capita incomes and have grown faster. Economic transformation will vary greatly between African countries based on their current sectors of growth and their stage of organic development.

*Resource Diversification*
The African Economic Outlook Report (2015) emphasised that structural transformation must start with the natural resource sector, because of the fact that natural resources will remain the continent's comparative advantage for a long time to come. The overarching objective should therefore be to create a diversified resource-based economy. Poverty persists because there are not enough good jobs. African countries should diversify their natural resource sector in order to diversify their manufacturing. On the other hand, they have to achieve large-scale agricultural transformation. The Report recommends putting in place the right framework conditions for structural transformation, optimising the revenues from natural resources and investing them wisely into new diversification initiatives.

Agriculture is an important driver of growth in developing countries and can have a multiplier effect in reducing poverty because of its ability to create employment for local communities. Many African governments have put agriculture back on the top of their development agenda and have increased their budget allocations for this important sector. Private investment in African agricultural value chains have also increased in recent years paving the way for a renaissance in Africa's agro-food systems.

Development of the agricultural sector within broader economic development can have a number of outcomes: Urbanisation creates an exodus of people from rural areas allowing those remaining on agricultural land to become more efficient; trade of agricultural products allows for farming specialisation; regional trade increases the opportunity of becoming more profitable; opportunities arise for other types of agricultural businesses to emerge; technology usage improves efficiencies of scale; and the agricultural sector becomes a main-stream contributor to economic growth and development.

Growth in the agricultural sector has accelerated in countries like Ghana, Kenya, Zambia, Ethiopia and Rwanda in the last 10 years. A supporting economic, institutional and policy environment should be at the heart of an African agricultural revolution. This includes the need for domestic, African and international markets that can absorb the increase in production; the need to empower farmers with skills and technology; linking production to an agro-industry; and accommodating small-scale farmers in the process. China's development path and growth experience can provide valuable lessons for developing countries, especially those in Africa. A primary resource transformation process is illustrated in Fig. 3.2.

China's economic and social conditions were very similar to those of African countries when the People's Republic of China was founded in 1949. The government inherited a war-torn agrarian economy with high poverty levels for most of its citizens. In 1978, China embarked on an economic reform and development process, which started with agricultural reforms that progressed into industrial diversification and trade liberalisation. China has, through its household responsibility policy, improved agricultural productivity by giving farmers more freedom to experiment and produce. Unlike most African countries, the Chinese government played a critical role in facilitating and guiding this economic growth.

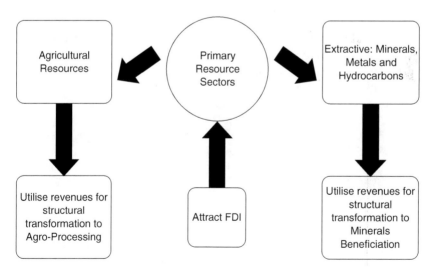

**Fig. 3.2** Primary resource transformation. (Authors' own)

## Industrialisation and Special Economic Zones (SEZs)

Africa has experienced a decline in manufacturing share over the last two decades. This failure to industrialise Africa can be attributed to insufficient infrastructure, ineffective industrial policies, small market size, low productivity, companies' orientation towards exports and limited firm capabilities. Manufacturing has provided a constant 6% of all jobs in Africa over the last three decades, failing to transfer job opportunities from the primary to the secondary sectors. African countries cannot afford to remain marginal players in manufacturing if they want to make progress in growth and development. One of the targets of the United Nations Sustainable Development Goals adopted in September 2015 is to encourage sustainable industrialisation that will increase employment creation as GDP, especially in least developed countries. Recognising the vital importance of industry for the economic development of the continent, the African Union in 2011 adopted the 'Action Plan for the Accelerated Industrial Development of Africa'. The main priorities identified in the Action Plan of the African Union are the creation of a relevant Industrial Policy, Institutions Infrastructure Development and Human Capital Development. "The rapid growth of developing countries like China makes it clear that constraints to manufactured-led growth are not insurmountable and can be achieved by certain African countries while other[s] may not be ready for that." This approach has the advantages of generating broad-based benefits because it creates many jobs, and enables rapid growth of the economy. One small African country, Mauritius, has already transformed itself from an impoverished sugar island to a middle-income diversified economy that is globally competitive in manufacturing.

About a decade ago China announced it would develop a series of Special Economic Zones (SEZs) in Africa to attract foreign investment, boost economic growth and facilitate trade in these countries. These zones provide various tax benefits and enable the setting up of business with streamlined bureaucratic processes for investing and operating in these zones. No less than 50 such economic zones were planned, but less than half of them are yet operational.

SEZs aim to make foreign direct investment (FDI) in industries attractive, which in turn will contribute to greater levels of employment, export-led growth and industrial diversification of the country. SEZs operate through different structures and include export-processing zones, economic processing zones, enterprise zones, free ports, free zones, foreign trade zones, industrial parks, single factories and specialised zones. China successfully introduced SEZs in the 1970s as part of its vision to open its economy to international trade. China first set up zones in the southern coastal areas, and Shenzhen, a small fishing town, became the first SEZ. It is now the most prominent manufacturing hub on the globe. China's success with their SEZs inspired African countries and became the benchmark for the establishment of so-called Chinese-driven SEZ developments in Egypt, Mauritius, Nigeria, Zambia and Ethiopia. More are planned and a Special Economic Zones Act was also recently approved and passed in South Africa (Kim 2015).

Industrial diversification was fundamental to China's African Policy 2016 and the African Union's Agenda. The Forum on China–Africa Cooperation (FOCAC) Summit in Johannesburg in 2015 identified action plans aimed at industry partnering and capacity cooperation between China and Africa to enhance the economic diversification initiatives for Africa. The cooperation also agreed to improve SEZs and jointly establish a number of industrial parks. In East Africa, pilot projects for industrial parks linked to specific economic sectors were established. These include manufacturing for export in Kenya as well as footwear production facilities in Ethiopia. Adeyeye (2016) offered several reasons why SEZs and Industrial Parks are still struggling in most cases to deliver the fruits enhancing diversification and ultimately the well-being of its citizens. According to Adeyeye, African countries should take responsibility and be more proactive on the following issues:

1. There should be a strong linkage between SEZs and local companies, especially small and medium-sized enterprises.
2. Industrial development policies and even laws should be adjusted to remove obstacles for investment and improve ease of doing business. (China improved the regulatory environment and tax policies for trade and investment to make its zones more attractive.)
3. Zone cluster development within the unique value chains of the specific country should be the central theme of these developments. (China and Singapore are good examples of where this was done effectively.)
4. Interaction with training institutes, research centres and universities should be encouraged to integrate research, innovation and technological advancement based on country knowledge and capabilities ('soft' structure is therefore important when it comes to attracting investors).

5. Development of zones should be linked to the longer-term vision of the region and country, and not be focused on the achievement of short-term gains.
6. Social and environmental effects that can arise if a zone is not properly managed must be considered.

Africa's cooperation with China in industrialisation should be welcomed; however, it should not be seen as a reason to be passive, but rather be proactive, to ensure that structural transformation is achieved in the correct manner.

## 3.2 Alternative Paths to Growth and Development in Africa

The organic growth in each country will be determined by a natural evolution that normally starts from an existing base of assets, structures and resources (roots) and then transforms, over time, to a more diversified and sophisticated system and structure, as it grows and develops. Governments must lead this structural transformation process with futuristic visions, strategic plans and policies that will promote manufacturing and industrialisation based on indigenous resources, country comparative advantages and capabilities of domestic firms. The process is depicted in Fig. 3.3.

The Strategic Process will start with an evaluation of the current structures, resources and industrial base, in terms of their current contribution to growth, future growth and employment potential, as well as policy frameworks supporting the relevant industries. Indigenous challenges and capabilities should then be considered in line with domestic and global market opportunities. The indigenous challenges and capabilities will be based on available assets, infrastructure and energy, education and skills levels, governance and policy, as well as productivity levels and technology available. Competitive advantages will first be developed in domestic markets with the potential to broaden benefits with exports to international markets. The industrial strategy and policy should link directly to the domestic economy to ensure that spillovers benefit other sectors in the economy. Existing industries should be further developed upstream and downstream, or new industries identified based on the level of diversification.

A dynamic industrial policy is required between the government and the private sector aimed at the successful implementation of an industrial

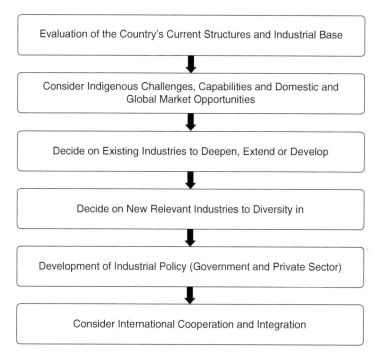

**Fig. 3.3** Strategic process for the industrial transformation of a country

vision and strategy. The industrial policy has to respond to the requirements of free markets and at the same time contribute to the social concerns and expectations of the citizens. Such industrial policies should also be aligned to other supporting policy areas such as macroeconomic and financial policies to improve successful execution. A critical evaluation of past policy successes and failures should inform every new policy cycle to enhance the policy-learning process. International cooperation and integration such as South–South or intra-African can now be considered based on industrial strategy objectives and funding requirements. The government needs to consult with the private sector when identifying new opportunities, markets and new sectors, in order to ensure private sector buy-in and support. Good governance is critical to the creation of an enabling environment for industrialisation and economic diversification.

As previously referred, Leke et al. (2010) identify four different growth trajectories for countries based on their levels of economic diversification and exports per capita as follows: Oil and Gas Exporters are countries such as Nigeria and Angola, which have some of the continent's highest GDP per capita, but are also the least diversified economies. Pre-Transition Economies are countries like Ethiopia and Mali, where the economy is still in a very early stage of development, and lacks some of the basic enablers of development, such as good governance structures and sustainable agricultural development. Transition Economies, for example Kenya and Zambia, have started with a process of diversification. Diversified Economies are Africa's four most advanced economies, Egypt, Morocco, South Africa and Tunisia, which are already broadly diversified, especially in the manufacturing and service sectors.

## 3.3 Organic Growth in Africa: Impact of China on Growth and Diversification

Many people in Africa have lost faith in the idea that economic growth can improve their lives. Instead of seeing value in economic growth and diversification, they see only uncertainty about their futures, growing inequalities and few social benefits. Too few people benefit and experience the fruits of economic growth and diversification, and too many face the spectre of conflict, mismanagement, corruption and poverty. With globalisation in retreat and nationalism on the rise, this pessimistic mood sometimes limits the potential of investment, growth and trade to improve the lives of the country's citizens.

Although economic growth in itself cannot solve all the problems of Africa, it is the most important cornerstone of the organic growth of any country, and therefore plays an extremely important role in uplifting any community. A poor economic foundation and lack of funds and investment have always been factors limiting development in African countries. Since 2009, Africa has seen a decrease in total inward total FDI, while China's share of FDI increased.

Manufacturing is one of China's main and growing focus areas for investment in Africa. Although the biggest investment by China is still in mining, China's investment in the manufacturing sector is growing. Chinese enterprises have also invested in other sectors in Africa such as finance, business services and science and technology services. By the end of 2012, China's direct investment in Africa's financial sector had reached US$3.87 billion. There are also many small and medium Chinese investors engaged in agricultural processing and production in Africa.

In this section of the chapter we will look at the impact of China on the growth trajectories of two African countries, more specifically their impact on the growth and diversification strategies, as well as the primary and secondary advantages, from this relationship. Let us start with Kenya, the leading economy in East Africa which has made great strides in boosting certain sectors like tourism and telecommunications. The other case study considers Nigeria, a leading economy in West Africa, an oil exporter achieving a certain degree of success in economic diversification.

## 3.4 The Case of Kenya

Kenya is the leading economy in East Africa, and its strategic location and well-developed business infrastructure make it an attractive destination for investment. Kenya is a politically stable country that encourages investment with its pro-business supportive stance. Although Kenya does not have the concentration of natural resources that China requires, it offers a gateway to East and Central African regions and markets. More information on the country is provided in Table 3.2.

Kenya lies across the equator on the east of the African continent. Its neighbouring countries are Ethiopia to the north, Somalia to the east, Tanzania to the south, Uganda to the west and Sudan to the north-west.

Table 3.2  Background to Kenya

**Population**: 46 million
**Cities**: Capital: Nairobi (population 3.4 million). Other major cities: Nakuru (1.3 million), Mombasa (850,000), Kisumu (650 000), Meru (250,000) and Eldoret (200,000)
**Ethnic groups**: Kikuyu 22%, Luhya 14%, Luo 13%, Kalenjin 12%, Kamba 11%, Kisii 6%, Meru 6%, other African 15%, non-African (Asian, European and Arab) 1%
**Languages**: English (official), Kiswahili (official), numerous indigenous languages
**Religions**: Christian 82.5%, Muslim 11.1%, Other 6.4%
**Government**: Executive (President and Cabinet), Legislative (Bicameral Parliament), Judicial
**Location**: Eastern Africa, bordering the Indian Ocean, and Ethiopia, Somalia, South Sudan, Tanzania and Uganda
**Climate**: Varies from tropical along coast to arid in the interior
**Terrain**: Low plains rise to central highlands bisected by Great Rift Valley; fertile plateau in the west
**Industry**: Manufacturing sector 14% of GDP

Authors' compilation from a variety of sources

The land rises from a low coastal plain on the Indian Ocean, in a series of mountain ridges and plateaus, to above 9000 metres in the centre of the country. There are eight main tribes, with each tribe having its own distinct cultural practices and unique language. Religion is integrated into almost every aspect of life with Christianity the most prevalent (82.5%). Islam comprises 11.1% of the population and is growing very rapidly with the immigration of many Somalian refugees to the country. The adult literacy rate is around 74%, while life expectancy is only 60 years of age. Over 40% of the nation is unemployed, and of those employed, 75% are in the agricultural sector and 25% in other sectors such as the manufacturing and services sectors.

### 3.4.1 Economic Growth and Diversification

According to the World Bank, Kenya's GDP was US$60.94 billion in 2014. The GDP annual growth rate in Kenya averaged an impressive 5.4% for the period 2004–2015. This economic growth was mainly supported by the expansion into agro-processing, construction, manufacturing, financial services, communications and information technology, and wholesale and trade. One of the previously stronger sectors of the economy, tourism, shrank by 11% since the Westgate Mall attack on 13 September 2013.

The Kenyan economy is more diversified than most of the economies in Africa. Tourism and agriculture are the traditional pillars of Kenya's economy, with tourism the strongest and with much potential for further growth. In agriculture, tea is Kenya's top agricultural product, while horticulture production is growing rapidly. Kenya is strategically well located on the Indian Ocean, facing Asia, with access to key shipping lanes between the Mediterranean and the Indian Ocean. This geographic advantage is an important consideration in the challenge of greater diversification of the Kenyan economy (Economic Diversification in Africa 2011).

Kenya has seen success in diversifying the agricultural and tourism sectors. The top export products of the last decade are tea, flowers, vegetables and coffee. Other successes include the diversification into financial services and information technologies. The East African region in which Kenya operates is relatively strong, diversified and well-integrated. The East African region includes three large states, namely Kenya, Tanzania and Uganda—countries well balanced in terms of size, economic growth and population, and that can therefore directly benefit from regional integration (Economic Diversification in Africa 2011).

The Kenyan government system has been relatively well developed, with solid policies and regulatory frameworks. The Kenyan government played an important role in the last decade to guide and support growth sectors. The Kenyan horticulture sector is a good example where government support of the sector helped it to grow to the extent that Kenyan flower exports have surpassed the traditional leading products of tea and coffee. The other important government initiative is Vision 2030, compiled in 2007, representing the government's main vision and policy for the future development of Kenya. The vision has economic diversification as the main thrust, and builds on the core economic capabilities of the country. The main aims and objectives of the vision are summarised in Fig. 3.4.

The vision is based on thee 'pillars', namely the Economic Pillar, the Social Pillar and the Political Pillar, and integrates the future growth prospects in a similar way to the 'African Tree of Organic Growth' paradigm

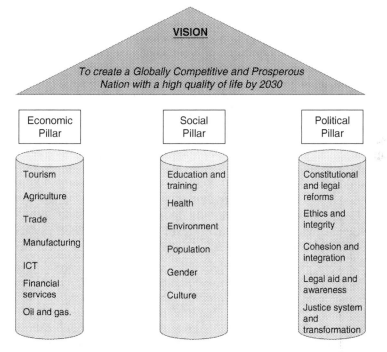

Fig. 3.4   Kenya Vision 2030. (Authors' depiction)

developed in Chap. 2 and used throughout this book. Kenya's Vision 2030 aims to transform Kenya into a newly industrialised middle-income country, providing a high quality of life to all citizens by the year 2030. The main economic target is to increase economic growth to an ambitious 10% per annum. The Economic Pillar aims at providing prosperity for all Kenyans while the Social Pillar seeks to build "a just and cohesive society with social equity in a clean and secure environment". The Political Pillar aims at realising a democratic political system founded on issue-based politics that respects the rule of law and protects the rights and freedoms of every individual in Kenyan society.

The public–private cooperation in Kenya is good and is represented in the National Economic and Social Council (NESC), which is directly linked to the office of the Presidency. The Kenyan Private Sector Alliance has been especially active in engaging with the government to create a stable environment to support business development in Kenya (Economic Diversification in Africa 2011). Existing transport corridors are being revamped with new government support. One prominent example is the transport corridor from the harbour of Mombasa in Kenya to Uganda, and eventually to Rwanda and the Democratic Republic of the Congo (DRC). Vision 2030 has been largely built around the Mombasa–Nairobi corridor and now includes a new northern corridor from Lamu on the north coast of Kenya into Sudan and Ethiopia. Vision 2030 has also capitalised from the Kenyan position vis-à-vis the Southern Corridor from Dar es Salaam to Burundi (Economic Diversification in Africa 2011).

Kenya's natural resources include rich biodiversity and natural attractions, which form the basis for their successful tourism sector. It also has a strong agricultural sector based on the quality of soil and arable land. Human capital development is good in Kenya with a literacy rate as high as 72%. Programmes are offered by the public and private sectors to build capabilities, especially in sectors like tourism. Kenya invests strongly in research and development and nurtures a healthy level of cooperation between universities and businesses. Growth strategies have been directly linked to human resource development.

Kenya is linked to its neighbours Uganda and Tanzania by their littoral positions around Lake Victoria. These countries had formed a regional relationship through the East African Community (EAC), and Rwanda and Burundi subsequently joined. The transformation of the EAC into a full common market in 2009 opened the way for east African economic integration as well as a diversified regional economy (Economic Diversification in Africa 2011). The regional integration provides wonderful opportunities for the Kenyan government to achieve greater diversification in its own economy. Kenya is also a leading country in the region in its dealings with the European Union, China and other key development partners. The Kenyan government has also emphasised good relations with other Indian Ocean countries in the Gulf.

### 3.4.2 Impact of China on the Organic Growth of Kenya

China views Kenya as an attractive country in Africa to do business with. The reason for this is that Kenya is a war-free country with a stable political framework and a good policy structure to support growth in the future. Kenya is strategically located and functions as the economic, technological and logistical hub of East Africa.

The relationship between China and Kenya can be divided into three historical periods as indicated in Table 3.3.

China's FDI Stock in Kenya has grown exponentially from US$26 million in 2003 to US$403 million in 2012. The provision of sufficient road infrastructure was, and continues to be, a top priority in the development of Kenya; China has seized the opportunity to build major transport links in the country. China's provision of finance capital for Kenyan roads began in 2003 and has resulted in the construction of 905 kilometres of road in 2006 and the investment of US$227.6 million to rehabilitate the Nairobi–Mombasa road. Chinese firms have also, for example, eased traffic congestion in Nairobi with the construction of several bypasses, as well as built a link road to the international airport. The China Road and Bridge Corporation is also constructing a 609 kilometre section of the Standard Gauge Railway (SGR) linking Nairobi and Mombasa for US$13.6 billion, while the China Communication Construction Company is building three berths at the port of Lamu Island for US$467 million (Sanghi and Johnson 2016). China has also significantly increased its funding of other Kenyan infrastructure projects including energy generation, modernisation of power distribution, electrification and a range of water projects (Mulinge 2012).

FDI to Kenya has increased significantly since 2010, topping US$500 million in 2013 and nearly US$990 million in 2014, of which China, the United Kingdom, the Netherlands and Belgium were the contributors. Most of the economic sectors are open for investment, although the

**Table 3.3** Summary of historical relations between Kenya and China

| Time | Relationship detail |
|---|---|
| 1963–1978<br>President: Jomo Kenyatta Era | Diplomatic cooperation between Kenya and China:<br>Anti-piracy cooperation<br>Bridges cooperation<br>Oil exploration cooperation |
| 1978–2002<br>President: Daniel Arap Moi Era | No new developments or further cooperation during this era |
| 2002–2013<br>President: Mwai Kibaki Era<br>2013–2016<br>President: Uhuru Kenyatta (son of Kenya's first president) | In this era, the cooperation between Kenya and China was deepened and expanded:<br>High-level political contacts and diplomatic relations followed by a series of agreements<br>Agreement covering official development assistance, investment and loans (EXIM Bank) for the following projects:<br>Road Infrastructure (2003, 2010, 2015)<br>Development of agricultural sector (2003, 2007, 2010)<br>Power distribution modernisation and strengthening (2005, 2007, 2010)<br>Standard gauge railway (SGR) (2013)<br>Telecommunications development (2005, 2007, 2009)<br>Government development and assistance which include office equipment (2004), technical training (2005) and e-governance (2010)<br>Economic and Technical cooperation (2005)<br>Drilling of 26 wells for geothermal energy (2014)<br>Social aid and assistance to Kenya which included an international Sport Centre (2003), Chinese courses (2003), Confucius Institute at Nairobi University and Eldoret Hospital (2010) |

Authors' own compilation

telecommunications sector has attracted the most foreign investment due to the arrival of fibre optics during 2009 and 2010.

The 'ease of doing business' increased substantially with the development of public–private partnerships based on 'Vision 2030', as well as their simplified procedures for business creation. Kenya currently has more than 400 Chinese firms spread across every sector. China invests mostly in metals, communications and automotive original equipment manufacturing (OEM).

One of the major concerns regarding Kenya's economy is its negative trade balance with net exports that have fallen by 14.74% per year between

2000 and 2014, reaching a low of negative US$12.2 billion in 2014 (Sanghi and Johnson 2016). The growing domestic market in Kenya is demanding more but instead of producing more they are importing more. According to Sangi and Johnson, Kenya's weak exports are directly linked to an underperforming manufacturing sector that has remained at only 10% of the GDP. Kenya still relies heavily on its agricultural and commodity exports like coffee, tea and flowers. Kenya's diversification is also concentrated on agricultural diversification like vegetable textile fibres, leather rawhide skins and flowers, and not enough on industrial diversification. Authors directly attribute this to insufficient infrastructure, high cost of doing business, and cheap imports and big trade deficit with China and India. Chinese imports have hurt textile and clothing producers, a sector that represents 20% of all manufacturing employment in Kenya. China is also selling a large amount of internationally branded second-hand clothing and shoes in Kenya. Although consumers in Kenya have benefitted from these cheaper imported products, the diversification into manufacturing has suffered due to the difficulty in competing domestically with these products. SEZs for manufacturing in Kenya have poor infrastructure and the infrastructure at the Port of Mombasa is problematic. Kenya's exports to China are insignificant—in the region of only 1%. The main reason for this is that Kenya is an oil importer and is a country that has relatively scarce resources.

It was found that Chinese businesses do localise their workforce—a term to describe the employment of local workers. China was the fifth largest creator of jobs, with India in the top position in this regard, for the period 2003–2015. Chinese companies hire fewer female employees at only 5%, compared to about 30% overall female employees in Kenya (Sanghi and Johnson 2016).

Workers are also trained in basic skills and safety, but technology and skills transfer in the larger projects are not always effective—as a result of Kenya not always maximising opportunities for local capacity-building. The language barrier obviously also represents a challenge in training (Sanghi and Johnson 2016).

Chinese companies identified corruption as the most significant obstacle to doing business in Kenya. Chinese companies in Kenya are also importing most of their inputs from China and buying less than 10% of their inputs from local suppliers, although this is mostly a function of availability and cost. Local manufacturers were, for example, only able to supply cement and a negligible amount of steel to the Single Gauge Railway

Project, while other inputs were mostly imported from China. Local manufacturers therefore missed a valuable opportunity for capacity-building, knowledge sharing and job creation.

Kenya ranks 109th globally in the 2014 Prosperity Index, an improvement of seven places from the previous year, showing that overall prosperity has increased. Kenya's best performance was in the Social Capital sub-index where it ranked 60th in 2014. Kenya's worst performance and ranking was in the Safety and Security sub-index where it ranked 132nd. This was a result of several countries issuing travel warnings in 2014 following several attacks by Al-Shabab militants on a shopping centre, police station and tourism resort in the same year. Unfortunately, things didn't get better with the attack at Garissa University College in the north-west of Kenya where 148 people were killed. One of Kenya's worst scores is in the Corruption Perception Index, where it is ranked 145th out of 175 and only 36th in sub-Saharan Africa.

The effect of China on the economic growth and diversification of Kenya is summarised in Fig. 3.5.

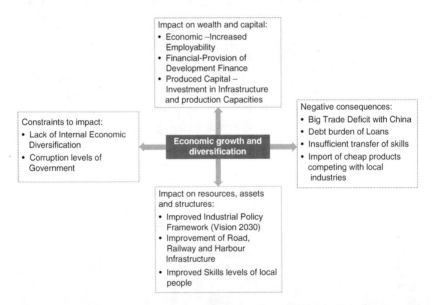

**Fig. 3.5** The impact of China on the economic growth and diversification of Kenya

Kenya is not endowed with natural resources such as oil and gas, although an offshore exploration deal was signed with China to drill exploring wells in six blocks in the country. China is providing critical funding and loans to several road, railway and other infrastructure projects in Kenya. One of the more recent is the US$13 billion railway project that will link Nairobi with the Port of Mombasa. It is hoped that the track will shorten the journey between the two cities from 12 to 4 hours. Passenger trains will travel at 120 kilometres per hour, and freight trains will be able to transport an estimated 25 million tonnes per year. The railway line is a direct link into the East African Railway masterplan and will create a direct link with Juba in Southern Sudan, Kampala in Uganda, Kigali in Rwanda and Bujumbura in Burundi, which aims to contribute towards a politically united and secure East Africa. The railway is being built by the state-owned China Road and Bridge Corporation (CRBC) and is being financed by the Exim Bank of China. The hope is that the new railway will also reduce congestion on Kenya's road network and promote tourism. Controversy has not been absent as the new railway will cut into Nairobi's wildlife sanctuary, and unrest erupted after local communities felt that not enough jobs were reserved for them in the project.

It is clear from the evidence provided in this section that China is funding the necessary infrastructure projects in Kenya. Not only is this providing an enabling base for economic growth and diversification as envisioned in Vision 2030, but it is also injecting real money into the economy.

Knowledge and technology transfer, which is critical to a developing nation such as Kenya, is not as effective as it should be—Kenya needs to be proactive in this regard to ensure that the benefits from the relationship are reaped and integrated. This can be done through strategic alliance or joint venture arrangements between Chinese companies and Kenyan counterparts, or by setting quota targets for local technical and managerial staff on infrastructure projects.

A map of the envisaged railway line connections connecting neighbouring Juba in South Sudan, Uganda, Rwanda and Burundi via Nairobi in Kenya to the Port of Mombasa is depicted in Map 3.1.

Agriculture is still the most important economic sector in Kenya and food processing the most important sub-sector. Coffee, flowers and tea are the most prolific export products. China's transition to a consumption-based economy by 2030 can benefit specifically the horticultural sector, which is already selling cut flowers directly to large supermarkets in Asia. To do this, Kenya should negotiate duty-free access for its cut-flower

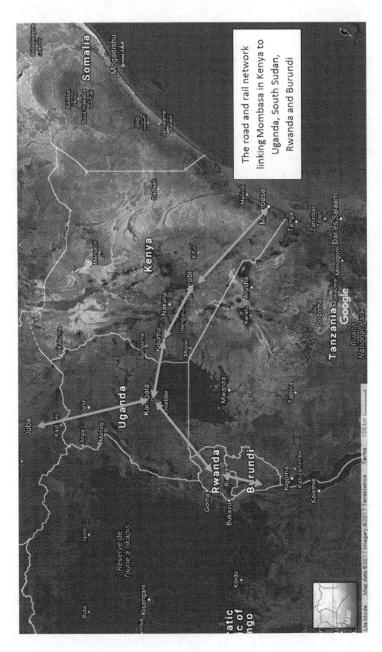

Map 3.1 Rail and road network linking the Port of Mombasa to the interior. (Google Maps)

exports to China. Leather products also show some promise and Kenya can develop this further by reorganising and supporting this sector. Kenya is still importing food, and should therefore not only find new markets for its agricultural products, but diversify into those food-processing sectors in which they have a comparative advantage.

The growing domestic market should be the first stop followed by other African markets, especially in East Africa, and then expand their footprint into international markets. China is unlikely to be a viable market for food products from Kenya as Kenya lacks a comparative advantage in China's main food imports such as beef, corn, wheat and soybeans.

Other important sectors identified for diversification in the 'Vision 2030' are tourism and financial services, both of which could benefit from the Chinese consumer. China has the biggest tourism market in the world, and tourism assets are one of the strengths of Kenya that should be further developed. Kenya has further developed innovative financial service products like MPESA that can be duplicated in other developing countries, as well as in China.

Kenya's trade balance reflects an urgent need for diversification that will produce exports for competitive markets. Rather than focusing on increasing exports to China, Kenya should build its own domestic markets and improve its competitiveness with export products in African and other international markets. An important factor that can enhance exports is access and improvements to the Mombasa Harbour. The infrastructure improvements will hopefully contribute significantly to achieve this objective, and are therefore of critical importance.

China has a comparative advantage in cheap manufactured goods and Kenya should protect infant industries that are strategic for development, and in which Kenyan businesses can develop a comparative advantage in the future. The apparel industry of Kenya, which is growing and supported by the United States' African Growth and Opportunity Act's (AGOA) renewal agreement in 2008, is such an example of an industry that should be protected in the short term. On the other hand, the import of certain cheaper supplies and consumer products from China and elsewhere that are needed in production and other economic activities is not in itself a problem.

Kenya's exports to China are small because it is an oil importer and has relatively scarce resources. SEZs should be developed in partnership with China, and in line with Kenya's development strategy, and barriers to production removed. Kenya should also aim to become the major supplier to

Chinese companies operating in Kenya, especially in its strong domestic industries, such as cement—instead of the current status quo of Chinese firms sourcing most of their supplies from China. FDI in the textiles and clothing sub-sectors is important for the creation of employment and should be developed further.

Corruption, safety concerns, barriers to production and insufficient infrastructure are still limiting FDI in Kenya, and should be improved. As detailed earlier, Chinese companies have identified corruption as the most significant obstacle to doing business in Kenya (Sanghi and Johnson 2016). China's investment can become more transparent and supportive of development if Kenya can reduce corruption and improve good governance. More reforms in the regulatory and especially the industrial policies will improve business effectiveness, while a focus by policymakers on labour-intensive comparative and competitive industries should support the improvement of employment levels.

China is quite active in the education sector in Kenya and provides a number of training programmes, university scholarships and language programmes. Language is an obstacle, especially in employing local communities in Chinese projects.

China is an important source for FDI, but Kenya needs to guard against a situation of being too dependent on China's investment, and needs to attract investment from other parts of the globe. An important development in this regard occurred in 2015 when Kenya signed deals with the United States and Japan that may see them working alongside China on certain projects. In one of these cases, Kenya entered into a deal with the United States' General Electric, to deliver trains for the new SGR.

## 3.5 The Case of Nigeria

While Kenya is the leading economy in East Africa, Nigeria is the leading economy in West Africa, and has the biggest population and largest economy in Africa. Nigeria has an important economic influence on the entire region, including the francophone region where it is significantly investing.

Nigeria's coastal boundary is delimited by the Gulf of Guinea in the South and it borders Cameroon and Chad in the East, Niger in the North and Benin in the West. Abuja is Nigeria's capital city in the middle of Nigeria, while Lagos is the country's largest city indicated on Map 3.2.

Nigeria is the most populated nation in Africa with a current population of more than 180 million people. The country is made up of people

ECONOMIC GROWTH AND DIVERSIFICATION FUELLING DEVELOPMENT... 61

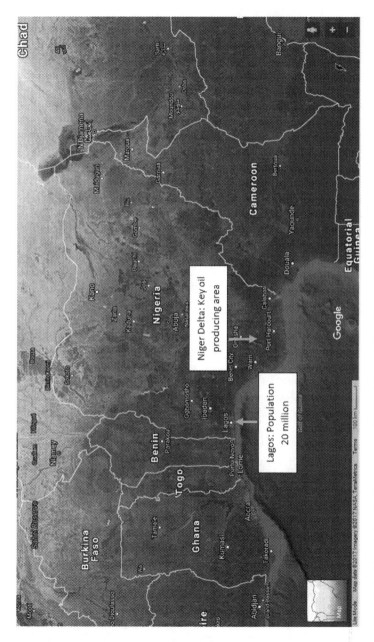

Map 3.2 Nigeria highlighting Lagos and the Niger Delta. (Google Maps)

**Table 3.4** Background information on Nigeria

**Land area**: 923,768 km$^2$
**Population**: 183 million in 2015
One in five Africans is Nigerian
**Diverse nation** with 250 ethnic groups: The three largest are the Hausa/Fulani (29% in the north and predominantly Muslim); Igbo (18% in the south-east and predominantly Christian); and Yoruba (21% in the south-west and a blend of Muslims and Christians)
**Political structure**: Divided into 36 political divisions called states and the Federal Capital territory located in Abuja
**Official language**: English. A modified form of English called 'Pidgin' is also used especially by some of the illiterate and semi-literate people
**Energy**: Major source of power generation is hydroelectric due to sufficient water supply
**GDP**: US$594 billion in 2014; US$521 billion in 2013
**GDP growth**: Q1 2014—6.21%; Q2 2015—5.54%
Well-educated and emerging middle class: about 20% of the population
Top 10% of earners responsible for 43% of consumption
**Major industries**: Agriculture, manufacturing, banking, mining, telecommunications, oil and gas
**City of Lagos**:
Largest population in Nigeria: 20 million people
Largest city in Africa and the seventh fastest-growing in the world
Largest port in West Africa
Nigeria's commercial, financial and industrial hub

Authors' compilation

of diverse cultures and religions and is also one of the richest countries on the continent endowed with natural resources of oil and gas. At independence from the British rule in 1960 the main source of revenue was agriculture and the extraction of minerals. The discovery of oil shortly thereafter led to an overdependence on oil and a gradual neglect of agriculture and the other sectors of the economy. Nigeria is one of the top ten countries in terms of gas and oil reserves in the world. From the early 1970s, Nigeria's oil exports became the main source of income for the country and the government. Most of this income has unfortunately been mismanaged through corruption and very little was utilised to diversify the economy. Detailed and further background information on the country is summarised in Table 3.4.

### 3.5.1 Economic Growth and Diversification in Nigeria

Nigeria's economy can be described as a rapidly growing economy with an average growth of 6% in the past decade. Nigeria became the largest economy in Africa in 2016, taking South Africa's long-held position as the country with the continent's largest GDP. Primary production consists of agriculture, and mining and quarrying, which include oil and gas production—oil and gas dominate the economy with about a 60% share. The secondary sector is primarily manufacturing and construction with a 10% share, while the tertiary sector is dominated by telecommunications and retail with a growing 30% share.

In the 1950s and 1960s and the early part of the 1970s, agriculture was the main source of economic income and growth, employing the majority of workers in the country. The decline in the performance of the agricultural sector increased since the discovery of oil. The biggest decline was in 2003 when a sharp rise in the oil production took place because of favourable prices, and the share of agriculture output dropped sharply. This phenomenon was again reversed with the 2009 oil crises, when there was a decrease in the GDP growth of oil and an increase in the GDP contribution from agricultural production. Although overall agricultural production rose over the years, production per capita decreased as it failed to keep up with Nigeria's rapid population growth. The result: Nigeria, once a major food exporter, now relies heavily on food imports to sustain itself. Growth in the agricultural sector is also negatively impacted by factors such as subsistence-based farming, low productivity and low technology.

In 2015, the economy of Nigeria was still heavily dependent on oil, accounting for up to two-thirds of government revenue and foreign exchange earnings. Nigeria's oil is located in the area known as the Niger Delta, which supports a range of ethnic minorities who have over the years developed resistance to oil exploration in the region. This resistance and conflict are based on the negative environmental, social as well economic effects perceived by the local population. They feel that they bear only the consequences, and no benefits, from this exploration.

The positive returns and gains from the oil industry, unfortunately, led to a dependence of Nigeria on oil for economic growth. Although the Nigerian economy is involved in the primary, secondary and tertiary sectors, there is very little movement in terms of value chain integration between these sectors. These sectors were therefore developed almost independently, instead of through a natural organic process of resource, industrial and service diversification. The secondary sector which should consolidate and give enhanced value to the primary sector is not aligned and is poorly developed. Most of the outputs of the primary sector, such as agriculture and natural resources, are not further processed. The spillover benefits of the oil sector on other sectors, for example, are limited because the government has not adequately developed the capability to pursue value-added activities in the petrochemical value chain. The focus on oil has also adversely affected the sociopolitical stability of the nation because of strife among different sections of the nation to control the Federal Government and therefore the rewards from oil production. Government institutions have until recently shown very little interest and initiative to use the income of oil to diversify and grow other sectors of the economy. Other challenges that also contribute to this poor performance of industrialisation are poor infrastructure, lack of an educational orientation, corruption, macroeconomic instability and weakness of institutions and regulations. It is clear that the organic growth and development of the Nigerian economy will be dependent on the diversification of the economy away from oil and gas to related sectors based on the country's abundant natural resources and comparative advantage.

Nigeria recently changed its economic analysis to account for the rapidly growing contributors to its GDP, such as telecommunications, banking and its film industry. Nigeria used a new statistical base to measure its GDP from 1990 to 2010, resulting in an 89% increase in the estimated size of the economy. As a result, the country now boasts of having the largest economy in Africa with an estimated nominal GDP of US$510 billion, surpassing South Africa's US$352 billion (Suberu et al. 2015). This rebased data, using updated prices and the latest methodologies, also show that the economy is much more diverse than was previously thought. Nigeria's GDP has been increasing at about 6–7% in the last decade, and the good news is that although GDP is still dominated by oil production, most of the growth post 2009 has come from services, agriculture and manufacturing (Chen et al. 2016). Rubber and leather are both abundant resources that Nigeria can further diversify into promising sectors for manufacturing. Consumer electronics and automotive assembly were also identified as possible future growth sectors.

The Nigeria Industrial Revolution Plan, released by President Goodluck Jonathan in 2014, aims to establish Nigeria as a regional manufacturing hub in West Africa by increasing the manufacturing share of GDP to 10% by 2017 (Chen et al. 2016). Nigeria has also instituted a policy of import substitution for certain goods to encourage the localisation of manufacturing. Many household goods are prohibited from importing, and local content policies have also been applied with the purpose of building capacity and human capital in these sectors. A good example of this is the banning of furniture imports to boost the domestic furniture industry in the country. The Nigerian Automotive Policy of 2014 also raised import duties on fully assembled cars from 10% to 35% to incentivise the domestic industry for future growth. This policy directly resulted in a number of international auto manufacturers investing in assembly plants in Nigeria.

AGOA also opened valuable export opportunities to the United States for African countries. Nigeria has been a top exporter of oil under the Act but has not benefitted so far in other potential sectors such as textiles, compared to other African countries such as South Africa and Kenya.

Overall, despite the efforts and policies to increase manufacturing in Nigeria, most manufactured consumer goods are still imported from the European Union and the United States, followed by China. Nigeria's service sector has also been growing, especially in telecommunications, financial services and trade. Most of the employment growth in this sector require specialised skills and is therefore on a narrow wage base that does not lead to overall employment growth. Development and diversification face the challenge of poor economic and social infrastructure. The country needs to invest its resources wisely on technological development, education, human development and improved infrastructure (Anyaehie and Areji 2015).

### 3.5.2 Impact of China on the Organic Growth of Nigeria

In the first decade after independence, Nigeria and China had no diplomatic relations primarily because of the support of China for the secessionist state of Biafra at the time. During the 1970s and 1980s, Nigeria primarily traded with Europe and the United States, and China was an insignificant player. The last two decades, however, have witnessed renewed positive and mutually beneficial developments. Several diplomatic visits at the highest level took place and bilateral agreements were entered into by the two countries. A summary of the relationship between China and Nigeria is provided in Table 3.5.

Nigeria is currently the largest recipient of FDI in Africa. Investment from the United States, Europe and China grew significantly since 1999, as business confidence grew due to President Obasanjo's election (Ogunkola et al. 2008). During this time China set up over 30 solely owned companies or joint ventures in Nigeria predominantly in the construction, oil and gas, technology and services sectors. China's stock of foreign investments increased from US$3 billion in 2003 to US$10 billion

**Table 3.5** Summary of the relationship between Nigeria and China

| Time period | Relationship detail |
|---|---|
| 1960–1971:<br>The first decade after independence from British Colonial rule<br>Initially coalition government followed by cycle of military coups<br>Civil War 1967–1970 over secession of Biafra | No diplomatic relations in earlier years between Nigeria and China:<br>Nigeria recognised the Republic of China (Taiwan) as 'China'<br>Hong Kong Chinese firms invested in Nigeria's textile industry<br>Nigerian government hostile towards mainland China because of Mao's support for civil war of 1967–1970 of secessionist state in Biafra<br>Established first diplomatic relations in 1971 |
| 1971–1998:<br>Nigeria ruled by generally corrupt and authoritarian military regimes with international condemnation and isolation | A strong political alliance was formed with China after withdrawal of Western aid and support<br>China provided extensive economic, military and political support to Nigeria<br>Nigerian–Chinese Chamber of Commerce was founded in 1994 |
| 1993–1998:<br>General Abacha, one of the most notorious and corrupt leaders | China Civil Engineering Construction Corporation won a US$529 million contract to rehabilitate the Nigerian Railway System (project not completed)<br>1997 protocols signed for power generation, steel and oil production |
| 1999–2007:<br>Election May 1999 of General Obasanjo | General Obasanjo visited China twice in 1999 and 2001 and signed several economic, technical, scientific, trade and investment agreements resulting in the following:<br>Investment: An increase in 'Oil for Infrastructure' projects<br>Tourism cooperation<br>Health assistance<br>Cooperation in communications and space programmes led to the launch of Nigeria's first communication satellite in 2007<br>In 2006 China pledged finance for two Free Trade Zones (FTZs) in Lekki and Ogun states<br>Bilateral trade with China increased nine-fold from US$2 billion in 2004 to US$18 billion in 2007<br>Establishment of Confucius Institute<br>Loan of US$1.1 billion to Nigeria in exchange for increased oil supply |

(*continued*)

Table 3.5 (continued)

| Time period | Relationship detail |
|---|---|
| 2008–2010: President Yar 'Adua  2010–2014: President Goodluck Jonathan | Relationship was strengthened after election of President Goodluck Jonathan  2010 China declared new plan for strategic partnership with Nigeria  Cooperation in agriculture  Cooperation in manufacturing  Chinese companies set up Private Industrial Estates (PIEs)  Loans for infrastructure in airport terminals  Nigeria became China's second largest export destination in Africa  China became the largest single source of FDI in Nigeria |
| 2015: Election of President Buhari, the first transition of power to the opposition (APC) party | China–Nigeria cooperation at the United Nations  Military assistance by China against insurgencies in Niger Delta |

Authors' own compilation

in 2010 (Izuchukwu and Ofori 2014). In 2013, the Chinese government provided US$1.1 billion low-interest loans for the development of infrastructure in Nigeria, including funding for four airport terminals (Izuchukwu and Ofori 2014).

China also remarkably strengthened its agricultural cooperation with Nigeria after 1999. In the Agreement on Trade, Investment Promotion and Protection that was signed between Nigeria and China in 2006, both nations agreed to expand trade and investment in agriculture. Despite a number of initiatives by China to assist agricultural production and diversification in Nigeria, agriculture still reflects the lowest proportion of Chinese companies operating in this sector. The sector continues to lack investment resulting in the poor growth in employment in the sector. There is no doubt that Chinese investment and cooperation could contribute to agricultural productivity and the securing of food for the nation. Nigeria can also directly benefit from China's own experience in this regard. There is an urgent need to diversify agriculture further to contribute more to the economy, and, therefore, there is also a greater need for Chinese trade and investment in this sector.

The trade imbalance between Nigeria and China became an issue because of the import of sub-standard Chinese products at the expense of Nigeria's own industries. Nigeria's exports to China are dominated by crude oil, which made up more than 90% of exports to the country. On the other hand, more than 50% of all imports to Nigeria are from China, of which machinery and equipment represent the biggest category, followed by consumer goods such as textiles (Ogunkola et al. 2008). Nigerian trade unions have sometimes blamed Chinese imports for the loss of Nigerian manufacturing jobs, specifically in the textile sector. These imports directly led to the closure of 65 textile mills and the lay-off of 150,000 textile workers between 1999 and 2007 (Taylor 2007). China became Nigeria's biggest trading partner in 2015 surpassing the United States, which was for decades the biggest trading partner. The need to diversify export products may be an uphill battle, given China's preference to import oil and gas, the result of which is that the balance of payments position has consistently been in favour of China.

Chinese companies in Nigeria have been criticised for being 'closed' due to perceived low levels of employing local experts. There was even a submission that they sometimes maltreat their workers. According to some reports, the conditions of employment of Nigerians in certain Chinese firms conform neither to the Nigerian Labour Laws nor to that of the International Labour Organisation (ILO) (Ogunkola et al. 2008). This was highlighted when a number of Nigerian workers died after being trapped inside a locked Chinese-owned factory that caught fire in 2002.

A research study that analysed 16 medium and large Chinese companies in Nigeria found that an average of 84.9% of workers in these businesses are local and that Chinese manufacturers therefore do employ mostly local Nigerians (Chen et al. 2016). The study found that the high level of employment appears to be driven by economics, as labour from China has become increasingly expensive, thus making employment of Nigerian labour more attractive. It further concluded that local people are primarily employed on the factory floor with very few in technical and management roles.

Technology and skills transfer is therefore not happening to the extent hoped for, although some training and skills transfer took place in the automotive and construction industries. It was found that technology transfer did take place in cases where companies made use of imported manufacturing machinery and equipment from China. Formal skills training is very low in most Chinese firms, and language and cultural differences remain a barrier for this type of skills transfer.

Despite the vast differences in historical experiences and cultural traditions between China and Nigeria, China has been remarkably successful in its efforts to promote Chinese culture in Nigeria. Several initiatives like student exchanges, the establishment of a Confucius Institute and the establishment of a Chinese Cultural Research Centre are some examples of specific efforts to boost cultural and language synergy between the two countries.

Chines firms decide to invest in Nigeria for a variety of reasons, including lower costs, lower competition and the country's large and growing domestic market. The Ogun–Guangdong FTZ established by agreement between China and Nigeria is one of the fastest-growing industrial zones. The zone focuses on light industry manufacturing, including ceramics, furniture, paper and packaging. The zone produces predominantly for the local market and is attractive because of the incentivised tax rates compared to Lagos (Chen et al. 2016). Other zones have benefitted from Chinese investments, such as the Lekki FTZ, which was one of the first zones set up under the Chinese 2006 agreement, and the Calabar FTZ in the Cross Rivers State comprising about 75 firms in 2015 of which half are in manufacturing, including Chinese truck manufacturer, FAW. A study by Chen et al. (2016) found that Chinese manufacturing companies invested predominantly in the furniture, steel and construction, food and beverage, and automotive assembly industries, although Chinese firms appear to be making disparate products, rather than grouping in clusters or sectors, therefore limiting sector development.

The impact of China on Nigeria's economic growth and diversification is provided in Fig. 3.6.

Nigeria's quest for growth and development is yet to deliver on the ultimate goal of wealth creation and poverty reduction despite the pace of economic growth achieved in the past decade. The failure to successfully diversify the Nigerian economy, as indicated in this chapter, has led to the failure of the ability of the country to address the needs of the nation.

Unemployment increased because of the inability of the oil sector to employ more people. This situation created a growing divide between the very rich who benefitted from oil, including government agencies and their cronies, and the very poor. The economy does not emphasise productivity and wealth creation. It is important that Nigeria leverages its huge oil reserves to diversify the economy and create employment.

Challenges that hinder diversification should be confronted, and Chinese investment directed to the relevant sectors that will stimulate

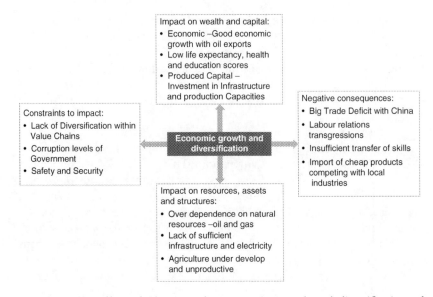

Fig. 3.6 The effect of China on the economic growth and diversification of Nigeria

growth, with the objective of lengthening and integrating value chains. An old Nigerian proverb states that "a man cannot sit down alone to plan for prosperity". It is therefore the Government of Nigeria's responsibility to plan for their nation's own prosperity and to make sure that the influx of Chinese funds and investment is contributing to this prosperity. Strengthening government capabilities will be essential to stimulate organic growth and diversification. Nigeria also lags relatively behind other developing countries in terms of their GDP spent on health and literacy. The educational focus tends to be bureaucratic, and not enough is being done for the development and transfer of technical and other skills.

## 3.6 Lessons Learned from the Kenyan and Nigerian Case Studies

The main development goal of any country is the continual enhancement of the quality of life of all its citizens, achieved through responsible and productive management of the country's resources and assets. Organic growth is a process of economic transformation in which the effective utilisation of resources, financial capital and investments, technology and skills, and institutional and governmental change, all work in harmony to enhance the current and future potential to meet human needs and aspirations. Economic growth and diversification are the drivers of organic growth in a country. Economic diversification can do this by extending the range of economic activities both in the production and in the distribution of goods and services. This process will result in the widening of the economy in existing sectors, as well as in new sectors, to create a broad base of economic participation.

Kenya is the leading economy in East Africa while Nigeria is the leading economy in West Africa. Both countries play a leading role in their respective regional economies in which they operate, and are therefore attractive destinations for FDI from the United States, Europe, India and, of course, China. Nigeria is one of the biggest oil and gas producers and exporters in the world, while Kenya is an oil importer. Both countries have access to a harbour, which facilitates and cheapens exporting. Both countries have a comparative advantage in agriculture, with Kenya being the more successful in terms of agricultural exports—coffee, tea and flowers are its biggest export products and agriculture its biggest economic sector. Agriculture is a big employer in both countries; yet remains relatively unproductive and subsistence-orientated. It has the propensity to employ more provided it is further developed, productive and diversified.

Both countries have a worrying trade deficit with China, with indigenous industries, such as the textile industry, suffering because of cheap imports from China. It seems that the government of Kenya is more proactive in protecting infant and indigenous industries against unfair competition from China, while Nigeria is less effective.

The growing domestic markets and good economic growth encourage China to invest in both countries. These countries are also popular destinations because of their potential to become important gateways to their regions, and provide access to landlocked countries that they border.

The development and diversification of the economies of both countries face the challenge of poor economic and social infrastructure. No country can achieve sustained growth without investing in its infrastructure, education and healthcare. Insufficient and poor road and rail networks, outdated harbour facilities, erratic power supply and low education and skills development levels are among the main constraints to economic growth and diversification in these countries. China is providing critical funding for the development of strategic road and rail links as well as other infrastructure such as airports and harbours in both countries, which is definitely contributing to an enabling environment for growth and diversification.

Nigeria has not been successful in the development of education and skills to support the growth of the economy. The educational system still produces graduates without skills, resulting in most of them remaining unemployed. Kenya, on the other hand, has an integrated approach to human capital development that has facilitated a reasonably good literacy rate of 72%. Programmes are offered by both the public and private sectors to improve the skills base in important sectors like tourism and there are good levels of cooperation between the university sector and business. Various researchers, however, have found that in both countries the transfer of skills and technology from Chinese projects and companies is not occurring at the level hoped for. Most of the higher-level positions are filled by Chinese nationals, first because some of these skills are not available in the local country, and second, because the respective governments are not providing the capacity and structures for the transfer of those skills.

Improved economic and social infrastructure will dramatically improve the capabilities of both countries to be more innovative and produce more with the same assets and resources. Chinese development finance has been a major contributor to the development of economic infrastructure in both countries.

Governments and supporting institutions are the main leaders and enablers of economic development and diversification in a developing country. It seems that in most developing countries there is a direct correlation between the development level of the country and the sophistication and ethical conduct of its government. The evolution of government efficiency is therefore a critical component of the organic growth process, and Nigeria is a very good example of how investment, growth and diversification improved dramatically after there was a significant improvement in the governance of the country (during the rule of General Obasanjo from 1999 to 2007). The situation was similar with the election of President Kibaki in Kenya from 2002 to 2013, when important improvements in governance and policy, such as the Kenya Vision 2030 project, kick-started a period of successful economic growth. These two periods are further characterised by massive inflows of foreign capital and investment, predominantly from the United States, Europe, India and China, due to the improvement in investment attractiveness of the two countries.

Unfortunately, both countries are still struggling with government inefficiency and corruption levels, which, if not improved, will continue to hamper growth and development. Corruption in both countries still makes it very difficult to manage the country's economy and to sustain policies that will transform the economy. Nigeria has had four different National Development Plans from 1962 to 1985 which did not achieve many of the planned objectives, mostly because of the lack of political will and due to corruption. Kenya is politically more stable than Nigeria, and the government is also more effective in the execution of industrial policy, such as the success of Vision 2030 in supporting economic growth and diversification. Safety and security are still one of the biggest barriers for business investment and growth, with both countries struggling with Muslim extremist groups which aim to destabilise them.

There is an urgent need for Nigeria to diversify its economy and develop its agricultural potential. Agriculture still plays a fundamental role in development and employment creation in Africa. Nigeria, which claims to be the giant of Africa, is undoubtedly lagging terribly behind in the area of agricultural development, which ought to be the cornerstone for national development.

China's contribution to investment in Nigeria has boosted primarily the extractive sector, at the expense of the agricultural sector. China's trade and investment in the agricultural sector is substantially low. The Nigerian government should consider including agricultural and human capital development as major components of all trade agreements. Value should be added by extending and integrating the agricultural value chain—this will broaden the economic base and reduce poverty. There should be more partnerships between farmers, government, non-governmental organisations (NGOs), local businesses and Chinese multinational corporations to accelerate growth in the agricultural sector. This will require addressing risk and profitability issues that may inhibit the supply and demand of technological inputs, as well as the implementation of subsidies to incentivise the private sector, to strengthen potential supply and value chains.

Chinese manufacturing FDI is important, because it can directly contribute to the diversification of the economy, and therefore facilitate a broader base of employment. It was found that the employment levels of local communities in Chinese firms are high in both countries, although managerial positions and jobs that required technical skills are mostly occupied by the Chinese. The contribution of manufacturing to GDP in

Nigeria and Kenya is 10% or less, thus proving underperformance. Nigerian and Kenyan governments need to be more proactive in determining the outcomes of Chinese manufacturing investment in their countries. The governments can introduce more effective industrial and other policies to support infant indigenous industries and direct FDI into priority sectors. This implies working with a range of role players, including the private sector, to shape and direct Chinese investment in manufacturing, thus helping to achieve the goals of diversification, skills transfer, development and employment.

Nigeria needs to use the return on its primary resources, specifically oil revenue, to diversify the economy and to create jobs and satisfy the social needs for the nation. Kenya must continue with its diversification process in the agricultural sector and other sectors that hold promise, such as tourism. Value chains in existing sectors should be extended and integrated into other sectors in order to create a comparative advantage. Nigeria should also attend to its growing energy needs and its gas reserves can be utilised to achieve this.

FDI from China has had, and continues to have, a positive effect on the provision of infrastructure and economic growth in both countries. There is, however, a need for the governments of Nigeria and Kenya to maximise the complementary effects of these investments. Effective diversification for poverty reduction will require not only collaboration with China, but strong coordination of institutions and resources—all of which should aim towards a common industrial growth trajectory.

Nigeria ranks among the most richly endowed nations of the world in terms of natural, mineral and human resources. It has a highly entrepreneurial, hardworking, largely youthful population of over 170 million. With such an abundance in human and natural resources, Nigeria has the potential to become one of the most diversified and competitive countries in the world. Kenya, on the other hand, is an economic powerhouse in East Africa, which has even in the absence of an abundance of natural resources, managed a more successful integration of their organic growth since 2000.

Despite the concerns voiced by certain groups within Kenya and Nigeria, most Africans recognise that China's growing presence in these two countries was overall more beneficial than harmful. Many Chinese entrepreneurs cited the growing domestic market of Kenya and specifically the massive market of Nigeria as one of the biggest factors to become involved in these countries.

## References

Adeyeye, A. 28 July 2016. SEZ's and the Industrialisation Drive in Africa. *AfricaBusiness.Com*. [Online]. Available from: http://www.africabusiness.com/2016/07/28/sezs-and-the-industrial-drive-in-Africa/ (accessed: 11 Feb 2017).

African Economic Outlook. 2015. AFDB, OECD, UNDP, page 75. [Online]. Available from: http://www.africaneconomicoutlook.org/sites/default/files/content_pdf/AE2015_ENpdf (accessed: 24 June 2017).

Africa Infrastructure Development Index. 2013. [Online]. Available from: http://www.afdb.org/fileadmin/uploads/afdb/Documents/Publications/Economicbrief (accessed: 24 June 2017).

African Tourism Monitor. 2014. AFDB, OECD, UNDP, ANECA, 2014 page 58. [Online]. Available from: http://www.afdb.org (accessed: 24 March 2017).

Anyaehie, M.C. and Areji, A.C. 2015. 'Economic Diversification for Sustainable Development in Nigeria', *Open Journal of Political Science*, 5: 87–94.

Chen, Y., Sun, I., Ukaejiofo, R., Tang, X. and Bräutigam, D. 2016. Learning from China? Manufacturing, Investment and Technology Transfer in Nigeria. IFPRI Discussion Paper 1565. Washington, DC: International Food Policy Research Institute. Reproduced with permission from the International Food Policy Research Institute www.ifpri.org. The original text is available online at: http://www.ifpri.org/publication/learning-china-manufacturing-investment-and-technology-transfer-nigeria.

Economic Diversification in Africa: A Review of Selected Countries. 2011. [Online]. OECD. Available from: http://www.oecd.org/daf/inv/economic-diversificationinafricaareviewofselectedcountries.htm (accessed: 27 March 2017).

Izuchukwu, O. and Ofori, D. 2014. 'Why South-South FDI Is Booming: Case Study of China FDI in Nigeria', *Asia Economic and Financial Review*, 4 (3): 361–376.

Kim, Y. 2015. What Africa Can Learn from China's Special Economic Zones. [Online]. Available from: http://www.The conversation.com/what-africa-can-learn-from-china's-special-zones-5157 (accessed: 15 Feb 2017).

Leke, A., Lund, S., Roxburgh, C. and Van Wamelen, A. June 2010. Excerpted from "What's Driving Africa's Growth", McKinsey & Company, www.mckinsey.com. Copyright © 2017 McKinsey & Company. All rights reserved. Reprinted with permission.

Mulinge, E. An Analyses of China—Kenya Bilateral Relations on Infrastructure Development. The Kenya Institute for Public Policy Research and Analysis Discussion Paper no 34, 2012. 3 (5): 529–537. [Online]. Available from: http://www.kippra.or.ke/index.php?option+com_docman&task+doc_view&gid+275&itemid+ (accessed: 28 March 2017).

Ogunkola, E., Bankole, A. and Adewuyi, A. 2008. *China-Nigeria Economic Relations*. African Economic Research Consortium (AERC).

Sachs, J. and Warner, D. 2001. 'The Curse of Natural Resources', *European Economic Review*, 45: 827–838.

Sanghi, A. and Johnson, D. 2016. Deal or No Deal: Strictly Business for China in Kenya? World Bank Policy Research Working Paper 7614. © World Bank. Accessed from: http://documents.worldbank.org/curated/en/801581468195561492/pdf/WPS7614.pdf (accessed: 17 February 2017). License: Creative Commons Attribution License (CC BY 3.0 IGO). (http://creativecommons.org/licenses/by/3.0/igo/).

Suberu, O., Ajala, O., Akande, M. and Adeyinka, O. 2015. 'Diversification of the Nigerian Economy Towards Sustainable Growth and Economic Development', *International Journal of Economics, Finance and Management Sciences*, 3 (2): 107–114.

Taylor, I. 2007. 'Governance in Africa and Sino-African Relations: Contradictions or Confluence', *Politics*, 27 (3): 139–146.

Zamfir, L. 2016. Africa's Economic Growth: Taking Off or Slowing Down. European Parliament Research Service Blog 2016. [Online]. Available from: https://www.epthinktank.eu/2016/0106/africas-economic-growth-taking-off-or-slowing-down/ (accessed: 4 March 2017).

CHAPTER 4

# Infrastructure: The Most Important Enabler of Organic Growth in Africa

Infrastructure is usually described in terms of physical structures such as roads, sewerage works, power plants, dams and communication towers. Yet this is insufficient to comprehend the fundamental contribution infrastructure makes in terms of development. It is perhaps better to consider infrastructure as the essential 'building-blocks', which, when combined, result in a facilitating environment for business to function, the state to govern and for people to be provided with the services essential for their well-being. While economic growth and diversification can be regarded as the 'fuel' for development, infrastructure is the 'engine' that powers growth. Africa's structural transformation and organic growth are hampered by a range of natural and man-made constraints of which infrastructural constraints are one of the most pertinent (Fig. 4.1).

## 4.1 The Impact of Infrastructural Utilities on Organic Growth

Ultimately infrastructure should improve the well-being of people: Access to running water and power in the home; sanitation and clean water to ensure health; transport infrastructure to be able to go to school and work. At the end of the day, infrastructure should make life easier and more comfortable. From an economic perspective, infrastructure should create a facilitating environment for business, the fuel for development, failing which, economic growth is stifled.

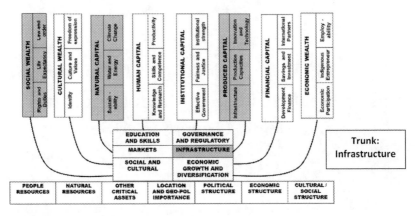

Fig. 4.1 The African Tree of Organic Growth

Considering The African Tree of Organic Growth, infrastructure contributes to social wealth in terms of a myriad of factors related to the wellbeing of the populace, and contributes to natural capital in terms of the efficient use of natural resources such as water and electricity that support a sustainable future. From a capital perspective, infrastructural projects should improve knowledge, support skills transfer and engender productivity; increase produced capital through improved production capacities; and improve financial capital with greater foreign direct investment and international partnerships in such projects, and the enabling environment of infrastructure should encourage private investment. Ultimately, economic wealth could and should be derived from infrastructural development. From a root perspective, the core competencies of the country would be improved in the long run, provided infrastructure is properly maintained and managed.

The case studies introduced in this chapter detail transport infrastructural projects in Africa which have been facilitated by the Chinese. Transport infrastructure is one of the fundamental requirements for economic growth, hence this emphasis. Transport provides the opportunity for market expansion by improving 'city transport networks that convey people from their homes to places of work and goods from their source of production to their distribution network; it connects rural communities to other rural communities and to cities where they can find a market for their goods or find gainful employment; it allows for mining operations in far-off places; it facilitates agricultural development due to speedy access to consumers; and it allows for regional development with trading partners in neighbouring countries. And of course, transport infrastructure provides access for better healthcare, education and other service delivery priorities.

It is also worthwhile to note that a critical aspect of infrastructural development that needs to be considered is the maintenance and management of these utilities, especially in view of the historic degeneration of infrastructure in Africa. Policy development and implementation needs to consider the best way to manage these critical assets. There are many options in this regard, but some models that African governments could consider involve community participation, community management with state funding and state contracting maintenance to private firms.

## 4.2 Infrastructure Shortcomings in Africa

Undoubtedly, suitable infrastructure in Africa is lacking in many circumstances. Power shortages are common, roads are sometimes in horrific condition, road and rail networks are insufficient and water and sanitation facilities are a health concern. It is not uncommon to see women walking many kilometres with water canisters poised precariously on their heads, fetching water for their families.

It is important to note that Africa's main development constraint is the development of infrastructure. Africa is trailing all the other nations of the world in terms of facilities for transportation, for energy production and for communication. For Africa to overcome these constraints, it needs to develop an effective network of infrastructure to meet these needs. Alexis Habiyaremye (Personal interview, 2016)

Vivian Foster and Cecilia Briceño-Garmendia, authors of *Africa's Infrastructure: A Time for Transformation* (2010) published by the World Bank, provide some valuable insights into the stocks of infrastructure in Africa. Their findings are summarised in Table 4.1.

In order to better understand the infrastructural stocks and shortages within Africa, the *Handbook on Infrastructural Statistics* (African Development Bank Group 2011) was consulted for more specific details per utility. These are detailed in the following sections (statistics are based on data available prior to publication in 2011).

**Table 4.1** Infrastructure in Africa

Infrastructure has been responsible for **more than half** of Africa's recent improved **growth performance** and has the potential to contribute even more in the future
Africa's infrastructure networks increasingly **lag behind** those of other developing countries and are characterised by **missing regional links** and **stagnant household access**
Africa's **difficult economic geography** presents a particular challenge for the region's infrastructure development
Africa's infrastructural services are **twice as expensive** as elsewhere, reflecting both **diseconomies of scale** in production and **high profit margins** caused by lack of competition
**Power** is by far Africa's largest infrastructural challenge, with 30 countries facing regular **power shortages** and many paying **high premiums** for emergency power
The cost of addressing Africa's infrastructure needs is around **US$93 billion a year**, about one-third of which is for **maintenance**
The infrastructural challenge **varies greatly by country type**—fragile states face an impossible burden and resource-rich countries lag behind despite their wealth
A large share of Africa's infrastructure is **domestically financed**, with the central government budget being the main driver of infrastructural investment
Even if major potential efficiency gains are captured, Africa would still face an **infrastructure funding gap** of US$31 billion a year, mainly in power
Africa's **institutional, regulatory and administrative reforms** are only halfway along, but they are already proving their effect on **operational efficiency**

Forster and Briceño-Garmendia (2010: 1–2)

## 4.2.1 Power

Power was identified by Forster and Briceño-Garmendia (2010: 1–2) as being the priority area for infrastructural investment in Africa, and this is confirmed by the findings detailed in the *Handbook on Infrastructural Statistics*: "At present rates of electrification, most African countries will fail to reach universal access to electricity even by 2050 … sub-Saharan power consumption, at 120 kilowatt-hours per person per year, is barely adequate to power one light bulb per person for two hours each day" (2011: 100).

In Africa, 30 countries experience chronic electricity shortages, resulting in an estimated economic cost as high as 5% of GDP. Businesses must often rely on back-up generators, which cost several times more than grid electricity. Grid electricity is also expensive in sub-Saharan Africa, which costs on average double that of more developed regions.

The *Handbook* estimates that about 7000 MW of new generation capacity is required per year to meet demand, yet Africa has only been able to expand capacity by 1000 MW per year (10-year average). The capital expenditure needed to achieve sufficient capacity generation is approximately US$40 billion per year—about three times more than the investment at the time of publication of the *Handbook*. Existing power utilities are also in a precarious position, with a revenue shortfall of US$8 billion annually due to underpricing and operational inefficiencies, a drain on resources available for investing in production capacity.

Sustainable and renewable energy production is an important factor to consider in Africa. In the effort to achieve the abovementioned much needed generation capacity, cognisance needs to be taken of the negative contribution this may have on global climate change, and the negative externalities that fossil fuel consumption poses. Consideration of renewable energy technologies such as hydropower, solar and wind energy, and the contentious use of nuclear energy, in the achievement of greater generation capacity, has to be prioritised.

### 4.2.2 Water and Sanitation

Due to the rapid rate of African urbanisation and continued limited investment in water and sanitation, water services are decreasing in Africa. Only five African countries had met the Millennium Development Goal for access to safe water. Access to piped water is mostly a luxury for the more affluent classes in Africa, and in rural areas about 40% of the population rely on unsafe surface water.

As for sanitation, there is even more cause for concern, with a third of Africa's population having no access to toilet facilities, and half only having access to elementary facilities. Sewerage facilities are mostly reserved for urban areas, with rural residents relying on their own resources and efforts to provide themselves with on-site toilet facilities.

An estimated US$22 billion is required annually to address the problem, but with a funding gap of US$11 billion, an operational capacity loss of US$1 billion, and an underpricing loss of US$1.8 billion, funding for this infrastructure is desperately needed.

### 4.2.3 Information and Communication Technology (ICT)

Africa has undergone an ICT revolution that has radically changed how people communicate, and information accessibility has blossomed. Much of the ICT investment has been private in nature, with giant multinational corporations from South Africa, Europe and elsewhere competing aggressively for market share in the lucrative African market.

An estimated cumulative investment of US$28 billion in new networks resulted in 300 million new mobile subscribers for the period 2000–2009, most of which were in prepaid cellular phones. Access to mobile networks for the African population grew from 20% to 70% for this period.

The cost of mobile services remains exceptionally high, about five times more expensive than that of South Asia. This is partly due to the lack of competition in most countries where three or more mobile operators would create a more competitive environment, but only a third of Africa's countries have that number of operators. Coverage would also increase if there was greater competition, and if regulatory restraints were removed.

Without investment in submarine cables and fibre-optic lines, international calls and Internet access remains expensive. This is changing as large-scale investment in submarine cables along Africa's coastline and the laying of fibre-optic cable backbones is occurring, and could reduce the costs by as much as half—provided there is sufficient competition to drive down the prices.

### 4.2.4 Transport Infrastructure

There has been notable investment in transport infrastructure in many parts of Africa.

While there is still much that needs to be done to improve the continent's road network, the quality and network of roads has increased dramatically and should reduce transport costs. However, the non-physical barriers to efficient and cost-effective transportation services, which impacts economic growth, are a concern. Border crossings, weighing stations, police checkpoints—all delay traffic and inflate costs. Cartels in the trucking industry sometimes found in Africa have the effect of preventing savings being passed onto consumers in the form of cheaper carrier fees.

Rural road infrastructure is a major concern in Africa—only a third of the African population have access to all-weather roads. To provide them with roads will be costly and take many years. Yet this investment is critical if agricultural development plans are to succeed.

Urban road infrastructure also requires substantial investment with many African cities experiencing poor or unpaved roads in urban areas, and poor town planning sometimes results in congestion as the number of vehicles increases with urbanisation. Public provision of bus transport is limited, resulting in the proliferation of minibuses and scooters as alternative means of transport, sometimes exacerbating the problem.

The use of the railway network in Africa has decreased, partly due to the improvement in the quality of the road network, and partly due to the deterioration of the railway infrastructure. Rail is, however, more efficient for the bulk transport of materials, and more convenient for the transport of passengers where road transport is underdeveloped.

Ports in Africa have rapidly experienced an increase in volume. The *Handbook on Infrastructural Statistics* (African Development Bank Group 2011) reflects that between 1995 and 2006, cargo volumes through African ports tripled. Intermodal transport is still a limitation. The ideal scenario of transferring containers from a ship to vehicle transport often doesn't happen; instead, containers are emptied at the port and repacked in other forms of transport.

Few ports are large enough to accommodate vessels from major shipping lines, resulting in traffic movement at many ports being relatively low. Some ports have become regional hubs, such as Durban in South Africa for Southern Africa, and Dar es Salaam for Eastern Africa, while other regions lack a suitable port and the capacity to implement a hub-and-spoke system. African ports tend to lag behind their international counterparts and are expensive, often with significant delays.

Air transport has flourished in some areas of Africa. Addis Ababa in Ethiopia, Nairobi in Kenya and Johannesburg in South Africa have developed relatively successful air traffic hub-and-spoke systems. Western and Central Africa air transport is less developed although the Southern and Eastern air carriers are beginning to expand into these markets. Investment is needed in modernising air traffic control and surveillance, which is sometimes non-existent, while certain airports need capital investment in better or parallel runways to ease congestion at airports. Air safety is a concern, with 4.3 aircraft lost per 1 million departures, compared to 0.7 elsewhere in the world. This is attributable to an ageing fleet of aircraft, although the purchase of new fleets of aircraft were evidenced, and to human error, suggesting that resources need to be made available for better training of pilots and tighter supervision by civil aviation authorities.

China has been implementing humongous infrastructural programmes in Africa, with much of China's policy towards Africa and the investment by Chinese companies in Africa revolving around infrastructural development.

The pertinent questions are what has been the impact of China on infrastructural capital in Africa, and how has this contributed to economic growth and development for African countries?

## 4.3 China: The World Leader in Infrastructure Investment

In order to answer the question posed as to what impact China has contributed to infrastructural development in Africa, it is necessary to first contextualise the capacity that China has demonstrated in its own country in infrastructural development, and the contribution this has had on its own socio-economic growth.

China has invested phenomenally in infrastructure which has contributed to its robust and long-term growth trajectory. Figure 4.2 provides a useful visual depiction of the high level of investment as a percentage to GDP.

In 2016, the investment as a percentage of GDP was 44.2%. This is significantly higher than many developed nations, such as Germany (20.9%), Norway (28.8%) and the United Kingdom (17.4%). The percentage is also much higher than many African nations; for instance, the percentage investment was only 14.8% in Malawi, 17.5% in South Africa and 19.8% in Tunisia. An exception to the rule is Algeria, with a 51.1% investment as a percentage of GDP.

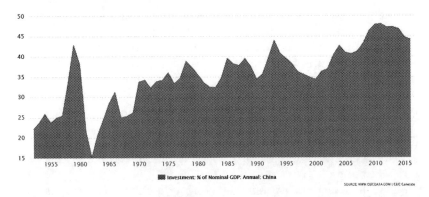

**Fig. 4.2** China's investment: percentage of GDP from 1952 to 2016. (CEIC 2016)

Intuitively, large-scale infrastructural investment should facilitate economic development. A number of studies have been conducted in this regard, with sometimes varied results. Two studies were consulted to shed some light on findings within China.

A vector error correction model was applied to a study spanning the time period of 1990–2013 by Yingying Shi et al. (2017) on the relationship between Chinese regional economic growth and infrastructural capital. The findings show that infrastructural investment did play an important role in the country's economic growth. The 13th Five-Year Plan for Economic and Social Development of the People's Republic of China of 2016 details a continued commitment by China to infrastructural investment. Agricultural modernisation, cyber economy, urbanisation and modern infrastructure networks are priorities in the plan. Transport is still a key consideration in the plan, with a focus on a modern, integrated, safe and eco-friendly transport system that connect regions, national and international routes, with the incorporation of multimodal hubs, and that provides more efficient service. The transportation projects detailed in the plan are quite momentous covering high-speed rail achieving 30,000 kilometres and connecting 80% of large cities; 30,000 kilometres of new and upgraded expressways; coastal and Belt and Road thoroughfares; 50 new civil airports; increased harbour and shipping facilities; city-cluster transportation; 3000 kilometres of new urban rail transit lines; rural transportation; the development of multimodal transport hubs; and Internet-based 'intelligent transportation'.

Energy investments will be geared towards greater efficiency, cleaner coal utilisation, renewable energy including the construction of 60 gigawatts of hydropower capacity, nuclear energy, oil and gas, improving energy transmission, storage and transportation routes, and improved energy technology and equipment. Water security projects include investment in large-scale irrigation zones, water diversion, construction of large reservoirs and water source projects, and better management of rivers and lakes.

On the domestic front, it is clear that China has invested and continues to invest in its infrastructure as a means of boosting economic growth. The lessons learnt from its own prioritisation of investment in infrastructure, and its growing global outlook, especially in Africa, suggests that China, as a successful developing country with strong infrastructural development capabilities, is a good candidate to offer these capabilities to other countries on the African continent.

## 4.4 China's Impact on Infrastructure Development in Africa

Africa has traditionally looked towards the West and the World Bank for assistance and financing of infrastructural projects, yet the results have been lacklustre at best. China, with its relatively recent foray into large-scale infrastructural investment and financing on the African continent, has provided an important alternative for African nations and, in doing so, has relieved some of the acute bottlenecks in infrastructural improvements.

The utilisation of the 'Angola-mode' framework agreements, effectively a swap arrangement of oil and mineral resources for infrastructure, was one of the unique ways that China engaged with Africa. "To a large extent it has been succeeding. Because China has been able to mobilise huge financial resources and human capital, from within its own construction industry, along with the labour sent to Africa to develop those infrastructures" (Habiyaremye, personal interview, 2016).

While there are concerns that these agreements have been vague and lack transparency, that there was not enough utilisation of local labour and local small to medium-sized enterprises (SMEs), that skills transfer didn't take place and that some African countries do not possess the capacity to manage and maintain the infrastructure, the benefits of these projects are undeniable when visiting African countries that have enjoyed such investment. Other concerns related to the Angola-mode framework agreements are in terms of creating 'resource dependency' and failure to diversify these economies. This may be true to some extent, although these agreements have evolved over the years towards a greater emphasis on industrial development, notably in countries such as Ethiopia. But as Alexis Habiyaremye cautions, "for the shift towards industrialisation to take place, people will really need to relinquish the idea that China is here to industrialise Africa. Africa should be here to industrialise itself" (personal interview, 2016).

The convincing nature of China's investment becomes abundantly clear when considering the proportion of infrastructural funding it provides in Africa. According to The Infrastructure Consortium for Africa (2015), the total funding for infrastructure in Africa in 2015 was US$83.5 billion of which US$20.9 billion was supplied by China and US$28 by African national governments themselves. In terms of each type of infrastructural sector, it is likely that the emphasis is to some extent driven by China's large investment: US$34.7 billion is invested in transport of which China contributed US$9.8 billion; US$34.7 billion in energy of which China invested US$10 billion; and US$2.5 billion in ICT of which China contributed US$1 billion. Total Chinese funding per region is as follows: US$14.1 billion in North Africa; US$15.2 billion in West Africa; US$4.9 billion in Central Africa; US$19.3 billion in East Africa; US$16 billion in Southern Africa excluding South Africa; and US$11.7 billion in South Africa; while US$2.2 billion is unallocated.

To better conceptualise the vast range of infrastructural projects that China and Chinese companies have conducted, financed and maintained throughout Africa, a 'snapshot' analysis was conducted on 2016–2017 media releases listed on the Forum on China–Africa Cooperation (FOCAC 2017) website that detailed such projects. The results are depicted in Table 4.2.

**Table 4.2** Chinese proposed, financed and built infrastructural facilities: Media releases by FOCAC during 2016 and 2017

| Infrastructure type | Country or region | Project details |
| --- | --- | --- |
| Power | Ethiopia | • US$230 million loan for an advanced electrical grid system for Addis Ababa<br>• Chinese firm to construct 120 MW wind farm<br>• US$14 million hydropower plant rehabilitation, by a Chinese company, financed with a government grant |
|  | Rwanda | • Hydropower plant to be built by consortium of two Chinese companies and an Austrian firm |
|  | South Africa | • China Development bank to finance US$500 million for Eskom's (power utility) capital expenditure programme |
|  | Kenya | • Opening of a Chinese-built electrical transformer-manufacturing plant<br>• Chinese firm to build 500 MW solar power plant |
|  | Côte d'Ivoire | • Final stage of construction of Chinese-built dam at a cost of US$571 million financed by the Chinese Exim Bank |
| Transport infrastructure | Africa | • Belt and road initiative (modern silk road) |
|  | East Africa | • China expressed interest in managing Air Traffic Control in East Africa<br>• Large-scale regional railway and road network, much of which is being financed and built by the Chinese |

(*continued*)

**Table 4.2** (continued)

| Infrastructure type | Country or region | Project details |
|---|---|---|
| | Kenya | • Chinese firm wins contract to repair Kenyan road<br>• Lamu Port project in Kenya constructed by a Chinese company |
| | Tanzania | • 680 metre long bridge built by a Chinese company at a cost of US$135 million and which connects Dar es Salaam with the outskirts of the city<br>• Inauguration of Chinese-built military airport |
| | Ethiopia | • Loans for two roads in Addis Ababa, one for US$102 million, the other for US$50 million<br>• The Ethiopian–Djibouti railway and several other railroad projects were reported upon that China and Chinese companies were involved in |
| | Rwanda | • Chinese company begins road upgrading in Kigali |
| | Liberia | • Chinese project to upgrade the Roberts International Airport Terminal |
| | Gabon | • China provides preferential loans for a perimeter highway project to be built around the capital of Libreville |
| | Nigeria | • Built by the Chinese, a 186 kilometre railway links the city of Abuja with the northern state of Kaduna |
| | Madagascar | • Chinese-built road inaugurated in Madagascar |
| | Mozambique | • Chinese-funded and Chinese-built bridge at a cost of US$15 million to reduce commuting time |
| | Sudan | • Partnership between Sudan and China to develop Port Sudan Harbour |
| | Angola | • Lobito–Luau railway completion—1344 kilometre line built by a Chinese company |
| ICT | Nigeria | • Chinese company launches digital terrestrial TV in an ancient town, one of 80 cities where the service has been enabled |
| | Tanzania | • Chinese media company contributing to Tanzania's migration towards digital migration |
| | Kenya | • Launch of Chinese digital TV project in rural Kenya |
| | Cameroon | • ICT training for Cameroonians in Shenzhen |
| | Malawi | • US$23 million agreement to boost Internet connectivity in Malawi |
| | Namibia | • Chinese firm signs memorandum of understanding with Namibia to drive ICT development and improve technological literacy |

(*continued*)

**Table 4.2** (continued)

| Infrastructure type | Country or region | Project details |
|---|---|---|
| Water and sanitation | Ethiopia | • A Chinese company institutes a harnessing of rainwater project to address a primary school's water shortage—a pilot project for an intended large-scale roll-out |
|  | Zimbabwe | • Chinese firms agree to construct Harare dam to augment water supply to the city<br>• Chinese firm to upgrade Harare's sewerage system |
| Agriculture | Nigeria | • China loans US$4.5 billion to improve local agricultural development |
| Other | Africa | • Several initiatives to develop and support special economic zones in Africa<br>• A number of government facilities built to support national and local governments in service delivery<br>• China was involved in various initiatives to support poverty alleviation, housing provision, and health, education and security services |
|  | Zimbabwe | • Completion of installation and training for a meteorological facility in Zimbabwe |

FOCAC (2017)

While this analysis does not intend to provide a comprehensive list of all the infrastructural projects China is involved in in Africa, it certainly provides a synopsis of the complexity and range of projects in Africa.

The FOCAC Johannesburg Action Plan (2016–2018) and outcome of the FOCAC 6th Ministerial Conference illustrate that China intends continuing with its massive infrastructural 'push' in Africa in the near future. Central to this effort is the acknowledgement that poor infrastructure is a key detractor to sustainable development on the continent. This is illustrated in the following excerpt from the Action Plan:

> The two sides agree that underdeveloped infrastructure is one of the bottlenecks hindering independent and sustainable development of Africa. The two sides will take concrete measures and give priority to encourage Chinese businesses and financial institutions to expand investment through various means … to support African countries and the African flagship projects in their efforts to build railroad, highway, regional aviation, ports, electricity, water supply, information and communication, and other infrastructural projects, support African countries

in establishing 5 transportation universities and facilitate infrastructure connectivity and economic integration in Africa. (The Forum on China–Africa Cooperation Johannesburg Action Plan 2015)

The Action Plan also details significant financial investment, much of which would be towards infrastructural development:

- Direct investment by China in Africa to increase to US$100 billion in 2020 from US$32.4 billion in 2014.
- China will offer African countries US$35 billion of loans of a concessional nature on more favourable terms.

In order to depict the compelling influence China has had on Africa's development through infrastructural investment, financing and support, an analysis was conducted on just one aspect of infrastructure development—transport infrastructure.

### 4.5 Providing Africa with Integrated Transport Infrastructure

The investment by China in Africa's transport is comprehensive. It is driven by China's own domestic agenda of a modern and effective integrated network of multimodal transport, linked to the global market through the One Belt One Road Chinese initiative. Chinese firms have built modern railway lines in Nigeria and Angola and are currently busy with the Nairobi–Mombasa line in Kenya which will link the capital with the port of Mombasa, and, eventually, to an array of regional destinations. The Ethiopia–Djibouti railway line linking Addis Ababa to the sea is also one of the latest and biggest railway projects by China in Africa. Three case studies showing the impact of Chinese transportation construction in Africa over time will now be described, namely the Tan–Zam railway line, Ethiopia's transport infrastructure development, as well as road construction in Lesotho.

#### 4.5.1 China's First Major Investment in Africa's Infrastructure: The Case of the Tan–Zam Railway Line

Tanganyika proclaimed independence in 1961, and after merging with Zanzibar, Tanzania was formed in 1964. During the same period, Zambia also proclaimed its own independence and formed the Republic of Zambia. Emboldened with these developments, the two countries aspired towards further economic development. Song (2015) describes how China's first major foray into Africa came about.

Zambia was, and continues to be, heavily dependent on copper mining in the 'copper belt' in the west of the country. Transport of copper from the copper belt was limited at that stage to transport through the colonial powers in the south, or the poorly maintained 'Great North Road' to the port of Dar es Salaam. The ideal alternative was a railway link between Zambia and Tanzania to the port of Dar es Salaam which would not only serve to transport copper but held promise of bringing development and trade to Zambia's Northern provinces. Map 4.1 depicts the eventual railroad built by China in the 1970s, one of China's first major infrastructural investments on the continent.

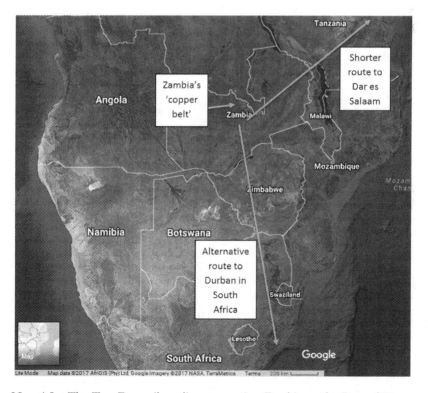

**Map 4.1** The Tan–Zam railway line connecting Zambia to the Port of Dar es Salaam. (Google Maps)

Applications by Tanzania to the United Nations and the United States for financing for the railway fell on deaf ears as the project was regarded as being risky and economically unfeasible. The United Kingdom and the Soviet Union also rejected their request. China, however, with a history of Chinese investments, interest-free loans and trade agreements, had a favourable dispensation towards Tanzania and was open to the idea. In 1965, Mao Zedong confirmed China's was committed to the railway for the Tanzania section.

Zambia at the same time was hoping the West would consider financing the railway in their country, and although with the conflict rising in Southern Rhodesia (now Zimbabwe), the British, Canadian and Americans were considering the project, but for a variety of reasons, including the proclamation of independence in Southern Rhodesia, China was asked to undertake the construction.

Construction of the railways, with the financial and technical assistance of China, began in 1970 and was completed five years later. China has assisted with the technical support and management of the railway since completion. The importance of the investment by China in the railway was significant for both countries, facilitating the movement of people with direct socio-economic benefits, whilst opening the region to trade both locally and internationally.

#### 4.5.2 Integrated Transport Infrastructure Development in Ethiopia

Ethiopia is one of the oldest and largest countries in Africa. Ethiopia is one of only two countries in Africa that was not colonised in modern times, although, sadly, it has a recent history tainted with famine and genocide, such as the genocide fuelled by ethnic conflict during the 'Derg' era.

Much has changed in the country: many international organisations are now profiled in Addis Ababa, including the headquarters of the African Union, housed in a Chinese-built skyscraper. Ethiopia also has a large and growing consumer base of about 90 million people, and is fast trying to change its global image from a country filled with drought and starvation to one that is filled instead with factories and railways.

The last 10–15 years have been characterised by a new drive to transform and develop the country. With the second largest population in Africa, and a much improved level of educated workforce, Ethiopia is poised to expand its manufacturing sector. The Chinese have realised this.

In addition to Tanzania, China has earmarked Ethiopia as an ideal country to implement their 'Angola-mode' framework agreement. However, instead of swapping infrastructure for minerals (of which Ethiopia has very little), China has opted for proceeds from the push towards economic diversification and industrialisation.

Cooperation between China and Ethiopia began in the 1970s and China has since contributed to numerous infrastructure projects. Transport, telecommunications and power provision were the sectors that benefitted the most from this cooperation. The sum of Chinese contracts in road and rail construction and electricity shows a remarkable increase in the last decade and many Chinese firms are currently engaged in the construction of transport infrastructure in Ethiopia.

*Africa's First Light Rail System in Addis Ababa*
Coupled to the urbanisation trend in Africa, Addis Ababa is bursting at the seams with its population of approximately five million people. The city's road network buckles under the pressure of a plenitude of cars and buses, and many outdated and barely legal Russian-built blue and white taxis, dubbed 'blue donkeys', dating from Ethiopia's communist past.

China's main contribution to modernising transport infrastructure in the city includes a new highway and the flagship light rail system dubbed a tramway. The Addis Ababa Light Rail Transit (AA-LRT) is an electrified rail system spanning some 34 kilometres, much of which is elevated above the bustling roads below. The two lines cross at Meskel Square, an iconic place at the city centre used for political demonstrations in the past. The trams are modern, clean, functional and fast—a classic engineering success by the Chinese (see Figs. 4.3 and 4.4). The cost of the tramway, most of which was financed by China's Exim bank, was US$475 million. The tramway was built by the China Railway Engineering Corporation (CREC).

It is a marvellous experience travelling on the tramway. Ticket vending is rather unsophisticated—the sales offices were blue containers positioned haphazardly alongside the stations (see Fig. 4.5). But with ticket prices at just a couple of US cents, it is affordable to most commuters. The pedestrian crossing crosses the railway line (with pedestrians not paying much heed to the tram, mind you) to the station and the other side of the road. It is obvious that attention has been paid to security and logistics. Security is high and officials actively monitor the flow of people in and out of the tram carriages.

Fig. 4.3 The sleek new Chinese-built trams in Addis Ababa

Even though the tramway has just recently begun operating, they were already jam-packed with commuters soon after the service began—a reflection of the speedy adoption of the tram as an alternative means of transport. Commuters had quickly learned the schedules and logistics of the tramway, and the speed of embarkation and disembarkation would rival that of the Western underground or Chinese MRT urban railway systems.

The positive impact of the tramway is abundantly clear. For the people of Addis Ababa, it provides a quick and affordable means of travelling long urban distances to work, or to conduct business, with its capacity of 60,000 passengers a day. It contributes to the alleviation of traffic congestion on the roads, and has limited negative environmental externalities. Skills transfer and job creation will hopefully be a long-term benefit,

**Fig. 4.4** Elevated tram system

**Fig. 4.5** The blue container ticket sales office on a busy Addis Ababa street. (The staff requested they not be photographed)

although it was noted that the tram drivers were all Chinese, 'assisted' by local Ethiopians, at the time of the authors' visit in 2015 (it was unclear whether they were training), and much of the building and maintenance that was still in progress was mostly conducted by Chinese teams. There are a number of other possible longer-term benefits of the tramway. Tourism is one that comes to mind. Tourism is in its infancy, yet Addis Ababa specifically and Ethiopia in general have an exciting array of tourist highlights and the largest airport node in Africa. Although the tramway is not currently linked to the Addis Ababa Bole International Airport, the tramway provides a prime opportunity to develop tourism corridors in the city and beyond.

The role that major urban rail transport systems play in urban economic growth and the well-being of cities' inhabitants is a topic that received attention at the 2011 International Conference on Green Buildings and Sustainable Cities, and can feasibly shed some light on the impact the Addis Ababa tramway has on the socio-economic well-being of the city. Chang-fu and Yuan (2011) describe the direct and indirect benefits of large urban railway transport projects. The direct benefits include economic opportunities for companies involved in the project such as civil engineering companies, equipment suppliers, brokerage firms, material suppliers, as well as general job creation. In the Addis Ababa tramway example, some of these benefits can be assumed to accrue to Chinese companies, although there is hope that there was some economic stimulation for the city during the project's progress.

Of more importance and long-term benefit are the four indirect effects Chang-fu and Yuan (2011: 523–524) spell out: the promotion of intensive utilisation of land and the progress of urbanisation; the provision of broad development space for the environmental protection industry; the transformation of economic development approaches; and the improvement of the city's 'soft power'. With regard to utilisation of land use, such rail transport leads to better and more intensive use of urban land—strategic planning of land use is conducted resulting in better coordinated results in more sustainable urban development. Rail transport is an environment-friendly way of providing commuters with transport at ten times the capacity of road transport; it contributes to the reduction of road transport, reduces emissions and noise pollution and opens up land space for urban greenery. In terms of economic development, such transport infrastructure can underpin the growth of the service industry, "breeds infinite business opportunities", and stimulates real estate development and increases government revenues through land taxation, amongst a plethora of other economic benefits. Soft power refers to the potential of the urban railway to energise the modernisation of the city and influence the city's culture, thereby "assembl(ing) precious and intangible assets for (the) city, indirectly improve the added-value of all sorts of existing assets of the city and enhance the city's comprehensive power and regional competitiveness".

*The Addis Ababa–Djibouti Railway Line*
China's newest initiative, a US$3.4 billion project, came in the form of a rail link between Addis Ababa and the Port of Djibouti in Djibouti as an element of developing the rail network in Africa (Map 4.2).

As a landlocked country, with coastal country borders of hostile Eritrea and conflict-ridden Somalia, Ethiopia has had to rely on the Port of Djibouti for exports and imports. Prior to the railway line, goods had to be transported by a poorly maintained 750 kilometre road that would take up to two days. The railway reduced this time to 12 hours, and is much more cost-efficient and environment-friendly. The new railway line gives Ethiopia access to international markets, while the tiny country of Djibouti gets easier access to 90 million Ethiopian consumers. It will make the region more attractive for investment and development. Incidentally, Djibouti also housed China's first overseas military outpost, a naval base that China insists is only a logistics hub for China's naval and trade presence in the Gulf of Aden.

The Addis Ababa–Djibouti railway line, the recent version of the Tan–Zam line discussed earlier, is similarly likely to stimulate economic growth and development and improve regional trade and integration. It is also envisaged to be one aspect of a transport network that will eventually also facilitate access between Ethiopia and Kenya and Sudan, probably funded in most part by China.

### 4.5.3 Can a Road Change the Lives of Poor Rural People in Africa? The Case of Lesotho

The Kingdom of Lesotho is a small, mountainous and landlocked country, completely surrounded by South Africa (see Map 4.3). It is classified as one of the least developed countries in the world. The majority of the

98  K. JONKER AND B. ROBINSON

Map 4.2  The railway line linking Addis Ababa and the Port of Djibouti. (Google Maps)

INFRASTRUCTURE: THE MOST IMPORTANT ENABLER OF ORGANIC... 99

Map 4.3 Lesotho landlocked by South Africa. (Google Maps)

population lives below the poverty line. It has a population of only 1.9 million with an annual GDP growth rate of less than 1%. The country is predominantly rural, with communities depending on subsistence farming for their livelihoods. With only 10% of the country suitable for arable agriculture, the country's income consists primarily of the Southern African Customs Union (SACU) receipts, the remittances of miners who work in South Africa and textile exports to the United States.

China is a significant investor in the textile industry, taking advantage of the United States' African Growth and Opportunity Act (AGOA), which allows Lesotho to export to the United States on favourable terms. In addition, China also assists the country with the roll-out of road infrastructure throughout the landlocked country. This case study contemplates how the new road infrastructure is fundamentally changing the lives of the predominantly rural mountainous Basotho people.

Lesotho conjures up images of the beautiful Basotho people; the smell of the horses on a 'pony-trek' up the mountains; colourful blankets worn on cold mornings; thatched 'rondawels' (houses constructed of mud, dung and wood); and mokorotlos (conical woven hats embodied on the national flag).

Two roads trips were conducted in 2014 and 2016 to evaluate China's road construction projects. A trip in 2014 took the route via the Sani Pass from South Africa to Lesotho. The strictly 4 × 4 route weaves up a narrow mountain pass, with motorcars slipping and sliding, reaching the summit, which boasts the highest pub in Africa. Travelling about 50 kilometres inland from Sani Pass towards Mapholaneng, the rutted, muddy road is transformed into a road construction site, with warning signs of impending road excavation explosions and road closures times. And then, Chinese trucks, Chinese heavy-duty road construction vehicles and a lot of Chinese—the entire workforce appeared to be Chinese, from truck drivers to engineers to the least skilled worker (see Figs. 4.6 and 4.7). Further on, a beautiful road lay beyond, a road intended to link the area to the north of the country and beyond.

Two years later, the new road between Roma and Ramabanta was explored. About 150 kilometres in length, funded by the World Bank, the Lesotho government and its development partners, much of the road was built by the Chinese: for example, China Geo-Engineering Corporation built the Senqu and Senqunyane bridges on the Roma and Ramabanta road—the same company which built the Mapholaneng to Sani Pass section described earlier.

INFRASTRUCTURE: THE MOST IMPORTANT ENABLER OF ORGANIC... 101

**Fig. 4.6** Road construction in Lesotho

**Fig. 4.7** Chinese contractors weaving the new road en route to Sani Pass

While the road may in the long term facilitate some cross-border transport with South Africa, it would be wrong to assume that the road was prioritised to link the landlocked country with different provinces (and ports) of South Africa with Maseru, Lesotho's capital. The road from Matatiele in South Africa to the border post of Qacha's Nek to Lesotho was unpaved and in poor condition (see Fig. 4.8). From Qacha's Nek the road was paved into Lesotho. Without investment by South Africa to pave their side of the border road from Matatiele, and for that matter the paving of the Sani Pass road, these investments will do little in terms of developing transit corridors (a priority of the Almaty Declaration on Landlocked Countries and the Southern African Development Community Regional Indicative Strategic Development Plan).

Looking at the mountains near Ramabanta, the beginning of the new road, it is difficult to even imagine a road traversing their peaks. Yet the Chinese succeeded, with the road winding sharply up and down, through the most spectacular scenery, and credit goes to the engineering and construction acumen involved in the project (Figs. 4.9 and 4.10).

**Fig. 4.8** Unpaved road on the South African side of Qacha's Nek border post

INFRASTRUCTURE: THE MOST IMPORTANT ENABLER OF ORGANIC... 103

**Fig. 4.9** A bridge on the new Roma to Ramabanta road

**Fig. 4.10** One of the twisting road passes on the Roma to Ramabanta road

However, it is difficult to imagine large trucks manoeuvring along these roads, and certainly no trucks were observed en route—a limitation to the propensity of the road being a trade route.

So has the M680 million (Basotho Loti which is linked to the South Africa Rand) spent on the road been well spent? From an economic perspective, there would be an expected trade benefit once the transit corridors are opened. But the immediate impact and value should be seen from the perspective of the well-being of these rural communities near the road.

Limited work opportunities may exist in the capital of Maseru, but most job-seekers join the migrant labour force in South Africa. But how do the rural communities access the job market if they can't get there? Prior to the Roma to Ramabanta road, the only means of transport was a 4 × 4 vehicle with a courageous driver and, of course, the reliable horse or donkey and the donkey cart. These communities would have had little, if any, access to education, healthcare facilities and, undoubtedly, no hope for formal employment.

The road has changed all that. Health and welfare facilities, many of them international aid agencies, are now able to provide services to the people along the road. There are many new schools and clinics being built, construction of which would have been very difficult without the road (see Figs. 4.11 and 4.12). Toilets were also being built at the time of the trip, with some villages sporting a new toilet for each home (see Fig. 4.13). Mobile phone coverage was relatively good suggesting that investment in mobile networks for the area had taken place. While there wasn't electricity provision, it is likely that the electrical grid could now be expanded to these previously inaccessible areas.

It was also evident that people were relocating from other areas to live alongside the road—many new homes had been built next to the road. And, very importantly, the roads now provide a quicker and more practical transport link for those wishing to work, to travel to Maseru or across the border to South Africa.

These roads are also an ideal opportunity for Lesotho to capitalise on the tourist industry. Prior to the many new roads, much of Lesotho was only available to the 4 × 4 offroad enthusiast or adventure biker (Prince William (prior to his marriage to Kate) and Prince Harry had lots of fun here). With its spectacular scenery (see Fig. 4.14), and the wonder of snowfall quite rare in Southern Africa, the roads now provide South African tourists with an alternative travel destination. Currently there are very few accommodation

Fig. 4.11 One of many of the new schools built near smaller communities

offerings in the country, but as tourism grows, this will surely change, and the labour-intensive tourism industry could provide numerous employment opportunities in the future.

One of the concerns regarding the new roads, and a concern echoed throughout Africa regarding infrastructural projects completed by the Chinese, is who is going to maintain these roads, and who is going to pay for such maintenance? In order to travel from Qacha's Nek border post to the new road, the older tarred A4 was driven upon. It was quite obvious that the road was not receiving any level of maintenance. In fact, the road was hair-raising to say the least, often with giant boulders from landslides many years before, obstructing much of the road (see Fig. 4.15). If maintenance does not take place on the new Chinese-built road, the forces of nature are surely going to erode all the advances the road has brought to the communities along its course.

**Fig. 4.12** A regular sight of schools and clinics alongside the road

**Fig. 4.13** Every home in this village has its own new toilet

**Fig. 4.14** A view only now accessible due to the new Roma to Ramabanta road

**Fig. 4.15** One of the many landslides along the older A4 road

So while some signs of progress may be quite melancholy, such as the beanie replacing the mokorotlo, the Chinese road construction interventions are having a dramatic impact on the lives of the mountain people of Lesotho. Provided they are well maintained, they can be a driver for socio-economic growth direly needed by the country.

## 4.6 The Contribution and Consequences of China's Infrastructural Investments

Infrastructure is a fundamental requirement to stimulate sustainable growth in African nations. China is contributing significantly to reducing the bottlenecks in infrastructural project construction and finance in numerous African countries. Expertise developed during China's own challenging trajectory of infrastructural development has been harnessed and applied to some of the development priorities in African countries.

In so doing, China has sometimes contributed to African countries' ability to improve their service delivery through the provision of access to basic needs. Infrastructure, such as power provision and road infrastructure, has improved the potential for industrialisation and access to global markets, thus facilitating economic growth. The large-scale construction projects that have utilised local labour and local suppliers have created jobs and facilitated skills transfer, and small and medium enterprise development.

One of the critiques against these Chinese-driven projects, though, is that the Chinese have perhaps not employed enough local labour, and in many cases, only employed local labour in lower-level positions, thus limiting the job creation benefits and skills transfer that these projects could have created. Similarly, the preference for Chinese suppliers could limit the benefits that may have accrued to small and medium-sized businesses. The increased debt burden on developing economies is a concern, and while Angola-mode type of framework agreements may reduce such a burden, it could have the negative impact of resulting in resource dependency and lack of economic diversification.

The importance of African nations themselves better managing the relationship and terms of engagement with China to leverage the best results from the large-scale infrastructural projects was emphasised.

A summary of the infrastructural aspect of the African Tree of Organic Growth is depicted in Fig. 4.16.

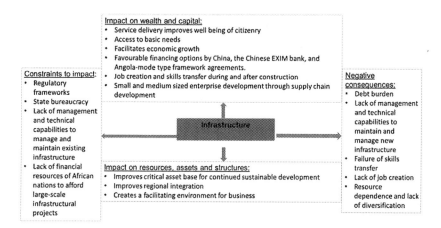

Fig. 4.16 Contribution of China's infrastructural investments to the African Tree of Organic Growth

# References

African Development Bank Group. 2011. Handbook on Infrastructural Statistics. Accessed from: https://www.afdb.org/fileadmin/uploads/afdb/Documents/Publications/AfDB%20Infrastructure_web.pdf (accessed: 28 May 2017).

CEIC. 2016. China's Investment: % of GDP from 1952 to 2016. Accessed from: https://www.ceicdata.com/en/indicator/china/investment--nominal-gdp (accessed: 13 July 2017).

Chang-fu, H. and Yuan, X. 2011. 'Research on the Role of Urban Rail Transit in Promoting Economic Development', *2011 International Conference on Green Buildings and Sustainable Cities*. Elsevier Ltd.

FOCAC. 2017. Latest News Releases: 2016–2017. Forum on China-Africa Cooperation. [Online]. Available from: http://www.focac.org/eng/ (accessed: 29 May 2017).

Foster, V. and Briceño-Garmendia, C. 2010. *Africa's Infrastructure: A Time for Transformation*. © World Bank. Available from: https://openknowledge.worldbank.org/handle/10986/2692. License: Creative Commons Attribution License (CC BY 3.0 IGO) (http://creativecommons.org/licenses/by/3.0/igo/).

Shi, Y., Guo, S. and Sun, P. 2017. 'The Role of Infrastructure in China's Regional Economic Growth', *Journal of Asian Economics*, 49: 26–41.

Song, W. 2015. 'Seeking New Allies in Africa: China's Policy Towards Africa During the Cold War as Reflected in the Construction of the Tanzania-Zambia Railway', *Journal of Modern Chinese History*, 9 (1): 46–65.

The Forum on China-Africa Cooperation Johannesburg Action Plan (2016–2018). 25 December 2015. FOCAC. [Online]. Accessed from: http://www.focac.org/eng/ltda/dwjbzjjhys_1/hywj/t1327961.htm (accessed: 29 May 2017).

The Infrastructure Consortium for Africa. 2015. Infrastructure Financing Trends in Africa—2015 Report. Accessed from: https://www.icafrica.org/fileadmin/documents/Annual_Reports/ICA_2015_annual_report.pdf (accessed: 17 July 2017).

CHAPTER 5

# The Role of Effective Governments and Institutions

Effective governance is one of the key facilitators of economic growth and development. China's engagement in Africa can either contribute to or detract from the ability of African countries to enable development through successful governance (Fig. 5.1).

Effective governance is informed by formal and informal institutions, while socio-economic development is a function of suitable public policy design, implemented by an efficient public administration infrastructure. This is represented in Fig. 5.2.

Many scholars have examined the conditions of poverty and underdevelopment in Africa and several causes have been identified. Among these are political opportunism and corruption, ethnic conflict and political violence, non-sustainable structures and policies, and military intervention in politics and governance. Underdevelopment in some of these countries can further be directly attributed to mistakes made by sometimes incompetent and ill-informed but well-meaning policymakers. A further obstacle of development in Africa is the absence of institutional arrangements that effectively guide and protect an ethical government process and prevent its agents, civil servants and politicians from engaging in rent seeking and political opportunism.

Government effectiveness in Africa ranges from many examples of notable successes to others representing horrifying failures: war and strife in the DRC and Burundi, famine in South Sudan and Somalia, thriving

© The Author(s) 2018
K. Jonker, B. Robinson, *China's Impact on the African Renaissance*,
https://doi.org/10.1007/978-981-13-0179-7_5

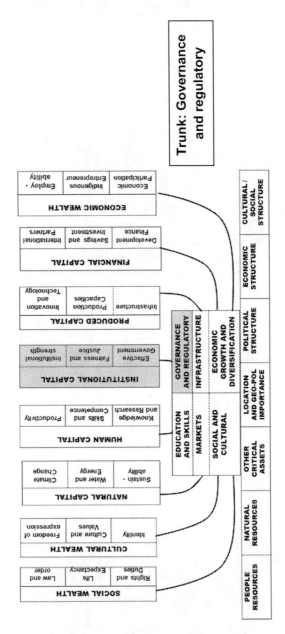

Fig. 5.1 The African Tree of Organic Growth

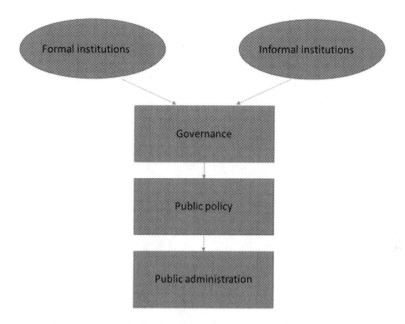

**Fig. 5.2** Organogram of effective governance. (Authors' own)

economies with strong governments in Botswana and Namibia. The question must be asked as to what are the governance factors that contribute to organic growth and development in some African nations, and what governance factors debilitate other African countries, and, finally, what is the contribution or detraction that China has regarding governance.

## 5.1 Democracy and Dictatorships

Governments can be constituted in many ways, and the debate about the efficiencies of different political systems is complex. In Africa, the political systems have mostly been inherited from both the colonial history of the country in question and the fight for independence, often supported by communist regimes such as Russia, China and Cuba. And unfortunately, sometimes, the political system is a function of the greed and powermongering of the country's leadership.

Without entering the foray of which is the better method of government, the West prioritises a system of democracy and their aid and investment in Africa is often conditional on free and fair democratic elections. China differs fundamentally in this regard, in that it has a 'non-interference' policy in the internal affairs of the African countries with which it engages. As a one-party state founded on Marxist and Maoist principles, democracy would not be a consideration in any case, yet often this non-interference policy is criticised from the viewpoint that China implicitly supports some of the most corrupt, warring, human rights–abusing leaders and governments in Africa.

Perhaps a more generic and useful approach to use in evaluating the effectiveness of government is its commitment to good governance, development and accountability. Governments are by their very nature accountable to the people of the country and are primarily responsible to maintain law and order and to provide public goods for the community. This entails that they should perform their duties in furtherance of the socio-economic-environmental needs of the general population, the country and the wider global community. It implies that government would perform an administrative role in developing policy, institutions and a regulatory environment to run the country. It would make laws and adhere to its own laws and constitution. It would be transparent in decision-making and enforcement. It should strive to meet the needs of society in an effective and equitable manner.

### 5.1.1 Losing Hope in Zimbabwe, Finding Hope in The Gambia and Savouring the Success of Ghana

If there ever was a lost opportunity, it was in Zimbabwe. In an unusual way, Cecil John Rhodes colonised the country in the 1880s under company rule for mining purposes, and the greater region, now known as Zambia and Zimbabwe, was named Rhodesia in his honour. An unpleasant colonial period followed that included the Matabele wars and the displacement of indigenous people in favour of Europeans. The country was later administered separately as Northern and Southern Rhodesia (now Zimbabwe), with Southern Rhodesia becoming a British colony in the 1920s, and in 1965, without the authority of the British colonial power, the country declared independence under Ian Smith. The 1970s were characterised by guerrilla warfare, with Robert Mugabe's Zimbabwe African National Union (ZANU) taking centre stage. Independence and democracy was eventually achieved, and in 1980 Robert Mugabe and his party achieved landslide victory at the polls.

Civil unrest followed until Mugabe reached a unity agreement that merged certain parties, and the ZANU-PF party was born.

Mugabe is a lucky man. Not only are Mugabe and the ZANU-PF still in power after 36 years, but Mugabe also won Z$100,000 in the Zimbabwean lottery in 2000. Speaking to Zimbabweans, or ex-Zimbabweans, Mugabe is described flatteringly in his early years of power. He guided the country through turbulent years and hopes were high that he would lead the country well. "We loved him, needed him, wanted him in the early 1990s", one Zimbabwean recalls. Infrastructure was good, the populace was well-educated, the economy was prospering, the mining sector was healthy and agricultural production was thriving. Initial indications were that he was adopting sound education, health and macroeconomic policies, while embracing non-racialism.

Poor decisions, policy failures, high HIV levels, election tampering and an increasingly autocratic leadership style followed. Land reform policies, initially on a willing seller–willing buyer basis, deteriorated to a point where Mugabe encouraged violent capture of land by war veterans, and included confiscations of white-owned land for redistribution to black farmers. Without the skills, finance and perhaps motivation, and accusations of favouritism, many of these farms achieved little success. Agricultural exports, previously the highest export sector, dropped drastically. Hate speech against whites, human rights abuses and anti-gay rhetoric earned him international condemnation. International sanctions followed the 'electioneering' fiasco that pervades the country. Inflation skyrocketed to trillion Zimbabwean notes, before the currency collapsed, and the country adopting the US$ as official currency, although it reintroduced controversial bond notes in 2016.

Mugabe seems to have lost touch with the people. Now known as 'Flying Mugabe' he travels the world in style and luxury, living the high life of a president seemingly not accountable for his people. His wife, Grace Mugabe, similarly enjoys the fruits of the position, infamous for her shopping sprees, earning her the nickname 'Gucci Grace'. The same Zimbabwean quoted earlier reflects that "people are worried, everything is upside down. People don't want him, even the war veterans (Mugabe's traditional support base) are changing their view."

Zimbabwe's failure in governance is abundantly clear in the critical role of providing free and fair elections, a cornerstone of any democracy. Table 5.1 reflects experiences of past elections and failures of the electoral commission.

**Table 5.1** Examples of Zimbabwe's failure to provide free and fair elections

**Presidential degree can amend the Electoral Act:** President Mugabe can bypass parliamentary authority on amendments for electoral changes
**'Vote buying':** numerous examples of vote buying though political gifts by Robert and Grace Mugabe
**Technical exclusion of voters:** Lack of transparency resulted in many urban voters being excluded from the voter's roll or being prevented from registering
**Voter roll errors:** Numerous errors in the roll
**Lack of funding for electoral process:** The Zimbabwe Electoral Commission (ZEC), the institution that is supposed to facilitate the elections, lacked the capacity to do so. It was underfunded, to the extent that the chairperson suggested the 2011 elections could not be held due to financial constraints
**Restriction of electoral support organisations:** The Zimbabwe Election Support Network was prevented from voter education in 2008
**Electoral commission politicised:** ZEC partisanship compromised its ability to be an impartial body in the electoral process
**Numerous breaches of the electoral Act by ZANU-PF:** In many instances the law and constitution were breached during elections
**Limited sanction for electoral irregularities:** The police and ZEC did little when electoral breaches were detected
**Lack of effective voter registration drive:** Not enough education and registration assistance was provided
**Lack of transparency of the voter's roll:** The voter's roll was not made available for public scrutiny
**Special votes contraventions**
**Media bias:** Media acted as a 'propaganda' mouthpiece for the ZANU-PF, and was instructed to 'attack' opposition party leadership in their media reports

Adapted from Hove and Harris (2015) commentary of elections in Zimbabwe

We now turn our attention to The Gambia, the smallest country in Africa. The Gambia hit news headlines in December 2016 when the 1 December elections saw the surprise defeat of long-term president Yahya Jammeh by the opposition candidate, Adama Barrow. Jammeh conceded defeat on 2 December. Celebrations were short-lived though, as on 9 December, Jammeh seemingly had a change of heart and rejected the election results, calling for a re-election.

In rare solidarity, the local populace, regional and international bodies condemned his renunciation of the election results, including the Economic Community of West African States (ECOWAS), the African Union and the United Nations Security Council. ECOWAS was particularly involved in attempts to solve what had now become a constitutional crisis. However, talks between Jammeh and ECOWAS representatives failed. Senegal, which surrounds the entire border of The Gambia, Nigeria and Ghana, formed a military coalition, and at a last resort was forced to invade The Gambia on 19 January 2017. Intense negotiations followed, and after a further two days, Jammeh relinquished control in favour of Barrow, and left the country to live in exile in Equatorial Guinea.

Jammeh was an unsavoury leader. He effectively ruled The Gambia from 1994 after a coup d'état to 2017. During his rule, elections were tainted with opposition intimidation, electoral engineering and intimidation of voters. The media was silenced or biased in favour of Jammeh and was used as a propaganda medium, resulting in the self-exiling of reporters and media outside the country's border. Prison terms were introduced allowing for the sentencing of journalists for reporting considered defamatory. Human rights abuses were prolific: for instance, Jammeh was vocal in anti-LGBTI rhetoric, threatening to behead gays and lesbians in the country. He fabricated claims that herbs could cure HIV/AIDS. Uprisings were quelled through force, with disappearances, killing and imprisonment being common occurrences. He has been accused of supporting Senegalese rebel forces and being involved in illegal money laundering and gun-trafficking with these groups, souring the relationship with The Gambia's most important potential trade partner. Corruption was rife under Jammeh's rule and the general consensus is that he benefitted enormously from his position and it is suggested that he was one of the wealthiest African leaders. It is unlikely that he will be sorely missed except by those who benefitted from his patronage.

While this rocky transition of power wasn't ideal, it does signify that a change of regime can occur through democratic processes, and that external regional mobilisation in Africa can enforce such processes when internal problems arise. There is a promise of hope for The Gambia.

Ghana was one of the first countries to achieve independence from European colonial powers in 1957, and, after a coup and various military and civilian government changes, the country achieved a state of political stability. Since then, Ghana has followed a path of good governance, which has resulted in relatively successful economic growth and development. One of the key success factors for Ghana has been the transfer of political leadership through democratic processes. President John Kufuor served the maximum two terms in office, having won the elections in 2001 and 2004. He was succeeded by President John Atta Mills in the elections of 2008. This also signalled the transfer of power from the New Patriotic Party of Kufour to the National Democratic Congress of Mills. Vice President John Mahama succeeded Mills in 2012. President Nana Akufo-Addo of the New Patriotic Party succeeded Mahama in the 2016 presidential elections. Both Akufo-Addo and Mahama signed a pact prior to the elections committing themselves to follow electoral rules and keep the peace.

The question that needs to be posed is what are the fundamental differences between these three countries? There are two ways of addressing this question: the first is to analyse whether free and fair elections took place, and second, whether there was ease of transfer of political power.

*Question 1: Free and Fair Elections*
Consider Bishop and Hoeffler's (2016: 609) definition of a free and fair election:

> 'Free-ness' means that all adult citizens must have the right to register and vote as well as having the right to establish and join parties and campaign freely within the country. 'Fairness' refers to the equal treatment of equals.

Bishop and Hoeffler presented ten variables to determine whether a free and fair election has taken place: the legal framework; electoral management bodies; electoral rights; voter register; ballot access; campaign process; media access; voting process; role of officials; and the counting of votes. An elementary comparative analysis in Table 5.2 indicates stark differences in the three countries against these ten prerequisites for a free and fair election.

Undoubtedly Zimbabweans and Gambians did not enjoy free and fair elections, while Ghanaians had a much greater opportunity to make their voice heard in their elections.

*Question 2: Ease of Transfer of Political Power*
Perhaps the more fundamental question is the ease of transfer of political power in these three examples. A comparison in this regard is made in Table 5.3 which considers the leader's willingness to concede power, and the level of internal and international influence on ensuring a regime change when relevant.

**Table 5.2** Comparative analysis between elections in Zimbabwe, The Gambia and Ghana

| Bishop and Hoeffler's (2016) variables | Zimbabwe (Hove and Harris 2015) | The Gambia | Ghana |
|---|---|---|---|
| Legal framework | President can unilaterally effect electoral changes | Unclear whether a satisfactory legal framework was in place | General perception of free and fair elections |
| Electoral management bodies | Restrictions of electoral support organisations, partisan ZEC | Electoral engineering | General perception of free and fair elections |
| Electoral rights | Technical exclusion of voters. Voter roll errors | Intimidation of voters | General perception of free and fair elections |
| Voter register | Voter roll errors, lack of transparency of voter's roll | Electoral engineering | General perception of free and fair elections |
| Ballot access | Electoral commission politicised. Breaches of the Electoral Act | Electoral engineering. Opposition intimidation | General perception of free and fair elections |
| Campaign process | Numerous breaches of the Electoral Act. Limited sanction for election irregularities. Media bias | Opposition intimidation, electoral engineering, intimidation of voters | General perception of free and fair elections |
| Media access | Media bias | Media silenced or biased. Prison terms for defamation | General perception of free and fair elections |
| Voting process | 'Vote buying'. Technical exclusion of voters. Special votes contraventions. Numerous breaches of Electoral Act | Opposition intimidation, electoral engineering, intimidation of voters | General perception of free and fair elections |
| Role of officials | Numerous breaches of the Electoral Act | Unclear whether election officials acted in a fair manner | General perception of free and fair elections |
| Counting of the votes | Unclear whether this was done fairly | Unclear whether this was done fairly | General perception of free and fair elections |

Authors' own analysis using Bishop and Hoeffler's (2016) variables

**Table 5.3** Comparative analysis between Zimbabwe, The Gambia and Ghana's leadership and internal and international influence

| Leadership and internal and international influence | Zimbabwe | The Gambia | Ghana |
| --- | --- | --- | --- |
| Leadership | Clearly President Mugabe has no intention of relinquishing power | Past President Jammeh was intent on holding on to his position even after being defeated at the polls | A commitment to a peaceful and free and fair election was the foundation of the election. Past President Mahama was prepared to abide by the election outcome |
| Internal and international action | Although elections have been marred by blatant election engineering, there has been a lack of sufficient internal and international action to affect a regime change | The regional commitment of neighbouring countries, including the use of force, was ultimately the factor that allowed for the regime change | Political stability and good governance supported a peaceful regime change |

Authors' own

The analysis in Table 5.3 indicates that when the conditions of a free and fair election are not in place, a regime change will only be possible if there is sufficient internal political activism to overthrow the government (as evidenced during the Arab Spring uprisings), or external support and action by the international community to force such a change. It also highlights the need for effective political institutions for guiding the transition of power.

China's role becomes relevant in supporting international efforts to address political instability in Africa.

### 5.1.2 Chinese Peacekeeping Efforts in Africa

There is no doubt that sustainable economic development is all but impossible when there is political instability or when conflict prevails—a fact China is aware of and which it highlights when the opportunity presents itself. Ambassador Lin Songtian, in his capacity as Director General of the African Department of the Chinese Ministry of Foreign Affairs, addresses this issue quite succinctly:

Peace and development are the two sides of one coin. Without a peaceful and secure environment, there can be no cooperation and development. Without cooperation and development, there can be no guarantee for peace and security. (FOCAC 3 2016)

The role that China is increasingly taking upon itself is actively addressing these problems through a range of peacekeeping efforts. While maintaining its non-interference policy, it hopes to influence problematic countries towards the maintenance of peace and stability. It does this through bilateral efforts and by participating in peacekeeping efforts of the United Nations and the African Union. In addition, China supports "Africa[n] countries to improve laws and regulations, to improve investment and business environment, helping African countries to enhance capacity building in law enforcement departments such as border defence, military and police, customs and taxation", in order to be able to achieve a safe and stable environment that supports growth and development (FOCAC 3 2016).

The People's Liberation Army (PLA) is China's military arm. Initially the PLA played a small role in international peacekeeping efforts, but this has changed, and China is now a significant contributor to peacekeeping operations throughout the world. It contributes the largest number of peacekeeping troops amongst the United Nations Security Council's Big Five (permanent members of the Council, namely China, France, Russia, the United Kingdom and the United States). China's peacekeeping efforts are also very closely aligned to its foreign policy agenda and is part of its diplomacy efforts.

China claims to have over 2600 peacekeeping personnel engaged in ten UN peacekeeping operations, including a certain number in strife-torn African countries. South Sudan is one of these. China has dispatched three peacekeeping infantry battalions to South Sudan since 2015, with the latest 120 members being dispatched to the capital city of Juba, which will be supplemented with a further 580 members at a later stage. This commitment took place even though China has suffered casualties in its peacekeeping efforts in the country—for instance, two Chinese peacekeepers were killed in 2016 in Juba (FOCAC 1 2016).

In addition to its involvement in the United Nation's Security Council, China actively supports the African Union in their efforts to stabilise conflict situations. In fact, China's commitment in peacekeeping efforts is conditional on the African Union and other regional communities mandate for such interventions—again an aspect of China's non-interference policy. Chinese President Xi Jinping pledged US$100 million in 2015 to the African Union with the specific purpose of establishing the Africa Standby Force. While respecting country sovereignty, direct bilateral mediation by China in attempts to resolve conflicts has also been claimed by the Chinese in countries such as Burundi and South Sudan (FOCAC 2 2016).

While there are philanthropic reasons for China's role in engendering peace and stability in Africa, there are also clear benefits to China itself: Its peacekeeping efforts demonstrate China's commitment to 'peaceful development' and a 'harmonious world', mitigating the fear that China would be an aggressor in its foreign policy. As the country's international role increases, China's national security increasingly becomes linked to global peace and stability. China's peacekeeping forces, working alongside other countries, will also gain invaluable experience and contribute to the modernisation and professionalism of the PLA, thus improving their own deterrent capacity (Huang 2011).

While this discussion indicates a resolve by China to positively influence peace and security in Africa to facilitate development, the concern can be raised that the non-interference policy of China could tacitly support some of the most corrupt and tyrannical regimes in Africa.

### 5.1.3  *China's Non-interference Policy*

China's non-interference policy is founded upon the Chinese 'Five Principles of Peaceful Coexistence', which detail the principles of mutual non-aggression; non-interference in each other's internal affairs; mutual respect for sovereignty and territorial integrity; equality and benefit; and peaceful coexistence.

The policy has found favour amongst most African Nations that were finding it difficult to comply with Western aid conditions of structural change. However, critics have vociferously condemned the policy as flawed and being misused, citing the following reasons and examples (Table 5.4).

There is no doubt that China is a significant global power in Africa, and the non-interference policy will continue to be a question mark in its interaction with African regimes. Yet the support that China provides through the United Nations Security Council and the African Union indicates that China is becoming more proactive in propagating peace and stability in Africa—the necessary conditions for sustainable economic growth.

**Table 5.4** Critique against China's non-interference policy in Africa

Policy designed to merely further China's economic and investment interests in Africa
The policy overlooks the reality of conflicts and sociopolitical realities in Africa
The policy is selectively applied and tailored to suit Chinese interests
The policy justifies the dealings of the Chinese with the elites
Questionable labour practices by Chinese companies, and the use of Chinese labour rather than local labour, has been sanctioned by the non-interference policy
China supplied the Sudanese government with arms and weaponry, which were used for persistent and systematic violations of human rights
In order to maintain a reliable source of oil, China is accused of manipulating political control in Sudan
Despite political instability in Guinea-Bissau, China has financed infrastructural projects and supported the government in return for exclusive deepwater fisheries and oil exploration rights
A high priority by China on preserving strong relations with African energy suppliers has supported some of Africa's worst dictators with poor human rights records, such as Sudan and Congo-Brazzaville, and allowed these regimes to ignore good governance standards

Adapted from Okolo's evaluation of the policy (2015: 39–41)

## 5.2 Core Institutions

The gradual, and sometimes rapid, decline of African nations is often symptomatic of the collapse of the institutional frameworks that are necessary for effective governance of nations. Institutions can be informal, such as the values, culture and rules of engagement in society, or formal, the regulatory environment of law and law enforcement, and the policy framework that guides the country in a particular path.

When healthy institutions don't exist, or when potentially supportive institutions are abused, they have the damaging propensity to seriously compromise any hope of securing well-being for the general population. What is the influence of China on the development of healthy institutions within Africa? Probably the greatest influence China can have in this regard is 'leading by example'. Through both its formal and informal institutions, China has transformed itself from one of the poorest countries in the world to the world's second biggest economy. It provides an example of a transitional economy that has progressed without property rights protection and sophisticated legal systems found in mature market economies.

Xu (2015: 534) describes the governing institution of China as regionally decentralised authoritarianism, where political power is highly centralised with the Chinese Communist Party having significant control, yet highly decentralised in administrative implementation and economic resource allocation. The huge party–state bureaucracy acts as the coordination mechanism with its top-down bureaucracy having state control over landownership and financial resources, and decentralised local administration and resource allocation. The judicial system plays an important role in the management of this bureaucracy.

In the face of a lack of market-related incentives, the success of the system relies on regional competition, which China has encouraged through the implementation of regional competitions—an aspect of the assessment of these regional competitions is how well these regional bureaucracies meet the GDP growth targets.

An important institutional contributor to governance in developing countries is informal institutions—the values and norms of communities and the wider society. China's Confucian ethos assisted it in historically governing the vast country and population, which emphasised communitarian ethics rather than individualism. Another informal institution that survives to this day is 'Guanxi', where economic transactions are informal and not reliant on formal contracts.

The Chinese model does have its problems and the sustainability of China's growth may depend on further radical reform including political and market reform and private landownership, including a move away from the dependence on regional competition as a primary 'incentive'.

African countries, in their various stages of evolutionary development, have different levels of formal institutional sophistication, and sometimes those in existence are counterproductive to development. While these formal institutions may take some time to be introduced or improved, this does not imply that growth and development cannot take place. Africa also has its own informal institutions, such as 'Ubuntu', 'Seriti' and 'Umuntu Ngumunta Ngabantu', traditional humanist philosophies that reflect a prioritisation of communities or society above the individual. If these informal institutions can be harnessed, they could support growth and development, and reject counterproductive formal institutions.

The evolution of appropriate formal institutions for African countries can be driven organically taking into account their own values and cultural and social structures—by doing this, the formal institutions will resonate with the informal institutions already in existence, thus contributing to the effectiveness of core institutions.

## 5.3 Policies for Development

One aspect of the heterogeneous nature of Africa is the varied evolutionary stages that African Nations find themselves in, in terms of their political and governance framework. Perhaps this is one of the reasons that Western interventions have sometimes failed in Africa, as these interventions were based on socio-economic assumptions of developed economies. Policies for development have to take cognisance of these stages, and a fit needs to be found that ensures the adoption of sound development policies that are practical to implement and that improve governance efficiency.

Effective policies can support growth and development, yet policies often fail because of inherent weaknesses in the design of these policies, and the lack of implementation of these policies. Even the best intentions in policy design will fail if there is no political willpower and if policies are motivated by the self-interest of policymakers.

Policy development and implementation are needed in almost every sphere of government. There are several specific policies that are utilised for advancing the development agenda. Some of these are described in the following sections.

### 5.3.1 Poverty Alleviation

Poverty alleviation or pro-poor policies are often in the form of targeted transfer programmes which aim to protect the most vulnerable of the population, the poor and people in need. These programmes can comprise either monetary benefits or products such as food for famine relief. The GDP growth of many African countries reached double-digit figures in the recent past, yet this paints a false picture of the well-being of the general population. Often there is no benefit of such growth for much of the population who remain in abject poverty. There is some debate as to whether cash transfers should be conditional or not. Conditional grants would stipulate how the funds are to be utilised, for instance the purchase of food or payment of school fees. Unconditional grants assume that the individuals whom the grant intends benefiting would be the most knowledgeable as to the priorities that the grant can finance.

### 5.3.2 Adopting a Workfare Approach in Job Creation

Mechanising job functions in the face of acute unemployment doesn't make sense. Replacing road workers with graders and bulldozers would limit the job creation possibilities of major construction projects. 'Workfare' is a term used to describe job creation policies, mostly employed in labour-intensive projects that use low-skilled labour to enhance employment levels. This would also apply to public works programmes where service delivery is coupled to job creation opportunities. One aspect of such a policy would be the requirement for foreign direct investment in large infrastructural projects to implement quotas of local labour and minimum job creation targets.

### 5.3.3 Infrastructure

Infrastructure enables economic growth: roads transport goods for sale; electricity powers factories; waste management manages the wastes from production. Infrastructure improves people's lives in many ways: sanitation and clean and accessible drinking water reduces disease; roads provide access to healthcare, schools and workplaces; improved communication access such as mobile networks improves access to information and social engagement.

Infrastructure policy in developing nations should identify the priorities in infrastructure investments, the most suitable funding options for large-scale projects and ensure the suitable management and maintenance of such infrastructure. Institutions are also needed to ensure transparent and cost-effective decision-making, honesty in the tendering and project-awarding process, and the long-term financing and administration of these assets.

### 5.3.4 Agricultural Policies

Developing the agricultural sector holds much promise for development in Africa. A carefully considered agricultural policy can go a long way towards developing this economic sector and contribute to the reduction of food insecurity. Land reform is often the first consideration, and the most controversial. The nationalisation of agricultural land and the expropriation of 'white-owned' farmland have historically been regarded as redistributed justice for colonial abuses of the past. As is evidenced in Zimbabwe, this has in many cases resulted in the collapse of the agricultural sector. Taxation of the sector has also been problematic, as it is often one of the main sources of government revenue in lesser diversified economies. Policy needs to find the balance between incentivising agricultural activities while generating revenues. Improving farming methods and the introduction of technologies to improve efficiencies of scale, training and support, research, agricultural development through consumer and producer subsidies, supply chain and beneficiation opportunities, and protection in the form of trade barriers are all important decisions in developing such policy.

### 5.3.5 Industrial Policies

Industrialisation is often regarded by economists as the key to economic growth. This may be true for some transition economies in Africa, while others may benefit from a greater reliance on agricultural sector development.

Industrial policies may consider the fundamental incentives for investment in industries. One such policy option is the introduction of Special Economic Zones. These have been introduced in a number of African countries following the successful utilisation of such zones in China in its path of economic development. The zones are geared towards providing suitable infrastructure, tax incentives and assistance in establishing companies and obtaining visas for expatriates. Basically, they have made doing business easier.

### 5.3.6 Education

There is no doubt that investing in the human capital of a nation can be a significant contributor to the upliftment of people and the global competitiveness of nations. Policy would focus on the priorities of primary, secondary and tertiary education and emphasis be placed on the skill set most needed by the country, for instance, mathematics and science as contributors to future engineers.

In developing countries, policy would often need to ensure the building of new schools, provision of textbooks and the allocation of competent teachers to these schools. In addition, practical issues may also need to be addressed, such as the provision of transport to enable children in rural communities to attend schools, or a feeding scheme to prevent malnourishment of poorer communities.

### 5.3.7 Health and Healthcare Finance

High birth, youth and maternal mortality rates; deaths due to diseases such as HIV/Aids, tuberculosis, malaria and Ebola; deaths due to malnutrition;

and premature deaths due to treatable cancer and cardiovascular disease are tragic realities in developing countries in Africa.

Health and the financing of healthcare to reduce the levels of premature deaths will always be important considerations in development policy. This type of policy should encourage healthier living habits, clinics should be established to provide primary healthcare and hospitals built to provide medical services.

There are numerous aid interventions available to African countries from non-governmental organisations (NGOs) and the global community. China itself is active in lending a helping hand in health provision in Africa.

### 5.3.8 Fiscal and Monetary Policies

Fiscal and monetary policies are important considerations for all economies, especially for developing economies. Monetary policy can be utilised to stimulate the economy, control inflation, encourage saving or spending, and encourage business investment. This is normally managed through some form of institution such as the central bank, which utilises the mechanisms of the discount rate or required reserves of commercial banks.

Fiscal policy relates to tax collection and government spending. A difficult budgetary balance needs to be achieved between collecting enough taxes without reducing the incentive for business and investment to take place, while ensuring adequate funds are available for financing development priorities such as health, education and transfer programmes. The level of debt, and the servicing of such debt, also requires careful consideration in order to enable the investment by the government in infrastructure, for instance, without crippling the economy for many years to come with burdensome debt repayments.

Historically the level of debt in many African countries has had a crippling effect. In 2005, at the Group of Eight Summit, the G-8 wrote off US$40 billion of debt, which benefited some of the poorest countries in Africa at that time, including Benin, Burkina Faso, Ethiopia, Madagascar, Mali, Mauritania, Niger, Rwanda and Senegal.

China has been at the forefront of debt cancellation in Africa. In 2009, China cancelled 150 mature debts of 32 African countries, followed by US$60 billion debt relief announced at the 2015 Forum on China–Africa Cooperation (FOCAC) Summit. Even with this contribution to debt relief, with China financing and undertaking numerous infrastructural projects, China will continue to contribute to increased debt burdens within Africa. Whether this is responsible lending for economic growth or whether it will create financial problems for some African countries remains to be seen.

### 5.3.9 Allowing the Market to Function

While China remains a one-party state with strong elements of a planned economy, it has realised the value of the market system, and has embraced the markets in supporting economic growth. An efficient market system is one of the central features of the 'trunk' in the African Tree of Organic Growth. While a chapter has not been dedicated to the topic, the importance of cultivating an efficient market system is paramount to fuelling economic and social development.

The government can either enable the market to function or create barriers to an effective market. Barriers could include crippling bureaucracy that makes it difficult for companies to be incorporated, obtain licences and rights, or purchase property—the red tape of doing business. And then there is, of course, the bureaucrats themselves, government officials who make every step towards a successful business venture more remote.

There is often an ominous reason for this. In many cases in Africa it is found that government officials are in cahoots with certain elements of the business sector, benefiting financially from the relationship. These government officials can influence the award of tenders, or create the already mentioned red tape, which effectively prevents a competitive market to function. One example is the influence the Gupta family have had in South Africa. Colloquially termed 'state capture', this wealthy family have close ties with President Zuma and his son, and it is alleged that they have influenced an array of state-owned enterprises and business decisions in their favour. An example was the purchase by the state enterprise Transnet of expensive harbour cranes for ports in South Africa from the Chinese company Shanghai Zhenhua Heavy Industries Limited, with Gupta-related firms allegedly receiving tens of millions of Rands for facilitating the transaction. Commentators have suggested that not only did the payment increase the price paid for the cranes, but the cranes purchased were not ideal for the particular purpose for which they were intended.

When the government places barriers to the possibility of an effective market, resources are drained away from the economy, while effective competitive markets act as a magnet to attract resources and investment. The relationship between the political institutions and market institutions is closely related.

## 5.4 Why Policies Fail: Poor Planning and Service Delivery Inefficiencies in Public Administration

As alluded to earlier, policy development and implementation can fail dismally, mostly due to poor governance. The most likely causes for failure are government inefficiencies and inability to provide effective service delivery, and, of course, the scourge of corruption.

Service delivery is a huge problem in Africa, often resulting in protests and more serious forms of conflict. African governments are infamous for overpromising, normally during election times, and under-delivering. There seems to be an endless list of the life-supporting priorities in Africa, such as housing, water, sanitation, power, education, health services, safety and security services. The media reports detailing the inability of the state to satiate these needs due to poor policy implementation are just as long.

A useful case study was conducted in Northern Uganda and Burundi that illustrates some of the challenges of service delivery. Chi et al. (2015) explored the barriers in providing emergency obstetric and neonatal care in these countries besieged with conflict. High rates of maternal mortality, 15% of pregnancies in developing countries experiencing pregnancy-related complications and 40% of deaths of children younger than five years due to neonatal problems are statistics that highlight the importance of access to emergency obstetric and neonatal care in developing countries. Compounding the problem was the conflict situation with the following consequences: lack of basic medication and equipment, depriving women and newborn babies of basic life-saving services; breakdown of the referral system due to roadblocks and travel restrictions that prevented access to women seeking specialised services in urban areas; poor communication between healthcare facilities; and personnel fleeing for their own safety.

Two themes emerged from their post-conflict research—first, human resources limitations, and second, systemic and institutional failures in providing emergency healthcare—both of which are illustrated in Table 5.5.

There are numerous examples of service delivery failures in healthcare throughout Africa, many resulting in death. Inefficient service delivery

**Table 5.5** Major themes and subthemes related to perceived barriers to the delivery of quality emergency obstetric and neonatal care services in Burundi and Northern Uganda

| | |
|---|---|
| Human resources–related challenges | • Acute shortage of trained personnel<br>• Demoralised personnel and perceived lack of recognition<br>• Perceived poor living conditions and poor remuneration for personnel<br>• High personnel turnover<br>• Increasing workload and high burnout<br>• High levels of staff absenteeism in rural health centres<br>• Poor level of coordination among key emergency personnel resulting in delays in providing emergency services |
| Systemic and institutional failures | • Poorly operational ambulance service for referrals<br>• Inefficient drug supply system<br>• Inefficient referral system<br>• Lack of essential installations, supplies and medications<br>• Poor allocation of limited resources<br>• Poor harmonisation and coordination of emergency training curriculum nationally<br>• Weak and incomprehensible training curriculum<br>• Poor data collection and monitoring system<br>• Inequity in the distribution of emergency facilities between urban and rural areas |

Chi et al. (2015: 25)

may not always be life-threatening, but can certainly impact the economic and personal well-being of Africans. Take the example of urban transport. Many if not most African capital cities are absolute chaos to navigate through, and probably 'life-threatening' if the driving is anything to go by, and pollution from all the vehicles' emissions makes travelling unbearable. Many of the infrastructural projects described earlier pertain to urban road and railway infrastructure. While these investments will go some way in alleviating congestion, an efficient public transport system is also key in this regard, and policymakers need to consider ways to implement such a system.

Accra in Ghana provides a useful example of urban policy implementation that has been disappointing in its uptake by commuters it was supposed to benefit. The city introduced the 'Metro Mass Transit' system for city commuters, which was 20% cheaper in price than traditional minibuses, yet the system is underutilised. Birago, Mensah and Sharma (2016) went about interviewing 134 commuters to find out why they weren't using the new public transport: Overcrowding, non-adherence to time schedule, long in-vehicle time, perception of lack of seats and comfort, non-availability of buses at origin and destination, long waiting time for buses and ease of accessibility of alternative transport options were all factors that resulted in non-use of the system.

South Africa also introduced a range of road and transport improvements and options. Lack of proper consultation and poor policy planning have sparked major protests. For example, minibus taxi owners rejected the notion of a rapid mass transport system in the Nelson Mandela Metropolitan Municipality in the city of Port Elizabeth, stalling the introduction of the system after a huge investment by the municipality in road infrastructure and new buses. Similarly, an e-toll road system in Johannesburg was met with 'drive-slow' protests disrupting the highways; non-registration and non-payment of toll fees; union action; and accusations of the government 'blackmailing' vehicle owners who already contributed to road infrastructure through its road tax regime.

### 5.4.1 Why Government Policies Fail: Corruption

Corruption diverts desperately needed funds in developing countries to political elites; public funds in public administration find their way into private hands; bribes compromise everyday life for those dealing with public officials; bribes affect the ability to do business efficiently; bribes raise the cost of doing business; bribes reduce the incentive to invest; while bribes to 'turn a blind eye' to illegal activities compromise the justice system and the safety and security of the people; and bribes that influence public spending, for example, influencing the tendering process, reduce the efficiency of public spending.

Transparency International publishes an annual Corruption Perceptions Index, which includes a world map. Africa is very 'red' on this map. The darker the red is, the greater is the perceived corruption in that country.

Botswana is perceived as the least corrupt country in Africa; even then, it ranks 35th in the world. Unfortunately, most African countries fall in the much lower ranks of the index, including the two appearing as the worst in the Corruption Perception Index, South Sudan and Somalia (Corruption Perceptions Index 2016).

Corruption is clearly a major problem. The question though is whether China exacerbates or alleviates this problem of corruption.

To answer the question as to whether China contributes to the problem or to the solution of corruption in Africa, the authors interviewed international thought leaders and academics to gauge their perceptions on the matter. Corruption in the roll-out of infrastructural projects was considered relatively insulated from corruption. As one professor from China highlights, these bilateral projects are critical to the African countries in which they take place and monitoring usually takes place by high-ranking officials. But possibly the main deterrent to corruption is often the mode of financing these projects. For example, the 'Angola-mode' framework agreements that China has used in some countries is effectively a swap agreement of mineral or energy resources in exchange for the construction of the infrastructural projects. Financing of the projects is usually in China through the Chinese EXIM Bank. In effect, money doesn't change hands in Africa, thus mitigating the risk of corruption to a large degree.

Private Chinese companies, as opposed to state-owned enterprises, are much more susceptible to corruption. At the time of the interviews, one of the thought leaders who was involved in researching the telecommunications sector described how some Chinese companies had been heavily involved in bribery in order to gain access to the market and secure contracts. Some companies and individuals had been prosecuted, with the representatives of companies sometimes being jailed. The involvement in corruption by Chinese companies can have serious repercussions. In the case of one of the bigger Chinese telecommunications companies, their corruption in Africa resulted in the Norwegian sovereign wealth fund, a major investor in the company, disinvesting from the company.

He also makes the point that Chinese companies do not undergo the level of public scrutiny of the West, and that there is less transparency for Chinese companies than a Norwegian or British company, for example—these firms would find it more difficult to be involved in corruption due to public opinion, civil society and the media.

While corruption in Africa can be said to be endemic in many countries, the same holds true for China, where corruption has infiltrated the country's huge government and bureaucracy. As one thought leader contended, "[c]orruption has always been a big issue. The Chinese are not unfamiliar with what corruption is. They know how to deal with it. The paradox is that China is a country that has managed to achieve tremendous things while not necessarily rooting out corruption."

Corruption is, however, a key focus of Chinese President Xi Jinping. He has embarked on a crackdown on corruption within his own Communist Party and the business sector with numerous arrests and sentences for those involved in corruption. In 2015, 26 state-owned enterprises were listed for inspection in the anti-corruption campaign of the President and its impact was quickly realised. Chang Xiaobing, chairman and chief executive of state-owned China Telecom was one of the 'fatalities' of the crackdown, resigning from his position at the end of 2015 for severe disciplinary violations and pleading guilty in 2017 for taking bribes. He was also expelled from the Communist Party.

While it would be impossible to quantify the level of corruption in the Chinese–African engagement, it would seem that the nature of investment in large-scale infrastructure projects and the efforts to reduce corruption by state-owned enterprises could together reduce some of the incentives to be involved in corruption. However, the onus is really on African countries themselves to combat the scourge of corruption through good governance efforts.

## 5.5 Concluding Remarks

There is a strong case for African countries taking a greater responsibility for their own futures. There are many informal institutions of cultural norms that already guide the cultures and communities in their rules of engagement. These can be leveraged, while formal institutions can be developed that are appropriate to their evolutionary development phase to support structural changes needed for such growth, provided, of course, that the very people tasked with institutional development do not manipulate these same institutional frameworks for their, or an elite's, benefit, thus depriving their own people of the benefits of such development. Appropriate institutions support effective governance and leadership, which in turn craft appropriate development policy and introduce public administration for successful service delivery.

China's government and Chinese companies operating in the myriad of African countries can support the stability and good governance of the countries in which they interact, thus playing an important role in the organic growth and development of these countries. Alternatively, they can manipulate the current weaknesses of governance, or take advantage and abuse the lack or failure of institutions—a reality in many African countries (Fig. 5.3).

## 5.6 China's Impact

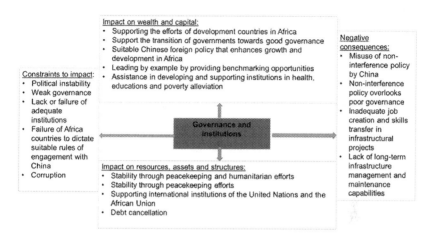

**Fig. 5.3** China's impact

## References

Birago, D., Mensah, S. and Sharma, S. 2016. 'Level of Service Delivery of Public Transport and Mode choice in Accra, Ghana', *Transportation Research Part F: Traffic Psychology and Behaviour*, 1–17.

Bishop, S. and Hoeffler, A. 2016. 'Free and Fair Elections: A New Database', *Journal of Peace Research*, 53 (4): 608–616.

Chi, P., Bulage, P., Urdal, H. and Sundby, J. 2015. 'Barriers in the Delivery of Emergency Obstetric and Neonatal Care in Post-Conflict Africa: Qualitative Case Studies of Burundi and Northern Uganda', *PLOS ONE*, 10 (9).

Corruption Perceptions Index 2016 by Transparency International Is Licensed Under CC-BY-ND 4.0. Accessed from: http://www.transparency.org/news/feature/corruption_perceptions_index_2016#table (accessed: 18 March 2017).

FOCAC 1. 5 December 2016. China Dispatches Third Peacekeeping Infantry Battalion to South Sudan. [Online]. Accessed from: http://www.focac.org/eng/zxxx/t1421391.htm (accessed: 18 April 2017).

FOCAC 2. 16 August 2016. FOCAC. China Making Efforts to Ensure Peace and Stability in Africa. [Online]. Accessed from: http://www.focac.org/eng/jlydh/mtsy/t1389422.htm (accessed: 18 April 2017).

FOCAC 3. 7 June 2016. The New Thinking and New Measures of China's Policy to Africa: Helping Boost Transformation and Development of African

Economy—Speech by Ambassador Lin Songtian, Director-General of African Department of MFA at the Policy Dialogue between China and IDA. [Online]. Accessed from: http://www.focac.org/eng/zxxx/t1370204.htm (accessed: 18 April 2017).

Hove, M. and Harris, G. 2015. 'Free and Fair Elections: Mugabe and the Challenges Facing Elections in Zimbabwe'. *International Journal of Human Rights and Constitutional Studies*, 3 (2): 157–170.

Huang, C. 2011. 'Principles and Praxis of China's Peacekeeping', *International Peacekeeping*, 18 (3): 257–270.

Okolo, A. 2015. 'China's Foreign Policy Shift in Africa: From Non-interference to Preponderance', *International Journal of African Renaissance Studies*, 10 (2): 32–47. Copyright © Unisa Press, reprinted by permission of Taylor & Francis Ltd, http://www.tandfonline.com on behalf of Unisa Press.

Xu, C. 2015. 'China's Political-Economic Institutions and Development', *Cato Journal*, 35 (3): 525–548.

CHAPTER 6

# A Skilled and Educated Workforce for Africa

Several authors have identified a direct correlation between the opportunities to acquire relevant education and skills in a country, and the rate of employment and productivity in that country. The International Labour Office (ILO) (2010) identified three cornerstones for developing a suitable skilled workforce: the availability of good-quality education as a foundation; a close matching of skills supply to the demands of the growth sectors in the economy; and the ability of workers and organisations to adjust to changing technology and markets and anticipating and preparing for the skills and competencies that will be needed for future growth. Recent evidence from emerging countries clearly demonstrated the fact that a knowledge-based economy is needed to develop innovation, create new jobs and support inclusive growth and sustainable development.

Good-quality primary and secondary education, complemented by relevant tertiary education, vocational training and skills development, will prepare future generations for their productive lives as members of their community, and will directly contribute to the wealth and produced and human capital of a country, as indicated in the African Tree of Organic Growth depicted in Fig. 6.1.

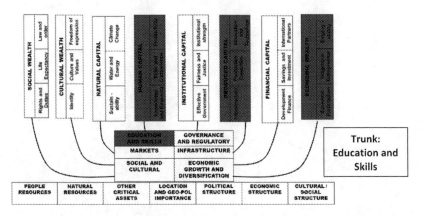

Fig. 6.1 The African Tree of Organic Growth

## 6.1 A WELL-EDUCATED AND SKILLED WORKFORCE: THE KEY TO SUSTAINABLE GROWTH AND PROSPERITY IN AFRICA?

There are several facilitators for the development of an educated and skilled workforce which are presented as essential ingredients to sustainable growth and development. These include good-quality and relevant education, with a specific focus on the youth—aspects discussed in more detail in the following section.

### 6.1.1 Quality and Relevant Education

Quality and relevant education are essential to realise Africa's organic growth and transformation, as envisioned in the United Nations Sustainable Development Goals. Better education and effective skills development constitute one of the cornerstones of economic transformation, and are therefore included in the trunk of the African Tree of Organic Growth. With the expanding youthful population in Africa and an abundance of resources, the opportunity for accelerated growth driven by skills, productivity and employment has never been greater. Education will not only better equip African people to find employment, but can also provide the foundation for innovative breakthroughs, spurring the disruptive solutions needed for sustainable growth in Africa.

Sub-Saharan African countries have recorded some of the greatest increases in primary school enrolment since the turn of the century according to a United Nations Educational, Scientific, and Cultural Organization (UNESCO) report published in 2015. UNESCO's 'Education for All: Global Monitoring Report' tracks the progress countries have made in reaching educational targets set at the World Education Forum in Dakar, Senegal, in 2000. The good news is that the number of children enrolled in primary schools in sub-Saharan Africa rose by 75% to 144 million between 1999 and 2012, which, according to the report, can be attributed mainly to the abolition of school fees in countries such as Ethiopia, Ghana and Kenya, as well as an increase in the number of teachers. It was, however, alarming that despite the increase in enrolments, there was still a very large number of 30 million primary-age children not attending school in Africa in 2012. In Nigeria, Africa's most populous country, 8.7 million children are not attending school (UNESCO 2015). According to the report, corruption, lack of investment and conflict in the country's northeast with Boko Haram have resulted in Nigeria having one of the worst educational systems in the world. In contrast, Burundi managed to double the proportion of primary-age children enrolled in school from less than 41% in 2000 to 94% in 2010, achieving the highest percentage point rise in Africa. Other countries amongst the top performers in enrolments were Niger, Mozambique, Guinea, Burkina Faso, Zambia and Ghana (UNESCO 2015). Sub-Saharan Africa has increased the number of primary schoolteachers from 1.9 million in 1999 to 3.4 million in 2012, an increase of 76%. Despite this, teacher shortages still remain a serious problem, and in 24 out of the 42 countries surveyed pupil/teacher ratios were above 40:1, with the ratio up to 80:1 recorded in the Central African Republic (UNESCO 2015).

Africa also has the world's lowest secondary school enrolment rates. An average of just 28% of youth are enrolled in secondary schools, resulting in over 90 million teenagers struggling for employment in low-paid, informal sector jobs (Thisisafricaonline.com 2013). It is estimated that a child entering the education system of an Organisation for Economic Co-operation and Development (OECD) country has an 80% chance of receiving some form of tertiary education, while the comparable figure for sub-Saharan Africa is only 6% (Thisisafricaonline.com 2013). Researchers identified several causes for this problem, of which inequalities, regional conflict, geographical location, lifestyle and traditions were found to be the most prominent. Africa has some of the world's starkest inequalities in access to education. Children from the richest 20% of households in Ghana average six or more years in school, compared to children from the poorest households having little or no schooling (Thisisafricaonline.com 2013). Conflict is another barrier to education. Many of Africa's out-of-school children from conflict zones, such as Somalia and the Democratic Republic of Congo (DRC), are living in refugee camps where they receive very little or no education. Some students have challenges enrolling for secondary education due to geographic location, lifestyles and traditions. In certain African countries, the majority of the population still lives in rural rather than urban areas, where nomadic lifestyles are prominent, and the subsistence economy does not demand a high level of education and skills.

The quality of the primary and secondary education received will also determine the potential of those who will progress to higher education, or find meaningful employment to successfully find gainful employment. The quality of primary and secondary education in most African countries is much lower than that found in the developed world, with many children exiting primary school not having any significant numeracy ability, and being unable to read or write. Inequality in access to education also mirrors the inequalities found in many Africa nations, with the wealthy being able to afford quality schooling, while the poor are often subjected to substandard teaching.

Educational systems in Africa are complex, sometimes being embedded in an unstable political, cultural and economic context. Poverty forces many children out of school and into employment. Gender roles in traditional communities could mean that young girls are removed from school to collect water or care for their siblings. Countries such as Niger, Chad and Mali have some of the world's highest number of child marriage, where many girls become brides before they have finished primary school. Quality of teaching and availability of handbooks are common problems. Studies in countries such as Lesotho, Mozambique and Uganda have found that less than half of the teachers could score in the top band on a test designed for 12-year-olds (Thisisafricaonline.com 2013). This is not a surprise if the situation is viewed within the African Tree of Organic Growth paradigm—in this paradigm, the teachers are a natural product of the system itself (or tree) in which they operate. Most of them have therefore not received a quality education themselves, and do not find themselves in an enabling or supportive environment to develop into good teachers.

The higher education sector, especially universities, has been criticised for not educating the youth for skills needed in Africa. A degree from a university is often seen as an entry requirement to a good government job, with little attention being paid to the specific skill set needed for the position. The African Economic Outlook study of 2012 claims that many African recruitment agencies believe that the most difficult sectors in which to find candidates with tertiary education are those that need specific technical qualifications, such as mining, logistics, the chemical and pharmaceutical industries, manufacturing in general and agri-business. It is disappointing to note that even with Africa's comparative advantage in agriculture and the great potential for international trade it has in processed agricultural products, there are a small number of graduates in the specialisation of agriculture.

The importance of capacity-building in agriculture is increasingly recognised in studies on inclusive growth and sustainable development in Africa. The African Union (AU) Heads of State Summits, held in Malabo, Guinea Equatorial in 2014, and in Addis Ababa, Ethiopia in 2015, have made clear decisions to enhance agricultural education, skills development and knowledge support. Based on the Malabo Declaration, the Agricultural Education and Skills Improvement Framework (AESIF) 2015–2025 was developed by NEPAD to address this issue (NEPAD 2015). According to the report, traditional agricultural training systems in Africa are outdated and do not fit the current end users' needs—these needs are for a more productive and knowledge-based agricultural system that will provide for future agricultural development and diversification. It was found that agricultural efficiency is knowledge-based and that productivity increases exponentially as the relevant level of education of practitioners increases. This shift requires an agricultural workforce with a different set of skills, competencies and mindset than what was needed in traditional agricultural systems. These skills include knowledge and competencies on aspects such as mechanisation, irrigation and modern production systems and methodologies such as horticulture and greenhouses. It was found that the agricultural technical vocational education and training in Africa were too theoretical and that the tertiary agricultural education institutions are embedded in rigid academic programmes, with financial constraints. In most cases their curriculum represents a mismatch between what the institution offers and what the industry requires. Curricula are still focused on farm production rather than encompassing all the segments of the agricultural value chain. Agricultural studies are also not a popular choice because such studies are still perceived as a path to poverty, and not as a key to success. As a result, agricultural enrolments are declining in most of these institutions.

Conditional loans from the Western world, and specifically institutions such as the World Bank and the IMF, have had a further negative impact in that they obliged African countries to focus their spending on primary, and not necessarily on higher, education. This resulted in a weakening of standards at universities in the postcolonial period. This scenario was further compounded by the marginalisation of universities by despotic African governments, who saw them as incubators of resistance and opposition, rather than as centres of knowledge. One of the World Bank's most shameful policies was to insist for decades that Africa did not need to focus on higher education, but on the school sector, the implication of which was that Africa was never going to fully develop (McGregor 2015). According to a report by McGregor (2015), this attitude has changed dramatically, and there is now high-level support for African higher education from Makhtar Diop, the World Bank's vice president for Africa. It is further estimated that the returns on higher education in Africa are now the highest in the world.

### 6.1.2 Preparing the Growing Youth Population of Africa for Growth and Employment

It is estimated that by 2025 two-thirds of the population of Africa will be between 15 and 24 years of age, compared to youth comprising less than a third of the rest of the world's population (The Brenthurst Foundation 2011). This group of young people will be the next generation of workers, technicians, engineers and decision-makers, and will be primarily responsible for the organic growth in African countries. The success of this 'African Youth Factor' will depend on the successful development of these people into economic actors with the necessary capabilities and skills to make a difference. This pool of young people can become Africa's biggest asset for growth if developed and harnessed, or Africa's biggest nightmare if they remain unemployed and fail to meaningfully participate in the future of their countries. Recent developments in North Africa have shown some of the potential consequences should young women and men in Africa not find meaningful employment opportunities.

Whilst Europe's and China's populations are aeging and the youth population shrinking, Africa's emerging young workforce represents tremendous potential competitive advantage for the respective countries—if the youth are properly developed and trained. Joblessness is endemic in Africa, especially among the youth. Youth unemployment and underemployment in some countries is as high as 80%. Zambia, for example, had 3 million people at independence of which 300,000 were in formal jobs. In 2011, it had a population of 13 million people, with only 500,000 in formal jobs (The Brenthurst Foundation 2011). Although most African countries enjoyed positive growth over the past 15 years, it has in most cases not translated into formal employment opportunities. There are numerous reasons for this, foremost among them being the lack of competitiveness and productivity compared to that of Asia and China; inadequate infrastructure; and a lack of skills and technical competencies. There are other institutional factors as well; for instance, South Africa has failed to increase formal sector employment, which is largely blamed on labour laws that have made employment less attractive for employers.

A youthful population gainfully employed will directly contribute to the lessening of inequality of incomes and access to opportunity, thereby enhancing the prospects for social coherence and stability—key ingredients for inclusive growth and development. The experience of the East Asian Tigers is highly indicative in this regard. Dividends of a sizeable youth population in the years 1965 and 1990 were captured in the form of better education and increased employment opportunities, leading to a strong and sustained economic upturn. Some scholars accredit as much as 40% of the growth in the region to the rapid expansion and development of the working-age population (The Brenthurst Foundation 2011).

An increase in the average income or economic prosperity of the citizens of a country is normally an indication that the economy of that country is in a growth phase. To increase the average income of people, two things need to happen: first, productivity needs to increase creating more overall income, and second, the resultant new income generated from their increased productivity needs to be returned to the workers in the form of higher wages. Although GDP growth in Africa averaged 5% per year in the period of 2005–2015 the real growth per capita achieved was only 2.1% (World Bank 2015). According to the World Bank report, the main reason for this phenomenon was that economic growth was not accompanied by an increase in productivity. African economies must therefore address the challenges of productivity and increased employment to enable them to achieve sustainable growth and eradicate poverty.

China has enjoyed significant increases in productivity over the last several decades. This drive to higher productivity started in the agricultural sector in the 1960s, and then spread to small businesses in townships and villages in the 1980s and 1990s. What make this so remarkable is that these productivity increases in China had a dramatic effect on reducing poverty in the country. A recent analysis of the impact of growth on poverty which compared China, India and Brazil found that China's economic growth reduced poverty at a rate of 50% more than that of Brazil, and even higher relative to that of India (World Bank 2015). Unfortunately, this reduction has not occurred in Africa, which lags behind in comparison.

## 6.2 China in African Education

The earliest form of educational cooperation between China and Africa consisted of an exchange agreement involving the outbound mobility of African students and inbound movement of Chinese teachers during the 1950s and 1960s. In the 1970s, short-term training programmes were established for African professionals in China. The first FOCAC Action Plan of 2000 reaffirmed China's commitment to increase the number of government scholarships and inbound teachers to Africa. The plan also makes provision for the establishment of an African Human Resource Development Fund to provide for the training of African professionals.

The third FOCAC Ministerial Conference contained Beijing's pledge to build 100 rural schools in Africa, while the fourth Ministerial Conference provided for the construction of 50 China–Africa friendship schools. China also provided some flagship educational infrastructure projects, including the Ethio–China Polytechnic in Addis Abba and the University of Science and Technology in Malawi (Obamba 2013).

At the last FOCAC Ministerial Conference in Johannesburg in 2015, Chinese President Xi Jinping announced ten major plans to boost cooperation with Africa over the following three years (FOCAC 2016) including the establishment of a number of regional vocational education centres that will train 200,000 technicians in Africa.

### 6.2.1 Higher Education and Academic Partnerships

Although mutual academic mobility has been a feature of Sino–African cooperation since the 1950s, very little inter-institutional engagement occurred from the 1950s to the 1990s. The 2006 Beijing Action Plan provided the first attempt to create institutional-level cooperation with the establishment of the Confucius Institutes at various universities in Africa (Obamba 2013). The 20+20 cooperation programme established in 2009 is another significant initiative. This initiative entails the launch of one-to-one partnerships between 20 Chinese and 20 African tertiary educational institutions, in order to promote capacity-building and sustainable development. This initiative proved to be a success with high-ranking universities taking part in the programme such as Peking University and Jilin University in China, and Stellenbosch University and Pretoria University in South Africa. At the last FOCAC Ministerial Conference in 2015 in Johannesburg, China offered students in Africa 2000 education opportunities with degrees and diplomas, and 30,000 scholarships (FOCAC 2016). The number of scholarships to study in China was thus increased remarkably from 18,000 in 2012 to 30,000 in 2015.

The fourth and fifth FOCAC Action Plans, issued in 2009 and 2012 respectively, portrayed a radical shift in the emerging trajectory of the Sino–African engagement. These blueprints demonstrate the emergence of a distinctive and dominant discourse of knowledge, science and technology, and its linkages to sustainable development and poverty reduction in Africa. Under this remit, China pledged to provide 100 postdoctoral fellowships for Africans, and to conduct 100 joint research demonstrations. The plans also made provision for three programmes that are of particular importance to the Sino–African development paradigm, namely The Technology Partnership Programme; The China–Africa Research and Exchange Programme and the China–Africa Think Tank Forum (Obamba 2013).

The Technology Partnership Programme focuses on technology development and technology transfer in areas that are critically connected to people's livelihoods—including agriculture, healthcare, environment, renewable energy and water development. The Research and Exchange Programme focused on joint research initiatives between institutions of China and African countries. The Think Tanks aimed to strengthen the knowledge base of the Sino–African cooperation agreements and projects.

### 6.2.2 *The Effectiveness and Role of Chinese Confucius Institutes and Cultural Centres*

The Confucius Institutes and Cultural Centres have been established by the Chinese government in order to promote the understanding of the Chinese language and Chinese culture worldwide. There are numerous

Confucius Institutes throughout the world, many affiliated to host country universities. Africa had approximately 60 institutes in 2014, although the numbers of institutes are constantly increasing as China continually invests in new institutes and centres.

Confucius Institutes are normally organised as joint ventures between Chinese and foreign universities. The institute in Grahamstown, South Africa, is a cooperation agreement between the local Rhodes University and Guangzhou's Jinan University. In Kenya, the University of Nairobi's Confucius Institute is partnered with China's Tianjin Normal University. The host university usually provides the premises for the institute and China the start-up funding for the first couple of years. It is this cooperative structure, and the resulting close relationship between foreign universities and the authoritarian Chinese State, which spurs critics to describe the institutes as either academic 'malware' or propaganda instruments of the Chinese Communist Party. For most universities in Africa, Confucius Institutes are the first and only contact point for people who want to learn more about the Chinese language and culture—numerous European and American universities have a long history of offering Sinology or Chinese Studies, but this is not the case in Africa (CPI 2016).

There are broadly two forms of partnerships that occur. One way is the establishment of a new Confucius Institute at a university, such as Rhodes or Nairobi, which has no previous instruction in Chinese language or culture. In this way, the Confucius Institute is responsible for introducing the study of Chinese at the degree level into the university system. On the other hand, when the Confucius Institute is invited to a university that already grants degrees in Chinese language and culture, it may supplement that instruction or offer a range of non-credit activities and programmes on Chinese culture and language (King 2014).

Although Confucius Institutes are classified by certain authors as a form of 'soft power', this view underestimates the need for this training, especially in Africa. The Confucius Institutes are primarily responding to a widespread vocational need for Chinese linguistic and cultural training, and not so much to adding another programme to the product range of the university. This need of training is inseparable from the presence of Chinese investment and companies in Africa, and their appreciation of local workers with Chinese language skills (King 2014). The evidence available shows that these institutes are playing a critical role in bridging the language and cultural gap for local workers and businesses in order that they may be more productive and involved in Chinese projects.

## 6.3  A Case Study on the Impact of China on Employment Creation and Technology Transfer in North Africa

China's rising involvement and investment in North African countries mirrors many features of the overall structure of economic relations across the continent. Energy and construction sectors dominate exchanges in countries such as Libya and Algeria; minerals like phosphates are a major export of Morocco; and fertilisers represent the bulk of trade with Tunisia. Manufactured items including electronics, textiles and clothing are the greatest proportion of exports from China to North Africa, while energy resources, minerals, and agricultural and food production constitute the bulk of North African exports to China.

Unemployment and underemployment problems are a persistent feature of the regional economies in North Africa, and are therefore a top priority for governments in the region. With an estimated 25% unemployment level amongst the youth, North Africa has a significant problem in this regard and the countries which have the most trouble with unemployment are those with the largest populations: Egypt, Algeria and Morocco. Egypt's population of 90 million is also the youngest in the region, with 30% of all youth without work. Algeria's population stands at 34 million with the latest report of the World Bank indicating that 26% of the youth are unemployed.

The two countries that will be evaluated to determine the impact of China on youth employment in North Africa are Egypt and Algeria. The conclusions of this evaluation are primarily based on an Economic Brief by the African Development Bank entitled Chinese Investments and employment creation in Algeria and Egypt (AfDB 2012). In both countries China has encouraged investment, initially in the energy and construction sectors. This has been expanded to the establishment of official Economic Trade and Cooperation Zones where Chinese and local firms have established manufacturing and assembly plants (AfDB 2012).

### 6.3.1  *The Case of Algeria*

Like most African countries, the relationship between China and Algeria dates back to the pre-independence days, with the newly established People's Republic of China providing diplomatic, economic and military support to the liberation movement, the Front de Liberation Nationale

(FLN) against French colonialism. Beijing was also the first non-Arab country to recognise Algeria's independence in 1962. Despite this positive start, it was not until the early 2000s that the two countries registered a boom in their bilateral economic and political relations (AfDB 2012).

In the 2000s, Algeria appealed to Chinese contactors to assist with the implementation of the Programme of Support for Economic Revival (2001–2004) and the subsequent Economic Growth Support Programme (2005–2009). These programmes were made possible after the country accumulated huge financial gains from oil revenues derived from the oil crises of 2003 (Pairault 2015). The goal was to make up for the time lost during the 1990s, when the oil prices were low and the struggle against terrorism was dominating their strategic priorities. When compared to other Sino–African relationships, the Algerian relationship with China shows certain distinctive differences compared to other African countries. The most important distinction is that the majority of infrastructure development in Algeria was self-funded, and not financed through 'Angola-mode' framework type agreements where infrastructure is traded for resources. Chinese companies were expected to tender for projects against other internal and external competitors, and projects were financed by the Algerian government (Pairault 2015).

By 2007, the value of contracts signed between Chinese companies and Algeria had reached the highest in Africa. These contracts led to an influx of Chinese migrants to Algeria. Between 2005 and 2011, Algeria was the African country with the most Chinese migrant workers, peaking at 49,631 in 2009. Many of these workers returned to China after the completion of their projects, and the number of migrant workers declined to 8646 in 2011 (Pairault 2015).

The Algerian government had to face two pressing political issues during this time period, namely housing and unemployment, which were both causes of endemic social unrest. To address them, the government followed two distinct approaches: they first relied on foreign companies to address the construction of houses; and second, they put policies and legislation in place to address the unemployment problem (Pairault 2015). One such policy was the imposition of a quota of a minimum of 20% Algerian workers to be employed on foreign projects. The issue of unemployment became central to the Algerian political discourse at the time, mostly due to the pressure put on the government by the largely unemployed youth component in the country (AfDB 2012). There was at the same time, a flood of criticism against Chinese enterprises, who were accused of increasing unemployment by importing their own workforce. One of the consequences of this social discontent was the unrest that broke out between Algerian citizens and Chinese workers during the summer of 2009, which was fuelled upon the perception that Chinese workers were taking job opportunities away from Algerians (Pairault 2015). Chinese companies contested that they had sometimes had very little choice but to import their own labour force, in order to meet the requirements of their contracts, such as low costs and short deadlines.

Since 2007, China expanded its investment in Algeria into new sectors, of which automotive and electronics were two key sectors. Algeria and Egypt were among the top 10 importers of Chinese cars in 2007, and China and Algeria entered into an agreement to establish a second Chinese Special Economic Zone in North Africa (The Jiangling Economic and Trade Cooperation Zone) with the focus on assembling motorcars. Several deals were concluded between Chinese automotive firms and Algerian partners in the industry, although this was short-lived when in 2009, the Algerian Minister of Industry announced that Algeria would prefer to attract automotive companies in Algeria that would manufacture cars, and not only assemble them in the country (AfDB 2012). As a result, all car assembling deals with China were suspended. The Chinese manufacturing sector in Algeria did not completely draw to a halt due to this, for instance in 2011, Groupe Mazouz announced that it had entered into a partnership with Chinese Higer for the assembling of the Higer minibuses in Algeria, an initiative that promised to create 1200 jobs. Investment by China also extended into electronics and in 2009 China Great Wall Computer Shenzen announced that it would open its first plant in Africa in partnership with the Algerian company EEPAD. The investment included factories that were expected to employ 3000 new workers.

The World Bank found that the potential of Chinese firms to reduce the unemployment challenges in Algeria was limited, for instance in the reduction of unemployment among university graduates. Unemployment was found to be more severe among university graduates than among the less educated labour. According to the World Bank, high unemployment of university graduates is also related to a disconnect between the skills they are taught at university, and the competencies required from the job market, thus requiring companies to retrain employees in certain skills that are needed in the workplace.

The evidence above shows that the type of employment that is needed to help Algeria deal with its high level of unemployment requires an investment in knowledge creation and skills development. The presence of Chinese firms in knowledge-intensive sectors has been limited, resulting in a lesser positive impact on the growing number of unemployed graduates in Algeria. The types of jobs created by Chinese projects tend to be for less educated professionals, but rather for male workers employed on construction sites. These jobs are not effective in addressing this dimension of the real unemployment crises in Algeria (AfDB 2012).

### 6.3.2 The Case of Egypt

With over 90 million inhabitants, two-thirds of whom are below 29 years of age, Egypt is Africa's most populous country after Nigeria and Ethiopia, and the largest Arab nation in the world. About 95% of Egyptians live along the Nile River, an area of less than 5% of the Egyptian territory, making the Nile area one of the most densely populated areas in the world. Egypt controls the Suez Canal: the shortest sea link between the Indian Ocean and the Mediterranean Sea. Unemployment in Egypt remains a persistent dilemma facing the Egyptian economy, and remains at the centre of policy debates since the January 2011 Egyptian Revolution. The high level of unemployment among the educated youth reveals that the labour market in Egypt is still suffering from a skills mismatch, fostered by the limited gains of formal education, and the ineffectiveness of current training programmes (Assaad and Krafft 2016).

The relationship between Egypt and China, like that of Algeria and China, has gone through periods of close political ties, but has only recently expanded into growing business interests between the two countries. Beijing recognised Egypt in 1956 a few years after independence, but the longstanding political, economic and military ties with the United States since the late 1970s, had caused Beijing to approach its ties with Cairo cautiously. These have grown in momentum since the 2000s, when China like in most other African countries, assisted Egypt to improve their infrastructure including that of roads, rail, housing and power, providing financing through the EXIM Bank of China, and Chinese companies contributing to the execution of the various construction projects. Egypt's long maritime coast and the economic reforms undertaken in the 1990s attracted foreign direct investment (FDI). China made significant investments in Egypt's port infrastructure, with joint ventures established with local companies to construct, operate and manage terminals at Egyptian harbours. In 2014, an agreement was signed with Egypt's Transport

Ministry for a high-speed train line covering the 900 km distance between Egypt's Mediterranean City of Alexandria and Aswan, close to the border with Sudan. Providing direct and spin-off local employment opportunities, the total cost of this project was estimated at US$10 billion (Scott 2015).

The bulk of Chinese products imported into Egypt are electronics, chemicals and textiles, while Egyptian exports include oil, steel, cotton and marble (AfDB 2012). Like many African countries, Egypt has been actively seeking Chinese investment, viewing it as an alternative to the conditional restrictions of western investment (Scott 2015). In August 2013, former President Morsi's visit to China resulted in investment agreements totalling US$4.9 billion; while President Al Sissi's visit in December 2014, produced 26 agreements, including 8 in transportation, 13 in electricity, 3 in tourism and 2 in the supply field, worth a combined value of US$60 billion (Scott 2015).

A notable trend in Sino-Egyptian relations is the push for technology transfer on the part of Egypt. China provided technology assistance and support in agriculture as well as technological assistance and joint production in other industries such as nuclear energy, aircraft flight trainers, as well as the development and establishment of the Egypt Suez Cooperation Zone. The zone, which was officially launched in 2009, is considered one of the most successful zones in Africa developed in partnership with China. The Chinese-backed trade zone differed from others, in that it not only enjoys the conventional duty-free privileges of a trade zone, but it also promoted Egypt as headquarters, and the gateway for Chinese companies investing in Africa and the Middle East. The aim of the zone from an investment perspective has been to encourage Chinese investments into sectors such as ICT, renewal energy, as well as the manufacturing of electrical equipment and automobiles. In 2012, the Jushi Group in China, the world's largest fibreglass manufacturer, started operating from the zone with an investment of US$225 million. It has since invested US$190 million, and is used by the Egyptian authorities to showcase Egypt as an attractive investment destination (Africa Business Magazine 2016).

The positive outcome of Chinese firms investing in the Egypt Cooperation Zone have led to further expansion, one outcome of which has been employment creation due to SME's setting up business in the zone. The Egyptian government stuck to its stipulation that only one out of ten employees could be foreigners—an approach that has yielded positive outcomes for local employment. Like Algeria, however, the immediate gains in areas like youth unemployment accrue to those who are less skilled and, therefore, offer little solution to the growing unemployed graduate component. Ensuring that Egyptians with high level of education and management skills are beneficiaries of Chinese investment, needs to be of equal priority as that of encouraging Chinese businesses to invest in the country.

Growing labour demand and increasing job creation is a necessary, but not sufficient, condition to solve youth employment in Egypt. Many employers reported having difficulty filling current job vacancies due to a skills shortage. A survey conducted among enterprises in 2008 indicated that the skills mismatch was among the top five constraints facing employers in Egypt (Assaad and Krafft 2016). A more recent study by The World Bank in 2012, showed that private sector firms were not able to find qualified candidates for 600,000 vacancies, despite the large pool of job seekers available. Evaluations of current skill development programmes indicate that they are fragmented and ineffective, a result of a curriculum that is supply-driven and outdated, as well as poor facilities (Assaad and Krafft 2016). Based on the Sustainable Development Strategy, a component of Egypt's 2030 Vision launched in 2016, the Government of Egypt intends introducing several reforms in their quest for inclusive sustainable growth. These reforms envisaged diversification and growth in certain economic sectors, as well as skills development programmes for workers to match the future skills anticipated in these sectors (Assaad and Krafft 2016).

## 6.4 A Case Study on the Impact of China on Local Employment in Angola and the Democratic Republic of the Congo (DRC)

Both Angola and the DRC are suffering from the consequences of civil wars over several decades and are in desperate need of reconstruction. Transportation, water and power infrastructure have been decimated by wars; education and healthcare systems are almost non-existent in most rural areas; hundreds of thousands of unemployed live in ghettos; and there are few secure and well-paid jobs, except in limited extraction industries. Both Angola and the DRC are troubled by huge foreign debts and corrupt governments, restricting their access to funds from western countries. Professor Xiaoyang Tang conducted an empirical research study on both countries on the impact of Chinese enterprises on employment of locals in Angola and the DRC in 2010. The results of Prof Tang's research serve as a foundation for the arguments presented in this case study, enriched with a personal interview between the authors and Prof Tang in Beijing, which also served to clarify details, and allowed for the incorporation of new observations.

### 6.4.1  The Case of Angola

Angola is potentially one of the richest countries in Africa because of its abundance of natural resources, primarily oil reserves, water resources, minerals, forests and vast tracks of land for farming. According to a report of the Angolan government on youth employment (Angola Country Report 2014), oil is the biggest economic sector of the country, yet, ironically, only employs 1% of the active population. The report further pointed out that the bulk of the skilled labour force does not match the needs of the Angolan economy.

The long civil war was directly responsible for the exclusion of an entire generation from any form of education and training. The percentage of unskilled labour was as high as 94% among the 15–19 cohort, 74% among the 20–24-year-olds and 68% among the 25–29-year-olds. The situation was further highly gender-biased, with 88% of women totally unskilled (Angola Country Report 2014). At the secondary school level, where students have a choice on the type of education they receive, students expressed a strong preference for technical training over generic choices. Unlike many African countries, technical education in Angola is seen as a path to a university education in engineering and sciences, rather than an immediate entry into the labour market.

China signed agreements of more than US$4 billion between 2004 and 2007, mainly for Angola's infrastructure construction projects including airports, railroads, schools, hospitals, telecommunication and water supply systems. Around 40 state-owned Chinese companies, mainly in the sectors of construction and telecommunications, entered the local market through these projects. After establishing a foothold in Angola, these companies expanded their businesses by obtaining contracts for other public and private projects in the country. Meanwhile the accelerated economic growth in the country also attracted private Chinese companies to invest in the country, mostly in consumer goods. A Sino–Angolan automotive joint venture was also established with a Chinese partner, Zhengzhou-Nissan, and the first car in the history of Angola was manufactured at the end of 2007 (Tang 2010).

The Angola Basic Private Investment Law Art 54/1 regulates all private business investments in Angola and prescribed that at least 70% of employees of these investment projects by foreign companies be Angolans. The definition does not include technical staff and managers, and refers only to non-skilled workers. The percentage of Angolan workers in the private sector is also higher than those in the government sector. The reason for this is that companies working on government projects are not covered by this legislation but are managed directly by the respective ministries. An analysis conducted on 13 sectors in 2007 showed that these conditions were met in most sectors, and that it was only in a few sectors such as communication and hydropower that the percentage of local employees dropped significantly below 70%. The overall average for the 13 sectors was 61.8% local employment (Tang 2010).

The availability of technicians is identified as one of the problematic areas in employing Angolans, evidenced by the low local employment scores for the two most technology-dependent sectors of power generation and telecommunications. Tang (2010) found that local workers make up between 70% and 80% of labourers in the 'low-tech' industries such as agriculture, catering, trading and commercial housing—a result of the low level of skills training required—and that the wages on these levels are more competitive and comparable to the average Chinese wage for comparable jobs. Chinese managers struggle to find Angolan workers for skilled positions, and those who are available, tend to be much more expensive and sometimes less productive than their Chinese counterparts. As a result, most Chinese companies prefer to bring as many skilled staff as possible, from plumbers and carpenters to electricians and engineers, from China to ensure progress and quality in their projects. The legal quota requirement that is also only applicable to low-skilled workers makes this strategy an attractive one for them to pursue.

Although the salary paid to Chinese expats is higher than the comparable salary packages in China, Chinese companies' cost structures cannot afford to pay similar expat packages as American, European and South African companies that operate in Angola (Tang 2010). An expensive city such as Luanda, with poor social services and limited entertainment for Chinese employees, offers little in making the lives for these workers a pleasant experience.

Tang found that Chinese workers, including managers, are not willing to stay overseas after their contract term, which is usually a two or three-year period. Chinese employers acknowledged this problem and have put strategies in place to replace Chinese workers with Angolans. This is being done mainly through two approaches: First, training programmes are utilised to raise the skill levels of local workers; and second, more local managers are employed to improve the communication, integration and productivity of the local workers. Several African countries experienced that language barriers remain a problem for efficient communication in Chinese companies. Tang found that 93% of the 73 Chinese companies interviewed in Angola have training programmes in place, and that those that do not are mostly newcomers in companies engaged in smaller short-term projects. Intensive training programmes are usually provided at the beginning of employment for workers to acquire the necessary level of skills, and at the end of the construction phase to train staff for post-construction maintenance. In the energy and telecom sectors where Chinese engineers are the major workforce for construction, Chinese companies preferred to train Angolan engineers to do the maintenance after the companies' exit. Overseas training is rare, given the immense costs involved. Therefore, overseas training only occurs in industrial sectors that require high-profile employees like engineers and managers. The Sino–Angolan automobile joint venture CSG, for instance, sent 50 Angolans to the company's headquarters in China for in-house training.

Tang (2010) also found that the recruitment of local engineers in Angola is constrained by the limited availability of Angolan university graduates in technology, and second, the fierce competition by companies for the limited number of local engineers dramatically raised the salary levels of these individuals. The localisation of management differs according to the demands of the structure and the sectorial context of the organisation. In the Sino–Angolan joint ventures, it was found that Angolans are integrated into management positions, especially in the trading, construction and restaurant sectors. A few Chinese companies use people from a third country, for example South Africans, who identify with the multicultural complexity of doing business, to help manage and contribute to the requisite skills. This is a common practice among multinational companies, such as European and American companies sending staff working in Portugal or Brazil to the Portuguese-speaking Angolan companies due to their linguistic and cultural similarities.

The subcontracting of work to Angolan companies and the use of local suppliers is another effective way to have a positive impact on the transfer of technology and skills and the creation of employment in the country. The large Chinese construction projects in Angola provided ample opportunity for Angolan subcontractors to become involved, to create jobs for local workers and to contribute to the long-term development of Angola's construction sector—the Angolan government has also stipulated quotas in this regard. Using Angolan subcontracting companies has added advantages such as knowledge of the supply chain, construction location, an understanding of local customs and traditions, and competencies of working within local bureaucratic systems—these can be leveraged to the advantage of Chinese companies. They have the further advantage of having large construction apparatus on location, while Chinese companies would have had to transport these from China at a huge cost. The research conducted by Tang (2010) indicates that the proportion of local subcontractors never exceeded 40%—the main suggested reason for this is that many Chinese companies perceive that local subcontractors are sometimes unable to meet the quality standards expected of them. Chinese companies also find it difficult to find local suppliers for certain products—a result of the manufacturing sector still being at a low 5% of Angola's GDP, hence very underdeveloped. Most of the construction, telecom and manufacturing equipment and inputs are therefore imported from South Africa (Tang 2010).

The Angolan government in the Angola Country Report (2014) confirms that youth unemployment is not a one-dimensional problem and that solutions to the problem must be considered within the broader context of human capital development. It is therefore not sufficient to only focus on the creation of more job opportunities, but to also improve access to quality and relevant education, and skills improvement through apprenticeships and internship opportunities. China has contributed in this regard: Construction agreements with China in the period 2006–2009 include the construction of 34 technical institutes aimed at improving the level of technical training in the country (Angola Country Report 2014).

### 6.4.2 The Case of the Democratic Republic of the Congo (DRC)

The DRC has been plagued with many years of ongoing conflict, which continues till today. Infrastructure has been destroyed, service delivery has been minimal, while supporting institutions have been crippled. One of the 'fatalities' of this ongoing conflict has been the educational sector. Most children do not attend school, and among those who do, very few attending primary school can manage even elementary literacy and numeracy exercises. The demand for education remains high though, as education is perceived as the road to better employment opportunities. Alternative training and education programmes have emerged, providing education and skills development for many of the uneducated youth and adults.

Economic cooperation between the DRC and China began in the 1970s with the construction of the national stadium and the Congressional Palace. In the 1990s, Chinese private and state-owned companies invested in the DRC in spite of the unstable political situation at the time. In 2001, Chinese telecom company ZTE formed a joint venture with the Congolese government, Congo China Telecom, which became one of the largest telecom operators in the DRC. It was in the 2000s that there was a remarkable escalation in Sino–DRC cooperation, for instance in 2007, China and the DRC signed a framework agreement of US$5 billion for massive infrastructure construction and the revival of the mining industry (Wild and Sguazzin 2007). This agreement followed the model of 'Angola-mode' Sino–Angolan cooperation, and was intended to be a vital part of the DRC's post-war economic reconstruction.

Chinese enterprises in the DRC are mainly in the sectors of mining, telecom, catering and textile trading, and the research conducted by Tang (2010) evidenced that the average percentage of employment of local people in the DRC was much higher than that in Angola—an average of 76.7%. Unlike Angola, the DRC has no legislation prescribing the percentage of local employment, and it seems that the high percentage of local employment is a function of economic considerations. One explanation could be that most Chinese companies in the DRC are not contractors, but are active in the trading and retail sector, and require local employees to do the sales and marketing of their products. A second interesting trend that was also observed by Tang is that the employment of local people increased over time, and that companies that are older than five years have more local people employed than those that are less than five years old.

Tang (2010) also found that the localisation of management and technical positions is also progressing with companies' growth. For example, during the period of his study, Congo China Telecom was sending about 20 Congolese engineers to China for training annually. These trainees were prepared with other local managers to take the place of their Chinese colleagues in the years to follow. The Company was also found to outperform its rivals in the telecom industry in terms of localisation and technology transfer.

## 6.5 China and the Development of a Productive Work Force for Africa: Closing Remarks

Africa has a large and growing youth population, and by 2050, it is expected to be larger than China's or India's population. Will it become an enabler of economic transformation and organic growth or will it become a social and political time bomb? The answer to this question lies in the individual responsibility of each African country, which will have to implement suitable policies, initiatives and actions to harness and maximise the productive potential of their youth. One of the major challenges for African countries is therefore to educate, develop and create employment for the growing youth segment that enters the labour market each year. This group of young people will be the next generation of workers, technicians, engineers and decision-makers who will directly contribute to the overall growth in African countries. Equipping this young and emergent workforce with the skills required for future growth and development is a strategic concern in the national growth and development strategies of all countries in Africa, and occupies a dominant place in the 'African Renaissance' narrative. Ultimately, each country's future prosperity will depend on how many of its people are employed and how productive they are—a function of them having and utilising relevant skills. To achieve youth development targets, governments, businesses and citizens must build an enabling environment that includes quality and relevant education, and the development of workforce capabilities and employment, in line with the growth requirements of the country as illustrated in Fig. 6.2.

Quality and relevant education is widely accepted as a primary building block for the growth and development of a country. In Africa where growth is essential, education is an imperative, especially in terms of creating employment and reducing poverty. Although the number of children enrolled in primary education in Africa has increased dramatically in the last decade, primary education still has some of the lowest completion rates in the world. Even more concerning is the fact that students who complete primary and secondary school do not necessarily receive a quality education. Scholars agree that secondary education in Africa does not sufficiently prepare all adolescents for adulthood and a future career. It is clear that there is no easy fix for the transformation of education, as each country's educational reforms are moulded according to the country's unique political, social and economic landscape.

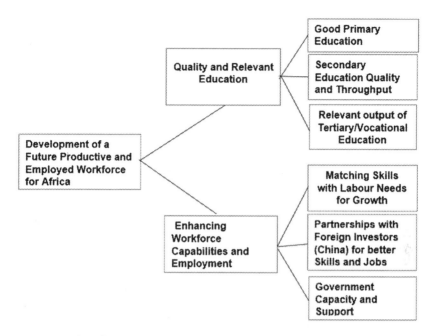

Fig. 6.2 The education and skills development dimension in Africa

It was found that the higher education system is equally inadequate in preparing young students for the workforce. It is claimed that African universities do not educate for African needs. Graduates in technical fields such as engineering, telecommunications and information technology find it easier to get employment than those from the social sciences or humanities, although the latter represents much higher numbers of students graduating from these universities. Given Africa's comparative advantage in agriculture and the great potential to trade in diversified agricultural products, it was also disappointing to note the low number of graduates that African institutions are producing in this area.

Chinese assistance for educational development has evolved over many decades and is currently quite diverse and institutionalised in its scope and format. Assistance includes the building of education infrastructure like schools, technical institutions and universities, as well as bilateral cooperation between universities in China and in African countries. The establishment of Confucius Institutes in African universities aims to enhance the understanding and comprehension of the Chinese culture and language in Africa. There has recently been a shift by China towards strengthening the science and technology capacity of Africans, with the ultimate goal of knowledge being applied to improving the lives of people living in Africa. This assumption suggests that the Chinese educational and scientific support may contribute towards achieving the United Nation's Sustainable Development Goals in Africa.

Equipping the emergent workforce with the skills required for the jobs of today and for the future is a strategic concern in the national growth and development strategies of all countries in Africa. Economic diversification and technological advancement require higher skills and productivity among workers, and the primary challenge for African economies over the next few decades will be to invest in the diversification of their economies, and generate productive employment for their growing youth population. This process can be accelerated by FDI and aid in infrastructure and industries identified for growth. Chinese investment in infrastructure and growth industry sectors can therefore make an important strategic contribution in achieving this objective. Partnerships with Chinese firms should therefore directly contribute to local employment and the transfer of technology in skills, to make sure that there is a positive labour impact in the longer term.

The case in Algeria is an example of how an African government can harden its demands from foreign investors over time, in terms of requirements for job creation and skills transfer. The formation of partnerships with Algerian companies and the provision of training and transfer of skills to local workers have been legislated and become central in the Algerian political discourse. It was, however, found that the contribution of Chinese firms in reducing the unemployment challenges in Algeria was constrained by the high level of unemployment among university graduates. In fact, unemployment is found to be more severe among university graduates than among less educated labour. The types of jobs created by Chinese projects tend to be for less educated professionals and largely male workers employed on construction sites.

The Egyptian government also stuck to its requirements that only one out of ten employees be foreigners, which created positive results for local employment with each investment in the country. Like Algeria, however, the immediate gains in the areas of youth unemployment accrued to those who were less skilled, and therefore offer little solution to the growing unemployed graduate component. To ensure Egyptians with advanced and management skills are beneficiaries of Chinese investment, their employment needs to be prioritised when encouraging Chinese businesses to invest in the country.

Both Angola and the DRC are suffering from the consequences of many years of civil war, and are in desperate need for reconstruction. Transportation infrastructure and water and electricity supply in both countries have been mostly destroyed by these wars, while the education and healthcare systems are almost non-existent. The Angola Basic Private Investment Law Art 54/1, which prescribed that at least 70% of the employees be Angolans, has contributed to employment levels in Angola. However, the availability of technicians and engineers was identified as one of the significant constraints to the Chinese hiring skilled Angolans (Tang 2010). Unlike Angola, the DRC has no legislation prescribing the number of local people to be employed, although there is a higher percentage of local employment, attributed to the consideration of economic needs—most Chinese companies in the DRC are not contractors, but are engaged in the trading and retail sector where they need local employees to conduct the sales and marketing function for their products. A second interesting trend that was also observed by Tang is that the employment of local people increased over time and that companies that are older than five years have more local people employed than those that are less than five years old.

Evidence from the four cases studies in this chapter confirm the observation made by other authors that there is a serious mismatch between skills and labour needs in most African countries. In Angola and the DRC, educational systems were destroyed by the years of civil war in these countries, and most of the labour supply is unskilled. Chinese companies in these countries therefore recorded relatively high employment of local people in unskilled positions, but find it difficult and expensive to find local workers at an affordable price in the high-tech industries. In Egypt and Algeria, where secondary education and university enrolment rates are higher than in the other two countries, we found that young workers are mainly in informal employment and in occupations that do not match their education. This has a negative impact on the workers' productivity and satisfaction, and indicates a severe mismatch between the skills of the labour force and those needed by the economy. This mismatch is primarily driven by a disconnect between education and training and the labour market's requirement for particular skills. Although Algeria and Egypt experienced a strong growth in university education in the last two decades, the technical and vocational education and training in both countries suffers from underdevelopment, apparently since it is perceived as a lower form of education.

Tang (2010) identified in his research two major patterns of Chinese investment regarding local employment and long-term benefits, both patterns being influenced by the urgency of infrastructural investment in host countries. The first one brings a large number of Chinese workers, technicians and engineers into the country to make sure that the project is executed effectively and quickly. This methodology has been termed the 'Bull Dozer' effect by Tang (2010) and is effective in least developed countries where there is not a big enough skilled workforce to help with the reconstruction of the country. Some of the big construction projects to restore rail and road infrastructure in Africa are examples of this. In such cases the temporary use of Chinese workers can speed up infrastructure development and, in so doing, stimulate further growth. The second model termed the 'Locomotive' effect "strive(s) to achieve maximum integration between China and the local community to get the maximum benefits for job creation and technology and skills transfer". Utilising the strengths of China, such as capital, technology and knowledge, this model can act as a 'locomotive', contributing to a much larger scale of growth and development, including indirect employment, supply chain development, training and poverty reduction. However, the choice of these models does not depend on China but is and should be decided by the African governments themselves. The stage of organic growth and the envisioned future should be determining factors in this decision.

Chinese investment can therefore be beneficial to the organic growth of an African country if the local government, local people and the Chinese companies work together to ensure a win-win situation for both parties. For African governments, the task is to create an enabling environment for investors to flourish and provide meaningful employment. A certain amount of local employment skills transfer and localisation ought to be demanded, but should allow enough flexibility to attract investment and stimulate growth in the country. Chinese employers are in fact eager to reduce their number of Chinese employees, as these expatriates are unwilling to stay for long time periods in Africa, and are often unsatisfied with the living and working conditions in these countries. Chinese companies feel that although this transition is relatively easy at a low skills level, technically competent staff is scarce and, if available, charge salaries that cannot be accommodated within their narrow cost margins (Tang 2010).

Universities should enhance their communication with Chinese enterprises to promote the employment of their graduates. Local vocation and education programmes should also be adjusted to meet the requirements of development, for example by adding Chinese courses. The quality of school education in Africa also requires attention. It is not simply school enrolment figures that are important, or even the percentage of GDP invested, but it is critical that the quality of the teachers and the quality of the education are improved. Major current concerns include the relevance of the fields of study, curricula and the quality of programmes and graduates. While the majority of students enrolled in tertiary education in fast-growing countries such as Korea, China and Taiwan are enrolled in science, engineering and technology courses, the figure is only about 20% for Africa. Achieving sustainable organic growth will require successful economic diversification and a productive and skilled workforce—quality education is the entry ticket for this road. More technical and vocational training programmes should be developed with the aim of increasing the growing demand for competent technical skills in these countries.

Stated bluntly, Africa cannot build growth and success on failing education systems. Neither can it generate the millions of additional jobs that will absorb the mass of young people entering the labour market in the future if they do not remarkably improve their educational systems. African governments also need to take responsibility for the development of effective skills development policies and action plans to promote active labour market programmes and decent work, especially for the upcoming younger generation. For the continent to be able to grow and deliver prosperity for all its citizens, there must be an increased investment in science and technology. African countries can benefit from China's various levels of technology, especially the low- to mid-range technologies, and should therefore do more to make technology transfer from China more effective. This can only be done if the host country's human resources have the desired level of competence so that these technology and skills can be transferred. This in turn can only be achieved with an effective investment in relevant and quality education and skills development as described in this chapter. African governments should take responsibility and a leadership role in ensuring that development partner investments, such as those from China, are complementary to their long-term skills development plan and growth vision.

## REFERENCES

AfDB. 2012. Chinese Investments and Employment Creation in Algeria and Egypt. [Online]. Available from: https://www.afdb.org/fileadmin/uploads/afdb/Documents/Publications/Brochure%20China%20Anglais.pdf (accessed: 17 April 2017).

Africa Business Magazine. 18 October 2016. Egypt Turning Towards China for Investment. [Online]. Available from: http://africanbusinessmagazine.com/region/north-africa/egypt-turning-towards-china-investment/ (accessed: 27 April 2017).

Angola Country Report. 21–23 July 2014. Republic of Angola: Country Report in Policies and Mechanisms for Integration into the Workforce and Job Creation. The 2014 Ministerial Conference on Youth Employment. Association for the Development of Education in Africa (ADEA). [Online]. Available from: http://www.adeanet.org/min_conf_youth_skills_employment/sites/default/files/u26/Angola%20Country%20Report.pdf (accessed: 28 April 2017).

Assaad, R. and Krafft, C. 2016. Labour Market Dynamics and Youth Unemployment in the Middle East and North Africa: Evidence from Egypt, Jordan and Tunisia. Cairo: Economic Research Forum (ERF) Working Paper 93.

CPI. 2016. China Policy Institute. [Online]. Available from: https://cpianalyses.org/2016/12/02/the-effectiveness-of-the-chinese-cultural-centres-and-confucius-institutes/ (accessed: 24 March 2017).

FOCAC. 2016. Xi Announces 10 Major China-African Cooperation Plans for Coming 3 Years. [Online]. Available from: http://www.focac.org/eng/zfgx/t1322068.htm (accessed: 23 March 2017).

International Labour Office. November 2010. A Skilled Workforce for Strong, Sustainable and Balanced Growth. Geneva. [Online]. Accessed from: http://www.ilo.org/skills/pubs/WCMS_151966/lang--en/index.htm (accessed: 26 April 2017).

King, K. 2014. China's Higher Education Engagement with Africa: A Different Partnership and Cooperation Model? The Graduate Institute of Geneva. [Online]. Available from: https://www.poldev.revues.org/1788 (accessed: 26 April 2017).

McGregor, K. 10 April 2015. Higher Education Is Key to Development—World Bank. University World News, 362. [Online]. Available from: http://www.universityworldnews.com/article.php?story=20150409152258799 (accessed: 23 March 2017).

NEPAD. 2015. Agricultural Education and Skills Improvement Framework (AESIF 2015–2025). NEPAD CAADP: 11.

Obamba, M. 1 June 2013. China in African Education—A Force for Good? University World News, 274. [Online]. Available from: http://www.universityworldnews.com/article.php?story=20130528175252513 (accessed: 23 March 2017).

Pairault, T. 2015. China's Economic Presence in Algeria. [Online]. Available from: https://halshs.archives-ouvertes.fr/halshs-01116295/document (accessed: 27 April 2017).

Scott, T. 2015. China-Egypt Trade and Investment Ties—Seeking a Better Balance. Centre for Chinese Studies Stellenbosch South Africa. [Online]. Available from: https://www.sun.ac.za/ccs (accessed: 27 April 2017).

Tang, X. 2010. 'Bulldozer or Locomotive? The Impact of Chinese Enterprises on the Local Employment in Angola and the DRC', *Journal of Asian and African Studies*, 45 (3): 350–368.

The Brenthurst Foundation. 2011. Putting Young Africans to Work: Addressing Africa's Youth Unemployment Crises. [Online]. Available from: http://www.thebrenthurstfoundation.org/.../Brenthurst-paper-2011-08-Putting-Young-Afric (accessed: 18 April 2017).

UNESCO. 2015. Regional Overview Sub-Saharan Africa: Education for All Global Monitoring Report 2015. [Online]. Available from: http://en.unesco.org/gem-report/sites/gem-report/files/regional_overview_SSA_en.pdf (accessed: 23 April 2017).

Wild, F. and Sguazzin, A. 18 September 2007. China Lends Congo $5 Billion for Mining Projects. Bloomberg. In Tang, X. 2010. 'Bulldozer or Locomotive? The Impact of Chinese Enterprises on the Local Employment in Angola and the DRC', *Journal of Asian and African Studies*, 45 (3): 350–368.

World Bank. 2015. Lessons for Africa from China's Growth. Speech Delivered by Akhtar Diop, World Bank Vice President for the Africa Region Beijing, China. © World Bank. [Online]. Available from: http://www.worldbank.org/en/news/speech/2015/01/13/lessons-for-africa-from-chinas-growth (accessed: 23 March 2017). Creative Commons Attribution License (CC BY 3.0 IGO). (http://creativecommons.org/licenses/by/3.0/igo/).

CHAPTER 7

# Developing a Sustainable Africa through Green Growth

There are compelling arguments for momentous growth and development throughout Africa. The conundrum though is that the negative externalities can be catastrophic for the environment and the society it is supposed to benefit. Hence the need for an integrated proposition, namely sustainable development.

Sustainable development is much more than a new buzzword. It is also not simply relegated to environmental protection. Rather an all-encompassing development approach incorporates three elements of environmental sustainability, social development and economic growth. Often it is referred to as 'Green Growth', a fitting analogy for the African Tree of Organic Growth, and is intrinsic to all levels of the paradigm.

This chapter will provide insight into the concepts of sustainability, within the context of global climate change, with specific reference to China and Africa. This is followed with case studies from East Africa, the Democratic Republic of the Congo (DRC), Lake Victoria and Mozambique, reflecting on sustainability in the context of pollution, energy, water, food and agriculture.

## 7.1 Interpreting Sustainability

The integrated nature of sustainability becomes apparent with the allocation of the United Nation's 17 Sustainable Development Goals, a useful benchmark to the themes of environmental sustainability, social development and economic growth as illustrated in Fig. 7.1.

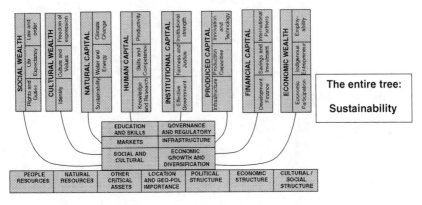

Fig. 7.1 The African Tree of Organic Growth

Figure 7.2 first illustrates the fact that sustainable development comprises all three themes of economic growth, social development and environmental sustainability. Second, it illustrates how many of the 17 Sustainable Development Goals transcend boundaries of themes and can be allocated to two or all three of the themes. Even goals such as eliminating hunger, while allocated to social development, would be dependent to a large degree on economic development to fund agricultural development or the importation of food, and agricultural development would in turn have environmental considerations.

The complexity of sustainable development aspirations is important to emphasise, as sustainable growth can best be achieved through understanding the interrelatedness and interdependence of the themes of sustainability.

The World Wildlife Fund (2016: 13) illustrates sustainability as an ecosystem between nature and people. From the ecosystem, food, raw material, medicinal resources and freshwater is provided. Efficient regulation of the resources ensures air and water quality, prevention of erosion, disease control, reduction of pollution and the moderation of extreme events. For this to occur, the ecosystem requires nutrient cycling, soil formation and photosynthesis. Because of this ecosystem, people derive a range of non-material benefits, such as health and recreation.

Economic growth and social development is covered in more detail in other chapters, while this chapter focuses predominantly on environmental sustainability. Three important considerations in achieving sustainable

Fig. 7.2 The integrated nature of sustainability. (Adapted from the United Nations' 17 Sustainable Development Goals per sustainable development themes (Sustainable Development Goals 2015))

development—climate change; pollution and waste; and energy, water, food and agriculture—will be evaluated in some detail.

### 7.1.1 The World at Risk in the Face of Global Climate Change

While some may still dispute the threat of global climate change, scientific enquiry suggests that greenhouse gas pollution is a serious contributing factor to climate change. Rising temperatures will have an adverse impact on ocean levels, ocean currents, the weather, ecosystems and compromise agricultural production.

**Table 7.1** Climate change observations

**Observed changes in the climate system:**
- Period between 1983 and 2012 warmest 30-year period in 1400 years in the northern hemisphere
- Ocean acidity has increased by 26% (as measured by hydrogen ion concentration) since the industrial era
- The Greenland and Antarctic ice sheets have been losing mass between 1992 and 2011 and at a greater rate between 2002 and 2011
- The global mean sea level rose by 0.18 m between 1901 and 2010, with the rate of increase since the mid-nineteenth century exceeding that of the previous two millennia

**Impacts of climate change:**
- Detrimentally affecting quantity and quality of water resources
- Land, freshwater and marine species have changed geographic ranges, seasonal activities, migration patterns, abundance and interaction
- Negative impact on crop yields

**Extreme events:**
- Cold days and nights have decreased and warm days and nights have increased, with an increased frequency of heat waves
- Heavy precipitation and extreme sea levels have increased
- Increased vulnerability to ecosystems and human systems has been attributed to climate variability

Adapted from the IPCC Climate Change 2014 Synthesis Report Summary for Policymakers (2014)

The United Nations established the Intergovernmental Panel on Climate Change (IPCC) in 1988 to track climate change and the results are startling, some of which are detailed in Table 7.1.

The IPCC findings reflected in the report summary presented in Table 7.1 depict a dire picture for the future, especially for disadvantaged people and communities, many of whom would be found in Africa. The international community has embarked on concerted efforts to reduce climate change, one of the more universally representative of which was the 21st Session of the Conference of the Parties to the United Nations Framework Convention on Climate Change (COP 21). Decisions made at COP 21 include the following: Limiting global temperature increases to well below 2 °C, preferably even below 1.5 °C; regular reporting by all countries of their emissions and progress made in implementing their nationally determined contributions (NDC); five yearly review of NDCs with progressive improvements; commitment of developed countries to assist the efforts of developing countries and encourage voluntary NDCs by developing countries; goal of US$100 billion per year contribution from

2020 through 2025 in support of the global climate effort; and mechanisms to address loss and damage as a result of climate change (Outcomes of the U.N. Climate Change Conference in Paris 2015).

## 7.2 Environmental Concerns in Africa

Environmental sustainability is a delicate balance, and Africa with its acute development problems is particularly susceptible to environmental problems. Some of the key issues, such as deforestation, desertification, pollution and waste, are worth debating in some detail.

### 7.2.1 Deforestation and Desertification in Africa

Africa, as mentioned earlier, is extremely susceptible to climate change. There are many examples in this regard (Table 7.2).

Of great concern is the level of deforestation and desertification in Africa, exacerbated by climate change. The United Nations Environment Programme (2016) estimates that forest cover will reduce to less than 6 million of its 30 million square kilometres by 2050. There are a number of reasons for this including climate change, overpopulation, demand for firewood, demand for wood for exports including the exotic and scarce woods, the conversion of land for agricultural purposes and the conversion of land for housing.

Table 7.2  Examples of climate change effects in Africa

| Area/Countries | Risk |
| --- | --- |
| North Africa and the Middle East | North Africa and the Middle East are the **most water-scarce regions** in the world and climate change could severely compound **water resources** (Terink et al. 2013) |
| East Africa | Malaria transmission in East Africa is likely to increase as **temperatures become warmer** in the vulnerable East African highlands (Onyango et al. 2016) |
| Malawi | **Maize production** in Malawi is expected to **decrease by 14% by mid-century, and as much as 33% by end century** due to climate change, noting that maize production accounts for **one-third of its GDP, 90% of its foreign exchange earnings and employs 85% of its labour force** (Msowoya et al. 2016) |

China imports substantial amounts of wood from Africa, and has sometimes been accused of contributing to the unsustainable harvesting of timber. The scale of China's involvement in the timber industry is enormous and the majority of timber exports in Gabon, Mozambique, Equatorial Guinea and the DRC find its way to China. Gabon, as Africa's largest timber exporter, alone provided about 5% of China's total timber imports.

Desertification refers to the degradation of land due to climate change, overgrazing, over water consumption, pollution, urbanisation, deforestation and soil erosion. The United Nations Environment Programme (2016) paints a troubling picture for Africa: Arable land is still a critical asset for agricultural production and economic development. Yet, it is estimated that 500,000 square kilometres of land is being degraded per year.

The result of this is the inability of such land to effectively support life and agricultural efforts and food production. The United Nations Convention to Combat Desertification (2017) estimates that two-thirds of the African continent is constituted of desert and drylands, often susceptible to devastating droughts. Desertification contributes to food insecurity, and failure to address the problem can significantly compromise development objectives in Africa.

Deforestation and desertification, at its most destructive, can contribute to devastating natural disasters. In 2017, for example, a landslide in the DRC killed an estimated 200 people, while destroying much of a small fishing village near Lake Albert. In Sierra Leone during the same period, another landslide killed more than 400 people in the capital of Freetown, with countless missing. While the heavy rains are a natural phenomenon, the deforestation on the outskirts of the city and the rise of informal settlements exacerbate the potential of landslides, and contribute to the likelihood of this happening again.

### 7.2.2 Pollution and Waste: Africa's Beautiful Sunsets and Toxic Air

Pollution and waste take many forms and it would be outside the ambit of the book to describe the multitude of problems, suggested solutions and the role China can play in reducing the impact. The important point to make is that the lack of development in African nations results in unique challenges that require unique approaches in addressing the problems.

Take the example of Rwanda, just recovering from a tragic genocide, with the government tasked with the monumental task of rebuilding the country. As the country grew, there would be greater access to goods such as found in supermarkets, and the use of plastic bags would exponentially increase. For many developing countries in Africa, limited facilities exist for waste management, which results in high levels of littering, with plastic bags being the biggest culprit. So, what did Rwanda do? They banned plastic bags. In addition, President Kagame introduced a compulsory day of cleaning in Kigali, which he himself adheres to. These are courageous moves by the government that resulted in cleaner cities, greater togetherness and, from an economic perspective, potential for development of the tourism sector as the country displays itself as a model clean country and generates savings from reduced waste management costs.

Another pollution example is that of Lake Malawi and Mount Kilimanjaro, two of the natural gems of Africa and certainly among some of the most beautiful places in the world. Lake Malawi with its serene, sometimes angry waters, beautiful beaches and unrivalled African sunsets, offers a natural wonderland to any visitor (Figs. 7.3 and 7.4). Mount

**Fig. 7.3** Invitation for sundowners on Lake Malawi

Fig. 7.4 Fishing boats on a serene Lake Malawi

Kilimanjaro, the highest mountain in Africa with its (diminishing) glacial caps, conjures up images of African explorers in bygone years. This is a popular tourist destination in Tanzania.

Sadly, both Lake Malawi and Mount Kilimanjaro highlight the endemic air pollution in East Africa. Those blood-red sunsets on Lake Malawi are due to smog, and Mount Kilimanjaro is invisible from Moshi, just a couple of kilometres away (Figs. 7.5 and 7.6).

Both Lake Malawi and Mount Kilimanjaro are in rural areas and far from urban cities and any form of industry, so industry and car fumes are not the contributing factor to the air pollution. Quite clearly, it is a result of bush fires prevalent in East Africa. The root cause of which is the production of charcoal for home use. Alongside roads, there are numerous vendors of large bags filled with charcoal. Fires are deliberately set, and the trees and bushes are later scavenged for charcoaled branches. So not only is the burning catastrophic for the air quality, but it is ravaging the natural vegetation (Fig. 7.7).

**Fig. 7.5** Fires on Lake Malawi's shore

**Fig. 7.6** View from Moshi of the mighty Mount Kilimanjaro in Tanzania is totally obscured by smog

Fig. 7.7 Vendors selling charcoal alongside the road in Zambia

It would be naïve to expect a quick and simple solution to the problem. Obviously, the charcoal is used for cooking and heating purposes, and the demand is unlikely to dissipate for the charcoal. The long-term solution is access to electricity, ideally through clean renewable energy solutions. Perhaps China can lend a helping hand in this regard.

## 7.3 China's Environmental Impact on Africa

China's environmental policies have gained momentum in an effort to address their own environmental problems, but increasingly, these policies frame the context of Chinese enterprises investing and operating in Africa.

### 7.3.1 China Takes Cognisance of Environmental Issues while Africa Lags Behind

With the phenomenal growth that China has experienced, it is of no surprise that the country contributes to greenhouse gas emissions and climate change, and that it also suffers from the consequences of climate change. For instance, near-surface air temperatures in China increased between 0.55% and 0.8% in the twentieth century and the frequency and intensity of extreme temperatures and weather have been growing. In addition, food insecurity is increasing with China's limited arable land and water resources, and resulting agricultural production in transition zones has been reduced due to climatic changes. The mounting air temperatures and air pollution have also increased morbidity and mortality amongst those with higher cardiovascular, cerebrovascular or respiratory diseases; and extreme hot weather directly impacts the productivity of the workforce and the cost of labour due to high-temperature subsidies offered in the country (Tong et al. 2016).

China, on its economic growth trajectory, acknowledges that carbon emissions will increase in the short term. However, at COP 21, the country made an important commitment in halting the growth of greenhouse gases by 2030. Later in March 2016, the Chinese government's Five-Year Plan included the goal of reducing carbon dioxide emissions by 18% by 2020 (Tong et al. 2016). Intrinsic to the plan is a deviation from pollution to an environment-friendly model that not only contributes to improving the well-being of the Chinese population, but also reduces the negative externality of climate change.

The lessons learned by China in addressing the consequences of climate change and reducing the country's negative impact on climate change can be an important guideline for African countries in their different stages of economic growth.

Learning from the Chinese experience is critical, as not only will African countries increasingly contribute to greenhouse gas emissions as they embark on economic growth, but they are extremely vulnerable to climate change and the consequences of deforestation and desertification.

One example of China's success in tackling deforestation and desertification can be found in the Loess Plateau in China (World Wildlife Fund Living Planet Report 2016: 24–25). The area once sported an extensive forest and grassland system, but early civilisation reduced the forest, biodiversity and organic matter, eventually resulting in the desertification of an area similar in size to that of France: An area characterised by cycles of flooding, drought and famine. An aggressive programme to restore the area began in the last couple of decades, with the designation of economic and ecological land, terracing, sediment traps, dams and an array of interventions to restore biomass and organic matter. A massive project of tree planting and ecologically supportive agricultural methods contributed to the effort. The area now has an ecological balance that supports economic development.

China can play a key role in addressing environmental sustainability in Africa through the technological transfer of innovations in reducing greenhouse gas emissions, focusing on renewable energy solutions and finding the ecological balance that supports economic development.

In fact, China is probably taking environmental issues more seriously than many African nations. Even the African Union's aspirations fail to prioritise environmental issues, although their Action Plan of the Environment Initiative of the New Partnership for African Development does raise certain environmental concerns. The Pew Research Centre's Global Attitude Project (Greatest Dangers in the World 2014) established that eight of the nine African countries surveyed ranked pollution and the environment as the least of the five greatest dangers of the world. In contrast, the survey found that pollution and the environment were ranked the highest of the dangers by other nations.

China seems to be actively pursuing greener growth in its engagement in Africa. The FOCAC Johannesburg Action Plan (2015) specifically refers to the intention of "environmental protection and tackling climate change". Chinese investments in Africa are also under increasingly stringent environmental requirements.

China's Green Credit Policy has prioritised environmental considerations in foreign direct investment (FDI) funding. It promotes 'green lending' in projects related to energy conservation, reducing emissions and environmental protection. Lending criteria are strict, requiring environmental feasibility studies; endorsement from host countries' environmental agencies; continued examination of environmental compliance during the project; and review once the project is complete. There is the expectation that Chinese companies will adopt Chinese environmental standards when the host country's standards are lower than China's.

The Chinese Exim Bank, one of the main sources of funding for Chinese companies in Africa, has an environmental policy guided by the Green Credit Policy and considers the environmental impact of investments, and requires companies to comply with host country policies in sustainable development and environmental protection. The China Chamber of Commerce for Minerals, Metals, and Chemical Importers and Exporters has also taken a tougher stance in regulating mining investments, especially around issues of environmental protection in addition to labour issues, supply chain management and human rights (Shinn 2016: 32).

Increasingly, Chinese companies have signed up to the United Nations Global Compact, committing themselves to furthering human rights, labour standards, anti-corruption and, last but not least, environmental protection. The World Bank's Equator Principles are also an important consideration in this regard.

### 7.3.2 Concerns Regarding the Negative Environmental Impact of China's Investments in Africa

Concerns do remain though. The temptation for China to move its polluting industries to Africa is high. Coupled to the fact that such industries create much needed jobs is the fact that investment in such industries is attractive to African nations wishing to address unemployment. There has been evidence of this happening in the steel and leather industries: Hebei Iron & Steel recently disclosed their interest in building a steel plant with the capacity of 5 million tonnes in South Africa; Sinosteel announced plans in 2015 to develop a steel plant in Kenya; and Sentua Steel Limited confirmed an increase in production at its steel plant in Ghana. In the leather industry, Chinese tanneries are known culprits of pollution: China–Africa Overseas Leather Products SC in Ethiopia was forced to close shortly after the commencement of operations due to complaints; and Jeronimo Group Industries & Trading PLC were accused of dumping waster in the local Somaliland River damaging the livestock industry (Shinn 2016: 40–42).

There are a number of other concerns, amongst which one is mining. Minerals and resources are often found in remote areas, offering opportunities for socio-economic growth outside of urban areas, but they are mostly situated in environmentally sensitive areas, and can have devastating environmental externalities, such as waste dumped into rivers. Chinese companies often negotiate mining permits with African governments, often with little consideration being given to communities and the environment, and environmental impact assessments are not always prerequisites for the commencement of operations. Overfishing is another concern. Approximately two-thirds of China's global catch is from around the continent, which can affect the smaller subsistence fishermen's capacity to support their families, thus contributing to food insecurity. Overfishing can also deplete marine resources, with Chinese companies sometimes being accused of failing to respect fishing quotas and staying within their fishing zones (Shinn 2016: 49).

Protecting Africa's wildlife from extinction is also a high priority. Poaching of elephant, rhino and abalone for their tusks, horn and exotic meat—much of which is destined for China—is a growing problem. The poaching and smuggling have often been perpetrated by Chinese nationals. The Chinese government has been slow in addressing the problem, but has begun banning the trade of endangered species' products.

While most large Chinese FDI in Africa are by state-owned enterprises, or under the influence of the state, these will likely follow China's environmental policies. Smaller, privately owned companies may not necessarily have these constraints, and their commitment to environmental protection may be lacking. It is therefore imperative that African nations also consider their own policies and legislation, funding and human resources needed to implement these policies to ensure environmental sustainability is prioritised.

## 7.4 Examples of China's Impact on Sustainability in Africa

A number of examples have already been given on the positive and negative impacts that China's investment and operations may have on environmental sustainability. What follows are three case studies that aim to provide better insight into the multifaceted impact China has on Africa's sustainability; depicts how African countries can benefit from the lessons China has learned through its own challenging growth trajectory; and the benefits Africa can accrue from the technological and financial investments by China in infrastructure.

### 7.4.1 Learning from China's Switch from Fossil Fuel to Clean Energy

Similar to the smog problem described in East Africa, when visiting China it becomes apparent that the strides of economic growth have also come at a price. Air pollution is rife. Economists would probably tell you this is a natural phenomenon illustrated in the 'Kuznets' curve: as an economy grows, negative environmental externalities increase, until such time that cognisance is taken of the environmental impact, and gradually environmental policies and controls are improved. China's industries and energy production were and continue to be fuelled by coal. In fact, coal consumption between 2001 and 2011 increased by approximately 10% every year. Using cleaner energy is therefore prioritised in China, and is expected to rise from just 9.8% in 2013 to 15% in 2020. So, while it is clear that fossil fuel usage by China is at a very high level, this trend is rapidly changing towards greater reliance on clean energy resources of hydro, wind and solar power, and, in addition, the country is continually improving energy use efficiency (Mathews and Tan 2015: 23–25). China utilises hydroelectric power more so than any other country with its target of 290 GW per year being achieved a year before the due date of 2015. Not only does China have the engineering expertise of hydroelectric dams, it has also been an innovator of electricity transmission required to distribute electricity over vast distances.

The Yangtze River is the longest river in Asia, and a bloodline for China. In Yichang, the water flows gently, and ships carrying precious cargo between Shanghai and Chongqing meander along the river. Just a bit further up lies the enormous Three Gorges Dam—a testament to the engineering supremacy of the Chinese. Possibly the largest construction since the Great Wall of China itself, it holds a number of world records. For instance, its 'shiplift' is the largest in the world capable of lifting ships weighing 3000 tonnes by 113 metres. Most importantly, though, is that with its 32 turbines, the 22,500 MW hydroelectric dam can produce as much electricity as 18 nuclear power stations (Fig. 7.8).

**Fig. 7.8** The 2000 metre Three Gorges Dam

## A Grandiose Plan: The Grand Inga Dam of the Democratic Republic of the Congo

Chinese state-owned enterprises have been very active in building hydroelectric dams in Africa. SinHydro, HydroChina and the Three Gorges Corporation are all actively involved in projects in Africa, often financed by the Chinese Exim bank, and further much of China's FOCAC commitments in Africa.

The hydroelectric capacity in Africa is enormous. The proposed Grand Inga Dam on the Congo River would shadow the achievement of the Three Gorges Dam with its generating capacity of 40,000 MW of electricity—nearly double that of the Three Gorges Dam. The electricity produced would not only power the DRC, but could also be exported to as far away as South Africa.

Financiers of the US$80 billion project could include the World Bank, the African Development Bank and the European Investment Bank. It is likely that the construction of the dam would eventually include one or more Chinese construction companies.

While the benefits of access to electricity in improving the quality of peoples' lives and supporting industrialisation is undisputed, it must also be taken into consideration that dams of this scale can have significant negative socio-environmental repercussions.

The Aswan High Dam in Egypt that was built in the 1970s is such an example. The Aswan High Dam was built to generate electricity, control flooding and serve as water storage for year-round irrigation. The irrigation would reduce the reliance of farmers on the previous year's flooding of the river and allow them to grow three or more crops a year. Without the flooding, though, the silt of the river, rich in organic matter, is no longer deposited in the agricultural lands. The result is that fertilisers must be used, which increases agricultural costs and contributes to the pollution of the Nile and damages the land itself, sometimes to the extent that the land cannot be used for agricultural purposes.

Returning to the Grand Inga Dam in the DRC, it is important to also consider the level of the country's development, and the impact this will have on the success and benefits of the project: the DRC has a pre-transition economy with some of the concerns detailed in Table 7.3.

China and Chinese companies' involvement in building hydroelectric dams can greatly support sustainable energy provision. Cognisance,

Table 7.3  Grand Inga Dam concerns

**Costs:** Expensive and risk of cost escalation
**Debt burden:** The cost of the project would be an enormous liability for a country struggling financially
**Lack of effective governance in the DRC:** Potential for corruption, which could further exacerbate cost of the project
**Ecological impact:** Nutrient and sediment trapping and loss of the Congo 'plume' (nutrient flow from the river) may cause loss of biodiversity and a shift of the dominant species
**Agricultural land flooding:** The dam would flood the Bundi Valley, affecting farming and the natural environment. It could also cause methane emissions, which would contribute to global warming
**Waterborne threats:** The dam may increase the threat from the likes of malanquin mosquitoes
**Deforestation:** The DRC is home to the world's second largest rainforest. Transmission lines would require large corridors to be cleared of vegetation
**Negative social impacts:** The dam and transmission lines could negatively impact the quality of living
**Displace communities:** The dam would displace communities
**Lack of benefits to the poorer communities:** There is little evidence that electricity would be provided to the Congolese people

Adapted from International Rivers (2016)

however, needs to be taken on the massive social and environmental threats that these megaprojects pose—especially when countries, such as the DRC, lack effective political governance and strong institutions to balance the needs for economic development, cleaner and sustainable energy provision, environmental protection and improving the wellbeing of its people.

### 7.4.2  Water: The Essence of Life

Water in Africa is a scarce resource for a number of reasons. Certain countries are naturally drought-prone with vast deserts; in others, water is abundant yet infrastructure to pump the water to households and businesses limits access to many countries' populace, and then, sadly, many of the continent's rivers and streams are strewn with litter, sewerage and waterborne diseases.

## Lake Victoria: A Man-Made Catastrophe

Another beautiful African lake is Lake Victoria. The lake belongs to Tanzania, Kenya and Uganda and supports millions of people along its banks.

The Nile Perch is a delicious freshwater delight; it is difficult to believe it is the cause of so much environmental damage at Lake Victoria. These fish are not indigenous to the lake, having been introduced by man to support fishing industries, and, in the process, the Nile Perch has decimated hundreds of species of native fish, many of which are now extinct. Algae-eating fish have been reduced, allowing for rampant algae growth, thus choking the lake. Oxygen levels in the deeper regions of the lake are being deprived, further exacerbating the survival chances of other species.

The local fishing industry is paying the price, with many communities surviving on their fishing activities being forced out of the industry. The Nile Perch damages traditional nets and only large-scale fishing companies can afford the equipment to catch the Nile Perch. The downward cycle perpetuates the problem. As the food supply chain dwindles, the Nile Perch numbers have also begun dwindling, with even the larger Nile Perch cannibalising the smaller Perch.

Then there is the curse of the water hyacinth. Raw sewerage directly entering the lake has increased nitrogen and phosphorous, which has resulted in an invasion of the hyacinth. This hyacinth depletes oxygen in the lake, congests boats and ferries, restricts hydroelectric power generation and compromises water access for industry (one 'positive' outcome is that the hyacinth may reduce fishing and contribute to fish growth). The hyacinth is a breeding ground for mosquitoes, including those that spread malaria, and snails that host bilharzia parasites, a parasite that attacks the liver, lungs and eyes of humans. Bilharzia is prevalent amongst children and people in the fishing industry alongside the lake. The threat of bilharzia also has a detrimental effect on the propensity for developing the tourism sector near the lakes (IRIN 2002).

Incidentally, one of the largest investments by China in Africa was destined for Lake Victoria in the form of the Lake Victoria Free Trade Zone. Announced in 2008, the so-called Sseesamirembe City was envisioned as an eco-city covering 500 square kilometres of land and included a solar-powered airport, various manufacturing and logistical facilities, agribusinesses and homes. Thousands of Chinese farmers were also expected to settle on the land and grow crops for export to China. This bold plan is now gathering dust on some forgotten shelf—the investment has failed to materialise (The Economist 2015).

While the free trade zone did not materialise, there are promising signs that China is contributing to alleviating the environmental concerns of the lake. There is a lack of a coordinated strategy by Uganda, Kenya and Tanzania in addressing development and pollution control of the lake. In addition, technologies for managing pollution in these countries are limited. One way the Chinese are contributing to a solution is through research and skills development. In 2016, it was announced that Chinese researchers had completed a field study on Lake Victoria, and had interacted with local government, academic institutions and civil society around the issue of the lake's development focusing on ecological protection. This was to be followed by technical training to improve the capacity of the affected countries, as well as pilot projects aimed at pollution reduction of the lake (FOCAC 2016).

Not only is China contributing to environmental protection, but it is also making strides in developing the local fishing industry. A US$5 million fish-farming centre has been established near Kampala in Uganda. Not only does it serve as a fish hatchery, but local Ugandan farmers are also trained in modern fishing methods. The experience of the Chinese in fish farming is also shared throughout East Africa, where basic technologies are shared on cage farming, selective breeding and nutrient supplements to boost fish growth (Ssekandi and Qing 2012).

While these may be considered small steps, the contribution that China can have in addressing the problems of Lake Victoria can be significant.

### 7.4.3 Food Insecurity in the Fertile Lands of Africa

The Chinese comprise 22% of the world's population, but China has only 7% of the world's arable land. Although a huge country, much of it is mountainous and not suitable for food production. Compounding the problem, it is estimated that erosion, pollution and other forms of degradation have compromised 40% of the arable land (Horta 2014). Even though agricultural technologies are continually improving and contribute to farming efficiency, in order to ensure food security, and feed the expensive tastes of a growing middle-class population, China has to look beyond its borders. Many African countries are in sight.

Yes, many countries in Africa are fertile, yet this resource is not always effectively managed, resulting in many cases of 'food insecurity'. For instance, hundreds of people were reportedly dying from hunger in 2017 due to drought in Somalia. Natural famines due to drought, plagues and natural disasters such as floods or earthquakes are terribly sad, especially considering the advances of logistics and modern food preservation that should contribute to food distribution throughout the year. Famines can be avoided if the political will is strong enough.

What is even more frustrating is man-made famine. Tchie (News24: 2017) describes the causes of man-made famines as extreme poverty, war, deliberate crop destruction and inability to distribute food. South Sudan is a prime example of a man-made famine. Years of conflict have destroyed the economy, its currency has devalued by 800% and food is simply unaffordable to many. The government is accused of preventing the delivery of food aid. What little money the government has goes into the purchase of weapons and waging war, and hunger prevails. As the situation continues to deteriorate, half of the country's population is expected to become food-insecure in 2017, with over 250,000 children severely undernourished at the time of Tchie's writing.

The balance between ensuring China's own food security and the temptation of 'land-grabbing' in Africa has been a matter of intense debate for some time. Deborah Brautigam and Sigrid-Marianella Ekman (2012) found discrepancies between reported conduct by the Chinese and the reality of the situation in Mozambique.

The purchase of large tracts of land by foreigners elicits concern of a loss of national control and reminders of Africa's colonialist past. In Mozambique, reports emerged of arrangements entered into between Mozambique and China allowing for the migration of thousands of Chinese farmers to produce rice for the Chinese market; these reports were followed by reports that protest action in Mozambique thwarted these plans; and, lastly, reports then detailed US$800 million worth of investment in rice farming for the Chinese market. Brautigam and Ekman found these reports to be far from real and that there was no evidence of the various claims made. Instead, they discovered a Mozambican government that was playing an assertive role with the private sector, working with multiple Chinese actors, to further

Mozambique's agricultural agenda. Brautigam and Ekman do not suggest that land-grabbing and exploitation do not happen, rather they reflect on Mozambique's increased ability to manage its engagement with China and other countries.

In conclusion, an integrated approach led by the host African country of leveraging the country's natural resources through Chinese skills and technological transfer, finance, direct investment and political 'friendship' can support the development of the agricultural sector and contribute to sustainable food security.

## 7.5  China's Impact

Environmental sustainability is a critical component of Africa's sought-after sustainable growth and development. In the face of a myriad of existing African environmental management concerns, such as poor policy and regulatory controls, a lack of coordinated environmental protection efforts, and poor knowledge and education on environmental issues, China, through its own hard-learnt lessons, may contribute some of the lessons that it has learned.

As the chapter has illustrated, China could contribute to a better quality of life for African citizens through its engagement in Africa, by reducing pollution, facilitating cost-effective access to water and electricity, and improving food security. From an economic perspective, the positive environmental impact, the development of agribusinesses with the potential for export growth and increased tourism potential could foster economic growth.

The transfer of green technology and engineering skills and resources could reduce the dependence on non-renewable resources, improve the efficiency of resource use and reduce the negative impact on the environment. Concerns do, however, remain that some of these megaprojects could be excessively expensive and result in debt burdens for some African nations. The social impact is also brought into question with the potential displacement of communities, the inability of communities to directly benefit from some projects, and then, of course, the contribution Chinese firms may have in exacerbating greenhouse gas emissions, deforestation and climate change.

A summary of the impact on the African Tree of Organic Growth is depicted in Fig. 7.9.

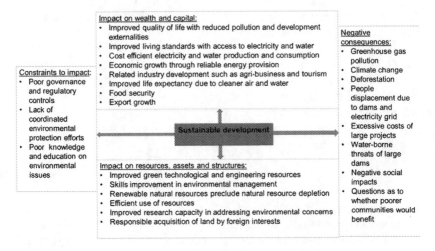

Fig. 7.9 Environmental sustainability and the African Tree of Organic Growth

REFERENCES

Brautigam, D. and Ekman, S. 2012. 'Briefing Rumours and Realities of Chinese Agricultural Engagement in Mozambique', *African Affairs*, 111 (444): 483–492.

Horta, L. 16 December 2014. Chinese Agriculture Goes Global. *Yale Global*. [Online]. Accessed from: http://yaleglobal.yale.edu/content/chinese-agriculture-goes-global (accessed: 2 March 2017).

FOCAC. 8 November 2016. China, Africa Cooperate on Freshwater Lake Protection. [Online]. Accessed from: http://www.focac.org/eng/jlydh/mtsy/t1413724.htm (accessed: 2 March 2017).

FOCAC Johannesburg Action Plan (2016–2018). 25 December 2015. Forum on China-Africa Cooperation. [Online]. Available from: http://www.focac.org/eng/ltda/dwjbzjjhys_1/t1327961.htm (accessed: 19 October 2016).

Greatest Dangers in the World. 2014. Pew Research Center. [Online]. Accessed from: http://www.pewglobal.org/2014/10/16/greatest-dangers-in-the-world/ (accessed: 17 November 2017).

International Rivers. 2016. Grand Inga Dam, DR Congo. [Online]. Accessed from: https://www.internationalrivers.org/campaigns/grand-inga-dam-drcongo (accessed: 16 August 2017).

IPCC Climate Change 2014 Synthesis Report Summary for Policymakers. 2014. *IPCC*. [Online]. Available from: https://www.ipcc.ch/pdf/assessment-report/ar5/syr/AR5_SYR_FINAL_SPM.pdf (accessed: 18 February 2017).

IRIN. 2002. Bilharzia Health Hazard Highlighted. [Online]. Accessed from: http://www.irinnews.org/report/29892/east-africa-bilharzia-health-hazard-highlighted (accessed: 1 March 2017).

Mathews, J. and Tan, H. 2015. *China's Renewable Energy Revolution*. Basingstoke: Palgrave Macmillan.
Msowoya, K., Madani, K., Davtalab, R., Mirchi, A. and Lund, J. 2016. 'Climate Change Impacts on Maize Production in the Warm Heart of Africa', *Water Resources Management*, 30 (14): 5299–5312.
Onyango, E., Sahin, O., Chu, C. and Mackey, B. 2016. 'An Integrated Risk and Vulnerability Assessment Framework for Climate Change and Malaria Transmission in East Africa', *Malaria Journal*, 15 (1): 551.
Outcomes of the U.N. Climate Change Conference in Paris. 2015. Centre for Climate and Energy Solutions. [Online]. Available from: https://www.c2es.org/docUploads/cop-21-paris-summary-02-2016-final.pdf (accessed: 18 February 2017).
Shinn, D. 2016. 'The Environmental Impact of China's Investment in Africa', *Cornell International Law Journal*, 49: 25–67.
Ssekandi, R. and Qing, Y. 30 August 2012. China Helps Boost Uganda's Fish Farming Industry. *FOCAC*. [Online]. Accessed from: http://www.focac.org/eng/zxxx/t964639.htm (accessed: 2 March 2017).
Sustainable Development Goals. 25 September 2015. United Nations. [Online]. Available from: http://www.un.org/sustainabledevelopment/sustainable-development-goals/#prettyPhoto (accessed: 19 October 2016).
Tchie, A. 4 March 2017. How South Sudan's Warlords Triggered Extreme Hunger in a Land of Plenty. *News24*. [Online]. Accessed from: http://www.news24.com/Africa/News/how-south-sudans-warlords-triggered-extreme-hunger-in-a-land-of-plenty-20170304 (accessed: 5 March 2017).
Terink, W., Immerzeel, W. and Droogers, P. 2013. 'Climate Change Projections of Precipitation and Reference Evapotranspiration for the Middle East and Northern Africa Until 2050', *International Journal of Climatology*, 33 (14): 3055–3072.
The Economist. 21 November 2015. Not as Easy as It Looks. [Online]. Accessed from: http://www.economist.com/news/middle-east-and-africa/21678777-western-worries-about-chinas-burgeoning-influence-africa-may-be-overblown-not (accessed: 2 March 2017).
Tong, S., Berry, H., Ebi, K., Bambrick, H., Hu, W., Green, D., Hanna, E., Wang, Z. and Butler, C. 2016. 'Climate Change, Food, Water and Population Health in China', *Bulletin of the World Health Organisation*, 94 (10): 759–765.
United Nations Convention to Combat Desertification. 2017. Annex 1: Africa. Accessed from: http://www2.unccd.int/convention/regions/annex-i-africa (accessed 16 August 2017).
United Nations Environment Programme. 2016. Land, Water, Biodiversity, and Air Quality Under Pressure in Africa: Global Environmental Outlook 6—Factsheet. Accessed from: http://www.unep.org/publications/ (accessed: 16 August 2017).
World Wildlife Fund. 2016. Living Planet Report 2016. Accessed from: http://awsassets.panda.org/downloads/lpr_living_planet_report_2016_summary.pdf (accessed: 20 August 2017).

CHAPTER 8

# Improving the Human Well-Being of All Africans

The importance of the leaves and fruit of human well-being in the African Tree of Organic Growth recognises the fact that integrated organic growth must prioritise the interests of the African people by creating equal economic opportunities, and generating social and cultural wealth and capital to a broad spectrum of the population in each country (Fig. 8.1).

Social wealth and capital on the macro level include human rights and duties, law and order, freedom of expression and access to quality health care and education. These factors are normally a direct consequence of good or

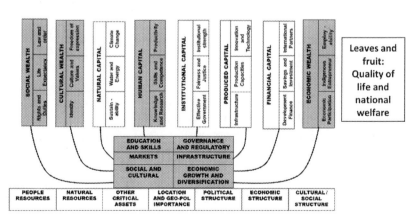

Fig. 8.1   The African Tree of Organic Growth

© The Author(s) 2018
K. Jonker, B. Robinson, *China's Impact on the African Renaissance*,
https://doi.org/10.1007/978-981-13-0179-7_8

bad governance and regulatory processes in place in a specific country. On the micro level, social wealth and capital refer to social cohesion and interaction, embracing diversity and human development and social justice. Social capital and wealth have direct and profound impacts on the organic growth of a nation as they form the base of human growth and development and represent the 'glue' that holds communities together. Human development seeks to enable people to lead full, productive and meaningful lives by raising their incomes and improving their standards of living, which include life expectancy, health, education, security and personal liberty and freedom of choice.

Cultural capital and wealth, on the other hand, builds positive self-esteem and cultural identity within communities. Culturally they contextualise all human development in the country by placing it in a historical and cultural context. The cultural landscape in Africa tells a story of underdevelopment, influences from colonisation, disregard of certain cultures and, in many countries, domination of one culture or race above the others.

There has been mixed progress with regard to social and human development in Africa. While poverty rates have been dropping, albeit at a slow pace, inequality remains high and is increasing in many countries. Probably one of the most important indexes, the Human Development Index, where the well-being of countries' people are ranked according to health, education and income, ranks most African countries sadly right at the bottom.

No African country features in the category of 51 countries in the 'Very High Human Development' index; Mauritius features at 64, Algeria at 83 (China slots in at 90), Tunisia at 97 and Libya at 102 in the 'High Human Development' index; African countries feature more in the 'Medium Human Development' index with the powerhouses of Egypt at 111 and South Africa at 119; and African countries dominate the 'Low Human Development' index of 38 countries, with the lowest ranking 15 countries all being African nations (Human Development Report 2016: 198–199).

From a regional perspective, East and West Africa rank the worst in terms of human development, with North Africa having the most countries in the higher level of human development. Southern and Central Africa have a mixed bag of human development achievements, from low to high. Progress in human development also varies regionally, with higher levels of improvement achieved in North Africa and South Africa.

For the Baobab Tree to achieve its full growth potential, it has to sprout the leaves and fruit that cover not just a few twigs or branches, but the entire canopy in rich foliage, absorbing the sunrays, energising it for the future. Africa's renaissance has to benefit and improve the well-being of all its people, as this is paramount for a sustainable future envisioned by the African Union Agenda 2063, the United Nations 2030 Agenda and the United Nations 17 Sustainable Development Goals.

The metaphor of 'treating the symptoms and not the cause' is very apt when it comes to human development. Here is the all-important proviso: Fundamental to human development is the need for broad-based economic growth and diversification, suitable and accessible infrastructure, sound and effective government leadership and suitable policy implementation—these are the roots and trunk of the organic tree that facilitate long-term well-being when these fruits can be distributed for all to benefit. Failing which, human development efforts will be unsustainable and remain at the elementary stage of 'handouts'—desperate attempts by the international community to avoid humanitarian crises so often seen in Africa.

Another metaphor, which is just as apt to this argument, is that in order to stimulate the production of more fruit, it is important to prune the nutrient-draining deadwood and dead leaves and flowers. These are the inefficiencies of the economic system, the misuse of resources, the corruption of power and the drain of the country's resources and assets to increase the stupendous wealth of a few. When these problems are addressed, there will be a greater opportunity for the tree to produce more fruit for all.

## 8.1 Towards Improved Well-Being for Africa

While the Human Development Index is a useful benchmarking framework that ranks countries' human development according to health, education and income, these are just some of the many attributes that contribute to the well-being of countries' populations.

The World Happiness Report 2017 (Helliwell et al. 2017) commissioned by the Sustainable Development Solutions Network uses economic and some further interesting variables to measure happiness amongst people in different countries: GDP per capita in terms of Purchasing Power Parity; life expectancy at the time of birth; social support from relatives and friends; freedom of life choices; generosity in giving donations; perceptions of corruption ; positive effect of laughter and enjoyment on the previous day; and the negative effect of worry, sadness and anger on the previous day.

A previous World happiness Report in 2015 illustrated the 'geography of happiness' in Map 8.1. Green reflects relative happiness, while red

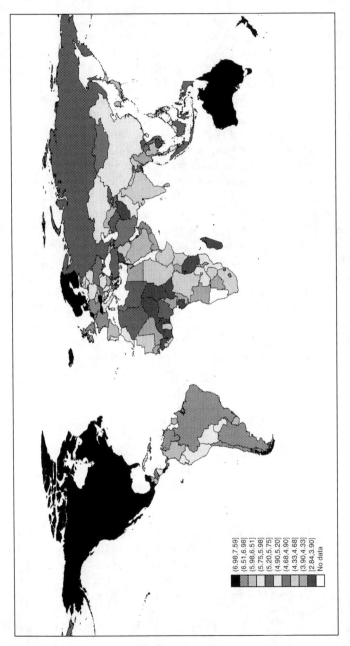

Map 8.1 The geography of happiness. (Helliwell et al. 2015: 20)

reflects relatively low levels on the happiness index. The deeper the red, the less there is happiness. Africa starkly stands out as the red continent. The World Happiness Report of 2017 (Helliwell et al. 2017) dedicated a chapter to determining the causes for the 'happiness deficit' in Africa. Correctly, they introduce the topic by describing the vast differences between the numerous countries in Africa and the 'inequalities' of happiness within countries themselves. However, they suggest that the greatest contributor to the happiness deficit is that "African people's expectations that they and their countries would flourish under self-rule and democracy appear not to have been met" (Helliwell et al. 2017: 110).

In understanding the elements of this happiness deficit, the authors of the World Happiness Report of 2017 describe the contributors to this deficit in Africa (Table 8.1).

Table 8.1 Causes of the happiness deficit in Africa

| Element | Contribution |
| --- | --- |
| Democracy | Democracy is weakly positively associated with happiness. The gap between preference for democracy and the satisfaction with its functioning depresses levels of happiness |
| Poverty | There is a strong negative relationship between happiness and poverty. Changes in reducing poverty over time increases levels of happiness |
| Infrastructure development and happiness | Infrastructure that results in access to electricity, roads, piped water, sewerage systems and cellular phone services increases happiness ratings. Lack thereof contributes to poverty, and, therefore, negatively impacts happiness |
| Corruption | Happiness improved significantly in countries where citizens saw a reduction of corruption by the country's leadership, and citizens noticed an effort by the government to fight corruption |
| Youth | The increase in the relative proportion of youth in Africa will be a future challenge and will have an impact on happiness levels. The youth have certain expectations of employment and living standards. Failure of this happening will contribute to poverty, unrest and the growing migration problem, and, ultimately, negatively impact the happiness levels of this growing segment of the population |
| Drought and extreme weather conditions | Recession and drought have historically contributed to unrest, such as seen with the Arab Spring and Ethiopian protests. Drought conditions affect food production and increase food prices, ultimately fuelling discontent |

Helliwell et al. (2017: 92–107)

Poverty alleviation, access to food and water, healthy lives, good living standards, security through law and order, the pace and level of urbanisation, population growth, the youth, human rights and equality, especially gender equality, are all factors that influence the well-being of people.

If one considers the seminal work of Abraham Maslow where he developed the pyramid of hierarchy of needs, achieving the level of self-actualisation is an impossible task without elementary needs being met. Physiological needs: without having a roof over your head, food in the tummy, a bed to sleep in and clothes to wear, individuals cannot hope to enjoy a 'normal' life. Safety needs: war, high levels of crime and poor legal institutions create an environment of insecurity and fear. Esteem needs can never be achieved without human rights and equality. While self-actualisation may be a theoretical concept, the assumption it makes is correct: without these basic needs being met, individuals will never have the opportunity to progress towards self-fulfilment.

### 8.1.1 Poverty Alleviation

The 'poverty trap' is the bleak reality for many in Africa: Unemployed, poor people, living in often inhumane conditions. The trap refers to the inability of the poor to improve their well-being. There are many reasons for this: Lack of access, such as transport services, to employment; lack of educational facilities and skills transfer to provide opportunities for gainful employment; lack of government social security support for the poor; ineffective policies and corruption; and the list goes on.

Pro-poor growth is a term coined to describe socio-economic growth that enhances the opportunity for those living in poverty to benefit from such growth, and, in so doing, contribute to sustainable development themselves. Pro-poor policies and strategies include transfer payments, government employment programmes, participatory development, community self-help, social upliftment, rural agricultural reforms and providing infrastructure to ensure the poor also benefit from services and have access to the most basic of life's essentials. Many infrastructure investments in Africa are motivated by the firm belief that they will lead to poverty alleviation and organic growth in the longer term. Amongst infrastructure, roads are considered one of the most critical in this process because they can have a significant and substantial impact on growth and poverty by providing access to jobs, services and markets.

## 8.1.2 Food Security

Food insecurity due to a wide range of phenomena, such as climatic conditions, natural disasters, climate change and the human factor of wars, conflict zones, overgrazing, deforestation and desertification, increases the vulnerability to famine in many parts of Africa.

There are certain short-term solutions to immediate crises, such as food and financial donations towards the purchase of food both by the relevant country's government and from the international community.

Eradicating food insecurity requires a long-term solution. With Africa's wealth of fertile land, reforms in the agricultural sector and modern farming methods not only hold the opportunity of reducing food insecurity and dependence on the international community for help, but the agricultural sector can be a pivotal asset as an economic growth sector.

In addition, many of the most food-insecure are small-scale subsistence farmers, extremely susceptible to shocks, such as drought or flooding, and who mostly do not have access to finance for investing in their farms or saving for the poor climatic seasons, do not have access to effective markets to sell their goods and generate income and do not have storage facilities, thus cannot store produce for long periods of time.

There are a number of policy options for governments. Landownership in many countries is contentious, with agrarian farming often being communal and property rights confusing. Land reform through privatisation or cooperatives could be considered. Subsidies and protection of local agricultural markets, marketing boards for particular products, microfinance, training in agricultural methods and modernising farming methods are some of the many policy considerations available to improve and support food security.

## 8.1.3 Health and Education Disparities

Health and education are marked by wide disparities in most African countries. The wealthy receive the best schooling and medical care, while many of the poor have to do without, or with sub-standard, services and education. Education is typically seen as a means of narrowing inequalities and concerted efforts have been made in the last two decades in many African countries to increase primary and secondary enrolments, with some success.

There were also significant improvements in the health conditions of the majority of African countries in the last four decades, yet life expectancy in most of Africa lags behind much of the world. While healthcare service provision has gradually improved in many countries, and life expectancy has increased, efforts to continually improve access to healthcare will always be a priority in human development. Interventions such as primary healthcare, access to care during pregnancy and child birth, access to health insurance, free provision of critical vaccinations and other life-saving interventions, and chronic and specialised healthcare provision all have the potential for addressing early mortality and life expectancy.

### 8.1.4 War, Law and Order

Living in conflict, fear of terrorism, kidnapping, vehicle hijacking, high crime levels, and physical and sexual abuse are some of the blights of the continent that are potential deterrents to achieving enjoyable productive lives.

National, regional and international interventions to prevent and manage conflict zones are of course critical. An effective, well-funded and efficient police sector, supported by legislation supporting law, order and human rights, access to the judiciary and fair and free treatment before the law are paramount for reducing crime and insecurity.

### 8.1.5 Living Standards

Standards of living are usually quantified on the Gross National Income per capita basis, where it is found that all African regions fail to achieve an acceptable standard of living. However, acceptable living standards cannot simply be quantified in dollars. It is difficult to put a valuation on having a decent home life. Consider having a home that is well positioned with a strong structure that can withstand wind and rain, and that is not in the path of wave surges, landslides and flooding rivers. Consider having clean drinking water, and water to bathe in and brush one's teeth. Consider free, solar-powered water heating for a shower and to wash dishes. Consider a house with electricity so that smelly and dangerous paraffin lamps and wood fires are not needed for lighting and cooking. Consider a hygienic toilet in or close to your home. Consider a paved road so you do not live in a dust bowl. Consider rubbish removal to keep you home and neighbourhood clean.

These may seem like very simple examples, but the reality in many parts of Africa is that people live in corrugated shacks that are boiling hot in the summer, freezing in the winter, damp and dripping in the raining season; electricity and running water are unheard of; positioned often where there is a vacant spot, with little thought to the threat of disease and natural disasters.

### 8.1.6 Economic Inequality

Examples proliferate in Africa of the rich getting exorbitantly rich in the 'leafy suburbs' of Africa (a reference to the wealthy suburb of Sandton in South Africa), presidents travel the world in luxury, and friends and families of the political elite become billionaires. Contrast this to large populations living in slums, without access to the very basic of life's needs. In Zambia, the richest 10% of the population earn a total income that is 42 times larger than the poorest 10% of the population. In Cameroon, a child born from the poorest 20% of the population has more than twice the probability of dying before the age of five years than a child who was born in the top 20% of the population.

Inequality is cyclical and difficult to break. As the poor continue to be prevented from accessing the fruits of economic growth, they will be unable to emerge from the trappings of poverty. If the wealthy, through manipulation of political and economic structures, continue to syphon the country's wealth, inequality will prosper.

### 8.1.7 Inequality in Human Rights and Human Capability

Inequalities in human rights and human capabilities often reflect inequalities in political power. Women, poor people and minority ethnic groups are often marginalised because they have weak political power and can be easily dominated by a majority. Sierra Leone had a very high level of inequality just before the outbreak of the ten-year-long civil war in 1989, inspired by young people who felt hopeless and powerless in their struggle for a better future.

Rwanda has set the benchmark on a number of fronts. From a gender equality perspective, it is the first and only country with the majority of parliament being female. So yes, certain African countries are making progress towards non-discrimination and the elimination of gender-based inequality, yet many others have a long way to go. Restrictive cultural practices, religious views, discriminatory legislation and male-biased labour markets restrict the economic benefits of women in many African economies. Yet women in Africa play a pivotal role driving socio-economic growth in Africa: they conduct most agricultural activities; they are central to the household economy; they care for their families; and they are leaders in their communities (African Gender Equality Index 2015: 5).

The African Gender Equality Index measures gender equality on three scales. First, equality in economic opportunities: Namely, whether men and women have equal opportunities in business and employment. Second, equality in human development: Are boys and girls given equal opportunity for schooling, and do women have access to reproductive health services? Lastly, equality in law and institutions: Are women and men equally well represented in institutions, do they have the same legal rights and do they have the same household rights?

The results paint an interesting picture. Overall, South Africa, Rwanda, Namibia, Mauritius and Malawi score the highest in that sequence. Yet Mauritius scores higher than South Africa for human development, but the least of the five countries in terms of economic opportunities. The lowest five in the index are Somalia, Sudan, Mali, Libya and Guinea, in that order. Yet Libya scores highly in terms of equality in human development, but extremely low in terms of equality in laws and institutions. These three scales and resulting indexes highlight the complexity of addressing country-specific gender inequality in Africa.

Another cause for concern is lesbian, gay, bisexual, transgender and intersexed (LGBTI) rights in Africa. While South Africa was one of the first countries in the world to entrench freedom from discrimination based on sexual orientation, the rest of Africa lags far behind in recognising the rights of the LGBTI community.

The death sentence for homosexuality exists in Sudan, Somalia and some of Nigeria, while in a number of countries, homosexuality is criminalised. In addition to legal discrimination, hate speech and violence against the LGBTI community is common. President Robert Mugabe of Zimbabwe, previous Gambian President Jammeh and Ugandan President Museveni have all publicly denounced homosexuality as wrong and have threatened retribution for these communities. So-called corrective rape has occurred in South Africa—a hate crime against lesbians intended to enforce heterosexuality.

## 8.2 Analysis of China's Contribution to Improving the Well-Being of African People

The Forum on China–Africa Cooperation's (FOCAC) Johannesburg Action Plan (2016–2018) provides some policy insights into China's commitment to the improvement of well-being on the African continent. A summary of the points in the Action Plan that could have a fundamental impact in this regard are detailed in Table 8.2.

To gain greater insight into the actual activities or projects that China has conducted in Africa that contribute to the improvement of the well-being of Africans, the FOCAC (2017) website's news releases were consulted to identify some of the interventions by the Chinese that have taken, or are taking, place in Africa. These are detailed in Table 8.3.

## 8.3 Case Study: China Makes a Decided Impact in Its Response to the Ebola Epidemic in Liberia, Guinea and Sierra Leone

The Ebola Virus Disease, to use its full name, is a highly infectious, killer disease, with fatality rates in past outbreaks ranging from 25% to 90%. While the origin of the disease is unclear, and its existence relatively recent—the first cases were discovered in 1976 in the DRC—the disease poses terrible risks in many of Africa's poorest nations with the least healthcare resources available to adequately care for those infected, and even less capacity to control the spread of the disease (Zhau et al. 2015).

The Ebola outbreak in West Africa was the most serious since the virus was discovered, and it affected Guinea, Sierra Leone, Mali, Nigeria, Senegal and Liberia in Africa, countries that have sometimes experienced years of conflict and instability, and many of which have inadequate healthcare and general infrastructure. When the Public Health Emergency of International Concern on Ebola was lifted on 29 March 2016, 28,616 confirmed and suspected cases of Ebola were recorded, with 11,310 deaths in total (World Health Organisation 2016). While Map 8.2 reflects the containment of Ebola with few new cases of Ebola at the time the map was published, the number of confirmed cases reflects the severity of the outbreak in Liberia, Guinea and Sierra Leone.

Liberia healthcare services were initially crippled by the Ebola outbreak. For instance, the period from January 2014 to March 2015 was character-

**Table 8.2** Summary of the FOCAC Action Plan points related to improved well-being in Africa

| Area of cooperation | Details of action plan |
|---|---|
| Agriculture and food security | Although classified under economic cooperation, the Action Plan emphasises safeguarding food security in the Comprehensive Agriculture Development Programme |
| Social development assistance | Refers to a commitment to increase assistance that improves people's livelihoods |
| Medical care and public health | China committed to develop Africa's public health systems and policies; to improve public health, surveillance, epidemiological and prevention systems; to strengthen prevention and treatment of malaria and other common infectious and communicable diseases in Africa; and enhance the assistance in maternal, child health and reproductive health. It also committed to supporting cooperation between Chinese and African hospitals, upgrading hospital departments, training public health workers and administrative personnel, and to send medical teams to Africa to provide free short-term medical services. It supported the building of the African Union Disease Control Centre. It would support investment by Chinese enterprises in the medical and healthcare industries in Africa. Infrastructure would be improved through Chinese construction, renovation and equipping of medical facilities |
| Poverty eradication strategies | The Action Plan refers to exchanging experiences on poverty eradication. One way was the joint organisation of the China–Africa Poverty Eradication and Development Conference to explore in-depth poverty eradication strategies and policies. China also committed to offering education programmes to train specialised personnel in the field of poverty eradication and development. In conjunction with African countries, China would implement village-community level comprehensive development projects. Resources would be mobilised, in conjunction with non-governmental agencies, to implement projects focused on women and children |
| Education and human resource development | A range of initiatives were detailed that addressed the shortage of professional and skilled persons that served as a major bottleneck constraining Africa's independent and sustainable development |
| Environmental protection and tackling climate change | A range of efforts were detailed in the Action Plan that addressed long-term sustainability issues that would impact the lives of people in rural and urban environments, including the implementation of clean energy projects, environment-friendly agricultural projects and smart city construction projects |

(*continued*)

Table 8.2 (continued)

| Area of cooperation | Details of action plan |
|---|---|
| Security cooperation | China committed to provide the African Union with US$60 million of free military assistance to operationalise the African Peace and Security Architecture. Mutual visits, training and sharing of technologies were detailed, as well as proposed intelligence exchanges and experiences to prevent and fight terrorism, ocean piracy and combat illegal trafficking of goods. It also committed to supporting the United Nations in playing a constructive role in regional conflicts in Africa |
| Consular, immigration, judiciary and law enforcement | Africa and China agreed to fight illegal immigration, transnational crimes, human trafficking, corruption and illegal trade in fauna and flora, to strengthen narcotics control, fugitive extradition and asset recovery, cyber security and law enforcement capacity-building |
| International cooperation | "To strengthen international coordination and to establish a new model of global development that is based on equality, accountability, mutual respect and that is more balanced, stable, inclusive and harmonious" |

FOCAC (2015)

ised by the highly infectious nature of the disease, which resulted in 815 local health workers being infected (Liu et al. 2017: 262). International assistance was desperately needed to support health services and mitigate the spread of the virus.

While American, European and Japanese countries were withdrawing aid workers in light of the outbreak in 2014, China announced it was sending 115 infectious disease experts to the region. The dispatch of the Chinese government of 480 People's Liberation Army medical staff to Liberia in November 2014 was a welcome intervention—the first time China had deployed a whole unit to combat an epidemic. The team established the 100-bed China Ebola Treatment Unit to treat suspected and infected Ebola patients. In addition, the unit provided public health and infection training to local healthcare providers. During the first two months, 112 Ebola-suspected patients presented at the unit, 65 were admitted, including 5 confirmed cases. The training was significant, with 1520 locals trained, which included healthcare workers, military care workers, staff at the unit itself and community members (Liu et al. 2017; Taylor 2015).

**Table 8.3** Selected FOCAC news releases in 2017 detailing interventions aimed at improving the well-being of Africans

| Country | Details |
|---|---|
| Africa | China has adopted a strategy of eradicating Malaria in Africa<br>China supports wildlife conservation in Africa through a commitment towards supporting African countries in responding effectively to wildlife crimes |
| Botswana | Chinese medical team contributes to Botswana's health sector |
| Central African Republic | China commits to support the United Nations to ensure adequate resources are made available for peacekeeping forces in the country |
| Ethiopia | Completion of clean water cellar project that saw the building of 41 water cellars in the Oromia region, benefitting 4000 people<br>Chinese embassy donates to child centre in Addis Ababa |
| Ghana | Donation of office accessories to the Office of the Attorney General in Ghana to build anti-corruption capacity and improve governance in Ghana |
| Kenya | China gives the World Food Programme US$5 million towards supporting the 420,000 refugees living in Kenyan camps<br>Chinese charity organisation donates to victims of fire in a Kenyan slum<br>Kenyan doctor to promote Chinese medicine in Kenya |
| Liberia | 140 Chinese peacekeeping police offices deployed to Liberia for a yearlong mission |
| Mali | Recognition of China's involvement in the United Nations' peacekeeping mission in Mali that was helping maintain national peace and stability while supporting the fight against terrorism |
| Morocco | 30 volunteers from a Chinese medical delegation in Morocco complete their two-year mission, with three new Chinese medical teams arriving in the country |
| Namibia | China donates rice to drought-affected communities said to benefit 600,000 Namibians<br>China to work with Namibia to combat poaching |
| Rwanda | 18th Medical group arrives from China in Rwanda. China credited for constructing the Masaka Hospital and constructing dormitories for medical employees at the Kibungo Hospital |
| Somalia | China provides 2800 tonnes food aid to drought-hit Somalia. US$1 million given to the United Nations Migration agency to support internally displaced persons and vulnerable communities in Somalia |
| South Africa | China pledges to deepen cooperation with South African women on women's affairs |

(*continued*)

## Table 8.3 (continued)

| Country | Details |
|---|---|
| South Sudan | China donates half a million boxes of anti-malarial medicine to fight the disease in South Sudan<br>A 15-member team of Chinese doctors donates assorted food items, school material and sports equipment to 48 children in an orphanage<br>China provides US$5 million to the World Food Programme to better respond to famine<br>China donates a batch of medicines and medical equipment to a children's hospital in Juba |
| Sudan | China's helicopter unit joins the peacekeeping mission in Darfur<br>The colloquially named Sudan–China Friendship hospital provides health services for thousands of poor patients in the area |
| Uganda | China donates 5900 tonnes of rice to Uganda as the country experienced food insecurity due to a prolonged dry season |
| Zambia | Chinese-funded handover of 420 boreholes to rural communities to improve their access to clean water<br>US$58 million made available to expand bed space at the Mwanawasa General Hospital to support better public health services in the country.<br>Medical teams donate telemedicine equipment<br>Zambia honours 18th medical team supporting healthcare services since the 1970s |
| Zimbabwe | 200 scholarships offered to students from the Harare Metropolitan Province by the Zhejiang Province in China<br>The Chinese Embassy in Zimbabwe donates US$1 million in funding and US$60,000 specifically for the provision of basic foods to assist local communities affected by floods in the southern part of the country<br>12,000 tonnes of rice donated to Zimbabwe to help alleviate food shortages |

FOCAC (2017)

Since the initial dispatch of healthcare workers, China has continued to offer support in Liberia and the entire region. In January 2015, a further 154 medical workers were sent to Liberia to support efforts in the fight against the disease. China had also provided US$121 million in cash and supplies to deal with the disease (Aljazeera 2015). Lin Songtian, the director general of China's Department of African Affairs, committed China to continued intervention until Ebola was effectively eradicated from West Africa (Taylor 2015).

China was able to apply its homegrown experience in combating infectious diseases to the Ebola crisis—China has had to combat the spread of Severe Acute Respiratory Syndrome (SARS) and Avian flu. Due to the

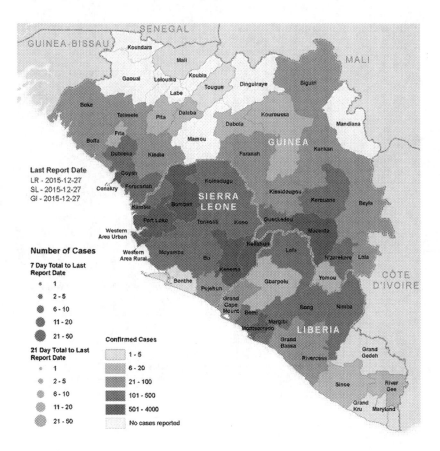

Map 8.2 Geographical distribution of new and total confirmed cases of Ebola: 30 December 2015. (World Health Organisation 2015)

meticulous infection controls adopted in Liberia, none of the Chinese, nor any of the staff at the China Ebola Treatment Unit, were infected during China's intervention in Liberia.

From a long-term perspective, China could contribute to the long-term eradication of the disease and prevent future outbreaks. A number of international efforts are in the pipeline to develop better diagnostic tools, services and vaccines, with China at the forefront in trying to find solutions to the disease. Chinese military scientists have developed a vaccine against the Ebola virus, and plans are in the pipeline to mass-produce the vaccine.

In addition to humanitarian interests, it is important to note that China did have economic and internal political reasons for responding to the crisis. China had significant economic investments in the region, and was a key trading and investment partner in the region: China's total trade with Sierra Leone was US$1.1 billion in 2013, accounting for 47% of Sierra Leone's total trade, making China its top trading partner; China's trade with Liberia totalled US$2.1 billion in 2013, accounting for 18% of the country's total trade; while in Guinea, US$823 million worth of trade with China accounted for 12.4% of its total trade, making it Guinea's second biggest trade partner (Taylor 2015). At the time of the outbreak Chinese firms were engaged in US$15 billion worth of investments in West Africa. China had also been an important influence on Liberia's peace-building efforts.

Thousands of Chinese workers had also been imported to work in the region. Some of China's initial response was to evacuate Chinese workers from Ebola-affected countries. One example provided by Taylor (2015) is the evacuation of workers contracted to build a road between Liberia and Guinea—this largest infrastructure project in Liberia ground to a halt. While figures are difficult to come by, it is estimated that half of the Chinese living in Ebola-affected countries left in 2014 (Taylor 2015: 49).

While China had a vested economic and reputational interest in containing the epidemic, it would appear that China's efforts went a lot further than protecting their own interests. China played a concerted and important role in controlling the outbreak, contributed to the reduction of fatalities, improved the long-term response capacity of West African countries and, possibly, will contribute to the eradication of the disease in its entirety.

## 8.4 Case Study: Caring for Displaced Somalians

In March 2013, an estimated 9 million refugees and internally displaced persons originated from East Africa and the Horn of Africa, with the region recording the largest increase in refugees globally in 2012 (International Organization for Migration (IOM) 2017). Armed conflict, acute poverty, drought and the absence of gainful employment are the major contributors to the problem, with people fleeing the DRC, Somalia and South Sudan and entering the 'safe havens' of Kenya, Ethiopia, Rwanda and elsewhere, contributing to the burden of these countries also in the flux of their own economic challenges (Map 8.3). Kenya, for instance, is estimated to host 600,000 refugees, most of which are from Somalia.

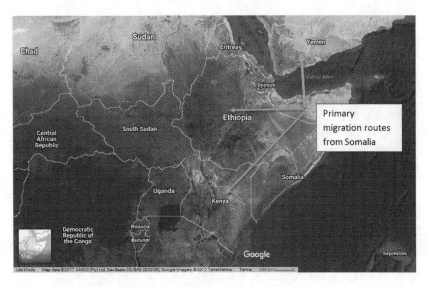

**Map 8.3** Somalia on the Horn of Africa. (Google 2017)

Within Somalia itself, the IOM estimated that, in 2015, 1 133,000 persons were internally displaced due to conflict and violence, as well as severe food shortages (International Organization for Migration 2017). The al-Shabaab has been waging a military insurgency in the country, often adopting terrorist tactics in their efforts, some of which are the worst that Africa has seen—in July 2015, 15 people were killed in a suicide attack at a hotel in Somalia, damaging the neighbouring Chinese Embassy and injuring some Chinese nationals, while over 300 people were killed in a truck bombing in Mogadishu in October 2017.

Trying to escape the horrors in Somalia, and often in search of greener pastures elsewhere, many Somalians have tried to leave the country, often with tragic results. One escape route is to cross the Gulf of Aden to Yemen and find their way to the Persian Gulf where the promise of work in the oil-rich nations beckons. The route is extremely dangerous. Smugglers are known to treat refugees terribly, sometimes even robbing them and, in the not-so-uncommon outcome, throwing them off the boats. Those who do reach the shores of Yemen alive are often sick from the stresses of the trip. Yemen itself has been crippled by years of war, and those Somalians who do make it to the shore face terrible hardship, and their chances of reaching Saudi Arabia are slim.

China's contribution to improving the lives of displaced Somalians has been multipronged: Diplomatic; food provision; support of refugee camps in neighbouring countries; support of efforts to repatriate Somalians living in other countries; improving homeland security; and support in the provision of housing and healthcare. China's Ministry of Foreign Affairs (2017) details some of the significant interventions China has made in Somalia and towards the migrant crisis facing the country (Table 8.4).

## 8.5 Case Study: A Critique of the Impact of Chinese Mining Operations on Social Wealth and Capital in Africa

There have been varied approaches by Chinese mining companies entering the African resource market, including the 'Angola-mode' framework agreements that saw the 'swap' of resources for infrastructure, financed mostly through the Chinese Exim bank, and which resulted in Chinese mining interests in Africa ballooning.

On the positive side, resource extraction can have beneficial externalities on the social upliftment of often remote communities where these resources are found. To enable mining operations, transport infrastructure has to be provided for by the mining companies to get the minerals to the closest port for export. Communities would benefit from these new roads and railway networks. The mines would provide a source for employment, and because mines often needs to provide some level of primary healthcare and education for both local and migrant employees, these services would often be made available to the wider community. Electricity, information and communication technology, water provision and sewerage are all prerequisites for mines to operate, again opening up the opportunity for local communities to benefit.

There are also obvious negative externalities. The peaceful nature of these rural communities will be forever changed by the mines and the influx of migrant workers and access to modern life extravagances. There have been numerous examples, not specifically from Chinese mining operations, but from a range of companies that have begun mining in rural areas where the impact on local communities has been extremely damaging: These negative effects range from loss of land and financial independence to social community impacts and damage of infrastructure and the environment.

**Table 8.4** Chinese humanitarian support of Somalia

| Chinese intervention | Details |
| --- | --- |
| Diplomatic interventions | China has been diplomatically working with authorities in Somalia, regional powers and the African Union in order to find a long-term solution to the woes of the country. China has also engaged the United Nations to increase the international communities' commitment to addressing peace and stability in Somalia. In 2016, China donated a range of equipment and supplies to the African Union for the specific purpose of capacitating the African Union Mission in Somalia |
| Support of the United Nations International Organization for Migration | China donated US$1 million towards the United Nations International Organization for Migration to support its efforts to help internally displaced people, vulnerable communities and Somalians returning to their country |
| Support of internally displaced people | China has contributed to support those who have been displaced due to famine and war. The migration of people to the capital of Mogadishu included many orphaned children, who had often no support, in a city characterised by warlords fighting over control. Orphanages, mostly established by concerned local citizens, were poorly equipped. China has made some direct donations of furniture, school desks, blankets and school equipment to help these orphanages provide a greater level of care |
| Support of refugees | China has supported both the care for Somalian refugees in refugee camps and of their repatriation. In 2015, China donated 5800 tents to Kenya to support the efforts of voluntary repatriation of Somalis living in Kenya's refugee camps |
| Famine and drought relief | The famine due to drought and the displacement of people due to conflict has been critical for some time. China has contributed financially to the World Food Programme and directly through food donations. For instance, in June 2017, China dispatched two shiploads of rice to Somalia as part of its US$300 million emergency food programme. The donation was expected to contribute to the feeding of 223,500 Somalis for a four-month period |
| Security in the Gulf of Aden | Pirate attacks on vessels off the coast of Somalia, including Chinese vessels, became quite commonplace, affecting the important trade route through the Gulf of Aden and the Suez Canal. China's military facilities in neighbouring Djibouti support efforts to deter criminal activity in these coastal waters |
| Healthcare | Also through China's support of the African Union Mission in Somalia, the Mission was able to provide medical support for Somalians in their local communities |

Source: China's Ministry of Foreign Affairs

Chinese companies have sometimes met criticism for their lack of community engagement when establishing mining operations in Africa. One prime example was the Jiuxing Mine in Soamahamanina, Madagascar. The mining company had negotiated their 40-year mining permit for gold extraction with the Madagascan government, and while there were some basic Corporate Social Investment (CSI) conditions attached to the permit, there was almost no engagement with the community. The mining company bought land voluntarily from many of the local community members, and set up operations.

Before the mine was able to begin operations in 2016, the community erupted in protest. Jiuxing Mine was accused of wanting to destroy the local church and school, eliminating the livelihoods of the local people, taking away their ancestral land and homes and damaging the environment. There were also accusations levelled at the mine and the government for corruption. Protest leaders were arrested, but protest action continued, until eventually, Jiuxing Mine was closed down. By mid-2017, mining operations had not recommenced, even though the mine management had suggested it would enter into further negotiations with the Madagascan government.

The DRC is a treasure trove of minerals and Chinese mining operations are quite extensive in the country. However, there have also been accusations levelled by Amnesty International and others at Chinese mining operations for human rights abuses in the south-eastern region (Katanga Province) of the DRC (Map 8.4). Take, for instance, the Congo International Mining Corporation (CIMCO), which forcibly evicted 300 families from the town of Luisha. Given a two-week notice period, the families were trucked to new sites and dropped off—with no housing or facilities. In the same region, COMILU, a Congolese–Chinese joint venture mining company, excavated a 3 metre wide trench that blocked access for the local communities to water and their fields. Protests were met by force, with police firing live ammunition, killing one protester (Amnesty International 2013).

Artisanal mining in the DRC is a common practice, with these miners often working with their bare hands in extremely hazardous conditions. They receive very little for the minerals that they sell, in a corrupt system of systematic exploitation. At the Tilwezembe Mine near Kolwesi, Amnesty International (2013) documented harmful labour conditions and ill-treatment, including fatalities from preventable landslides and falling boulders, and insufficient ventilation.

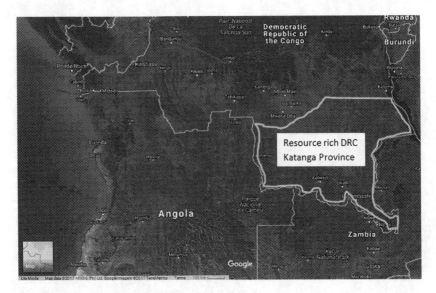

Map 8.4   Katanga in the Democratic Republic of the Congo

However, Chinese companies, just as their Western counterparts have been doing, have increasingly committed themselves to good corporate citizenship principles. Chinese mining companies have also been influenced by a greater prioritisation and legislation by the Chinese government on environmental issues in the mining community, as well as being more proactive in corporate social responsibility due to China's Social Harmony Policy. Sustainability reporting by mining companies is a key component to making the industry more transparent and accountable for their activities.

CSI activities are especially important in mining communities due to the finite nature of these non-renewable minerals and resources. Many mining companies globally focus their CSI attention on diversifying the local communities' economy in order to be sustainable after the mine inevitably closes.

It remains to be seen whether Chinese extractive industries in Africa adopt a more proactive role in community engagement and corporate social responsibility that truly makes a long-term, sustainable impact on communities in which they operate.

## 8.6 China's Impact

China, through its substantial humanitarian efforts, and by the very nature of its role in infrastructure and economic investment efforts, can and does contribute to improving the well-being of Africans throughout the continent. While Chinese mining interests have been tarnished by poor working conditions and lack of community engagement, efforts by the Chinese government and the necessity of community engagement to enable operations, may engender more sustainable mining operations in the future.

China's impact on the African Tree of Organic Growth from the perspective of well-being is detailed in Fig. 8.2.

In terms of the African Tree of Organic Growth, China is seen as having a positive impact on human development and social capital. The activities described in this chapter highlight that China is actively engaged in addressing urgent crises on the continent, such as drought, food security and famine; containing the outbreak of disease such as the Ebola epidemic; and through diplomatic and peacekeeping efforts, trying to find long-lasting solutions to conflict areas in Africa. Its investment in infrastructure directly assists African governments in providing better services to their people, including electricity, water, sewerage and other basic services provision. The wide range of efforts to engage culturally facilitates a better understanding and respect for the rich cultures of Africa and China.

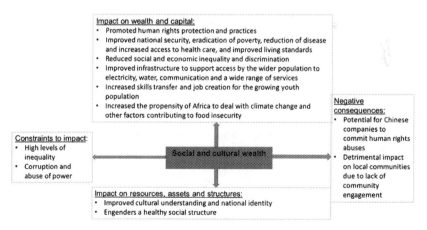

**Fig. 8.2** China's contribution to the well-being and cultural wealth in Africa

However, there has been evidence of human rights abuses by some Chinese companies operating in Africa, especially in the extractive industries, and an apparent lack of community engagement and a long-term sustainable approach to these communities. China seems to have committed itself to increased corporate social responsibility, which in the long term will hopefully reduce these negative impacts Chinese investments may have in Africa.

## References

African Gender Equality Index. 2015. Empowering African Women: An Agenda for Action. African Development Bank. [Online]. Accessed from: https://www.afdb.org/fileadmin/uploads/afdb/Documents/Publications/African_Gender_Equality_Index_2015-EN.pdf (accessed: 9 May 2017).

Aljazeera. 13 January 2015. China Sending Large Ebola Team to West Africa. Accessed from: http://www.aljazeera.com/news/africa/2015/01/china-ebola-west-africa-201511391645512136.html (accessed: 18 June 2017).

Amnesty International. 2013. Chinese Mining Industry Contributed to Abuses in Democratic Republic of the Congo. Accessed from: https://www.amnesty.org/en/latest/news/2013/06/chinese-mining-industry-contributes-abuses-democratic-republic-congo/ (accessed: 4 September 2017).

FOCAC. 25 December 2015. The Forum on China-Africa Cooperation Johannesburg Action Plan. [Online]. Accessed from: http://www.focac.org/eng/ltda/dwjbzjjhys_1/hywj/t1327961.htm (accessed: 19 June 2017).

FOCAC. 2017. The Forum on China-Africa Cooperation's Latest News Items. [Online]. Accessed from: http://www.focac.org/eng/ (accessed: 19 June 2017).

Helliwell, J., Layard, R. and Sachs, J. 2015. World Happiness Report 2015, New York: Sustainable Development Solutions Network. Accessed from: http://worldhappiness.report/wp-content/uploads/sites/2/2015/04/WHR15_Sep15.pdf (accessed: 21 August 2017).

Helliwell, J., Layard, R. and Sachs, J. 2017. World Happiness Report 2017, New York: Sustainable Development Solutions Network. Accessed from: http://worldhappiness.report/wp-content/uploads/sites/2/2017/03/HR17.pdf (accessed: 21 August 2017).

Human Development Report 2016: Human Development for Everyone. 2016. United Nations Development Programme. [Online]. Accessed from: http://hdr.undp.org/sites/default/files/2016_human_development_report.pdf (accessed: 9 May 2017). Creative Commons Attribution 3.0 IGO.

International Organization for Migration. 2017. East Africa and the Horn of Africa. Accessed from: https://www.iom.int/east-africa-and-horn-africa (accessed: 1 September 2017).

Liu, L., Yin, H. and Liu, D. 2017. 'Zero Health Worker Infection; Experiences from the China Ebola Treatment Unit During the Ebola Epidemic in Liberia', *Disaster Medicine and Public Health Preparedness*, 11 (2): 262–266.

Ministry of Foreign Affairs of the People's Republic of China. 2017. Somalian Press Releases. Accessed from: http://www.fmprc.gov.cn/wjb/eng_search.jsp (accessed: 3 September 2017).

Taylor, I. 2015. 'China's Response to the Ebola Virus Disease in West Africa', *The Round Table*, 104 (1): 41–54.

World Health Organisation. 30 December 2015. Geographical Distribution of New and Total Confirmed Cases in Guinea, Liberia and Sierra Leone. [Online]. Accessed from: http://apps.who.int/ebola/sites/default/files/thumbnails/image/sitrep_casecount_31.png?ua=1 (accessed: 19 June 2017).

World Health Organisation. 10 June 2016. Situation Report: Ebola Virus Disease. [Online]. Accessed from: http://apps.who.int/iris/bitstream/10665/208883/1/ebolasitrep_10Jun2016_eng.pdf?ua=1 (accessed: 19 June 2017).

Zhao, J., Dong, S., Li, J. and Ji, J. 2015. 'The Ebola Epidemic Is Ongoing in West Africa and Responses from China Are Positive', *Military Medical Research*, 2 (1): 1–6.

CHAPTER 9

# Integrated Organic Growth: The Cases of Cameroon and Mauritius

The baobab tree is a useful analogy for Africa's growth, development and well-being of its people—this time the tree analogy is utilised to develop an integrated framework of organic growth that can be applied to all African countries. The African Tree of Organic Growth paradigm used in this book further incorporates the 'African Renaissance' philosophy, a philosophy that suggests that African nations and their people shall overcome the current challenges confronting them on the continent by following a route of cultural, scientific and economic renewal. This renewal process implies that growth will be organic in nature, driven from within the countries themselves and by Africa's own people. The African Tree of Organic Growth that was developed for this book is depicted in Fig. 9.1.

This chapter will first analyse and evaluate the success of the internal growth processes in delivering a better life to the citizens of the countries studied, and second, the role that China plays and the impact it has in supporting or deterring the success of this process. The two African countries that were selected for this analysis are Cameroon and the island of Mauritius.

Zafar (2007) argues that China will have the greatest growth impact on resource-rich and oil-exporting countries in Africa, such as Cameroon, while smaller, resource-poor countries like Mauritius, will be detrimentally affected by the relationship due to a number of factors, including direct export competition with China in the textile and clothing sector.

African countries became responsible for their own growth and development after independence from their colonial past. China, on the other

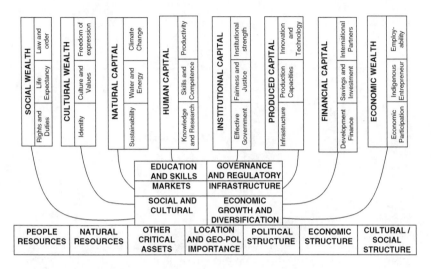

Fig. 9.1 The African Tree of Organic Growth

hand, has had the biggest influence on the growth of African countries after the 1st Forum on China–Africa Cooperation (FOCAC) Ministerial Conference in 2000. The analysis of the growth of Cameroon and Mauritius, and the impact that China has had in this regard, will therefore be focused on these respective periods of time.

## 9.1 The Case of Cameroon

Cameroon is situated in Central-West Africa and, as Map 9.1 illustrates, shares its borders with Nigeria, Chad, Central African Republic, Equatorial Guinea and Gabon. It has a population of 23.3 million people and the two regions of the country that border Nigeria are Anglophone, while the rest of the country is Francophone (World Bank 2016). Cameroon is a complex country that is home to more than 200 different ethnic groups—sometimes referred to as 'Africa in miniature' due to its myriad of cultural and geographic diversities. Cameroon has an abundance of natural resources, including oil and gas, minerals and an array of agricultural products such as coffee, cotton, cocoa, maize and cassava. It also has forests of exotic timber, and is the last country in the world where ebony can still legally be purchased to produce musical instruments.

Though Yaoundé is the country's official capital, Douala is the only port and the economic powerhouse of the country due to it facilitating

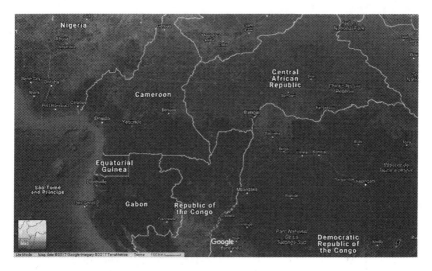

Map 9.1  Cameroon and neighbouring countries. (Google Maps)

trade with the world. This river-port is one of the most difficult to access in West Africa due to the low flow depth of the river.

Cameroon was first a German and then a French colony, before attaining independence in 1960. The country has officially been a democracy since 1990, when parliament endorsed freedom of association and allowed for the establishment of political parties. President Paul Biya has ruled since 1982 and his party, the Cameroon People's Democratic Movement (CPDM), has dominated the country's political landscape for the last two decades. Although the political situation in the country is relatively stable and peaceful, there is an indication that this may change in the near future with the increasingly worrying security risk situation developing in its northern regions on the border with Nigeria, where Boko Haram is currently waging a low-intensity war.

Cameroon is classified by the Mc Kinsey study (2010) as a 'Transitional Economy', an economy that is in the transitional phase from dependence on commodities such as oil and agriculture to becoming a more diversified economy. Agricultural, oil and mining resources still account for a large proportion of the GDP and exports of Cameroon. Agricultural production has increased to the point where the country is now self-sufficient in food production. Over two-thirds of the working population are employed in the agricultural sector, which contributes about 25% of value-added production to the economy. In comparison to other oil-producing countries, the economy is relatively diversified.

### 9.1.1 Historical Overview of Cameroon's and China's Relationship

China views Cameroon as an attractive African country to do business with and has, over a lengthy period, invested a substantial amount of political and financial capital into the country. The diplomatic relationship between the two countries was established in the early 1970s, but as with many other Sino–African partnerships, the Sino–Cameroonian one gained momentum in the late 1990s, and was quite intensive by the early 2000s (Cabestan 2015).

The relationship between China and Cameroon is summarised in the Table 9.1.

The close partnership with China could not have been possible without a strong political will on the Cameroonian side. Cameroon played a very

Table 9.1 Overview of historical relations between China and Cameroon

| Period | Years and leadership | Relationship detail |
|---|---|---|
| 1. | 1971–1982 President Ahidjo 1982–1999 President Biya | Diplomatic corporation between Cameroon and China: March 1971: Establishment of diplomatic relations 1973: Ahidjo visited China and became the first African president to visit China Several visible infrastructure projects were launched after a second visit to China: <br> • Construction of a new Presidential Palace (completed in 1977) <br> • National Congress Hall (Palais des Congress) in Yaoundé (inaugurated in 1985) <br> • The financing of a large hydroelectric project (Lagdo Dam) with a US$75 million loan completed in 1982 <br> The first trade agreement was signed in 1973 followed by a second in 1984 <br> A Cultural Cooperation Accord was concluded in 1984 <br> A Medical Assistance programme was launched and included building of two hospitals equipped with Chinese medical teams (1975 and 1976); and the development of a close relationship with China in the fight against Malaria <br> China's Premier Li Peng visited Cameroon in 1997 and signed a politically significant agreement for the reciprocal protection and promotion of Investments |

(continued)

Table 9.1 (continued)

| Period | Years and leadership | Relationship detail |
|---|---|---|
| 2. | 2000–2016 President Biya | After the first FOCAC Ministerial Conference was held in Beijing in 2000, the cooperation between Cameroon and China was deepened and became diversified: <br> In 2002 Premier Zhu Rongji visited Cameroon and signed an ambitious agreement to stimulate economic and commercial cooperation <br> In 2006, Cameroon was granted Approved Destination Status for Chinese tourism <br> Eight agreements worth US$129 million covering official development assistance, investment and loans (EXIM Bank) were signed during President Hu Jintao's visit in 2007 including the following: <br> • Technical and economic cooperation <br> • Construction of a gynaecological, obstetric and paediatric hospital in Douala <br> • Construction of two primary schools <br> • Agreement to secure China's participation in the oil sector <br> In 2010, China's Political People's Consultative Conference Chairman Jia Qinglin led a parliamentary delegation that resulted in the signature of eight additional agreements including a US$ 6.4 billion grant and interest-free loan of the same amount <br> In 2011 two other Chinese vice-premiers visited Cameroon: Hui Liangyu, in charge of agriculture and Liu Yandong responsible for education <br> In 2011–2016 China was involved in 70% of Cameroon's infrastructure projects and 90% of the road construction and restoration projects, which include the following: <br> • Water projects in Douala (2014) <br> • Kribi Deepwater Port (2014) <br> • The construction of 1500 low-income houses in Yaoundé (2014) <br> • The Lom Pangar Dam north of Bertoua (2016) <br> • The Mekin hydro-electrical power plant (2016) <br> • The Mevle'ele Dam in the South |

Compiled from Cabestan's (2015) discourse and other public information

active role in the FOCAC Ministerial Conferences, using the Forum as a platform for promoting Cameroon's role in Sino–African relations. President Biya has been a frequent visitor to China having travelled five times to the country since 1982 (Cabestan 2015) and has acknowledged China's role in improving the socio-economic conditions in Cameroon.

### 9.1.2 The Impact of China on the Integrated Growth and Development of Cameroon

The success of Cameroon's internal growth process will now be evaluated using the African Tree of Organic Growth framework developed in this book. The negative and positive influences of China on this organic growth process will also be considered.

#### The 'Root System' of Cameroon

The root system at the bottom of the organic tree provides nourishment, sustenance and stability for the tree. These are the core resources, assets and structures that the country will have in place at any point in time and will form the foundation of the country's integrated growth. The root system will therefore, like the balance sheet of a business, give a true reflection of the assets and liabilities of a country at any point in time.

An evaluation of the root system forming the base of the organic growth in Cameroon is given in Table 9.2.

#### People Resources, Natural Resources and Country Assets

The wealth of a country will, to a great extent, be determined by the effective development and growth of its people and the optimal utilisation of its resources. Cameroon is a low–middle-income country with a population of 23.3 million people and is home to more than 200 ethnic groups. The division of Cameroon into British- and French-ruled League of Nations mandates after the First World War, created the anglophone and francophone regions. The English-speaking regions consist of south-west and north-west provinces, where English is taught at school. The educational system and legal practices derive from those of England. The French-speaking region consists of the remaining eight provinces. Education is based on the French school system, while the legal system is based on the statutory law of continental Europe (Butler 2015). Tension between these two regions increased after the introduction of a multiparty political system in the 1990s. Cameroon is endowed with significant natural resources, including oil and gas, high-value timber species, minerals and agricultural products such as coffee, cotton, cocoa, maize and cassava (World Bank 2016). The economy of the country is heavily regulated and dependent on exports of commodities such as oil, timber and agricultural products.*

**Table 9.2** The 'Root System' of the African Tree of Organic Growth in Cameroon

| 'Root System' | Country evaluation: Cameroon |
| --- | --- |
| People resources | Cameroon has a population of 23.3 million people, divided as follows: Two regions are anglophone (English-speaking) while the other eight regions are mostly francophone (French-speaking) Cameroon is home to more than 200 different ethnic groups |
| Natural resources | Abundance of natural resources, including oil and gas, high-value timber species, minerals and agricultural products such as coffee, cotton, cocoa, maize and cassava |
| Other critical country assets and liabilities | Lack of infrastructure in roads and rail transport, harbours, schools, hospitals and dams<br>Good hydropower potential<br>Ineffective health and education system |
| Location and geopolitical importance | Wedged between Nigeria, Chad, the Central African Republic, Gabon, the Republic of the Congo and Equatorial Guinea<br>Cameroon has one major port of Douala which serves as the country's economic powerhouse due to its access to world markets<br>Cameroon is politically important as it is considered the natural leader of the Central African Economic and Monetary Community (CEMAC) |
| Political structure | The country is politically stable with a multiparty political system since 1992. Executive power is held by the president, who serves for seven years |
| Economic and business structure | 'Transitional economy': Growth primarily based on oil, timber and agriculture, although more diversified than other oil exporters<br>Exchange rate pegged to the Euro<br>Debt reduction as part of Heavily Indebted Poor Countries (HIPC) initiative<br>Inefficient parastatal companies in key industries |
| Cultural and social structure | Distinct cultural, religious and political traditions as well as broad ethnic variety<br>French and English are the official languages<br>There is a high degree of social inequality |

## Location and Geopolitical Importance

The location and geopolitical importance of a country will directly influence its ability to grow and attract foreign direct investment (FDI). Cameroon possesses 600 km of coastline but only one major port at Douala. Cameroon is politically important for the region as it is considered the natural leader of CEMAC of which it is a member. Cameroon is not only the major regional trading partner in this region, but its population represents almost 50% of CEMAC and accounts for almost 40% of the GDP of the group (African Development Bank 2009).

**Political Structure**
Many scholars who examined the causes or roots of poverty and poor growth in Africa have identified political opportunism, political violence and corruption as some of the main contributors to this negative scenario.

Cameroon has officially been a democracy since 1990, when parliament endorsed freedom of association and the creation of political parties with free and fair elections (African Economic Outlook 2013). The current ruling party of President Paul Biya dominates the political landscape and he has been in office since 1982. An April 2008 revision of the constitution now limits the presidential term to a maximum of two terms, a result of which will be that President Biya, who was re-elected in 2011, will now end his term in 2018 (African Development Bank 2009).

**Economic, Business and Social Structures**
Since devaluating the currency in January 1994, Cameroon's economy has rebounded to an annual growth rate averaging 5–6% during the last decade. Cameroon has an exchange rate pegged to the euro and a monetary policy controlled by the Bank of Central African States (BEAC), leaving fiscal policy as the government's main economic instrument (African Development Bank 2009). Although oil is still playing a dominant role in the economy, the government's ambitious infrastructure interventions to boost the agriculture and forestry sectors have also contributed to the strong economic growth cycle over the past few years.

The current strengths and weaknesses of the Cameroonian economy were described in an economic study by Coface (2017), and are depicted in Table 9.3.

Political stability and the longevity of President Paul Biya's rule have facilitated the growing involvement of China in Cameroon's development strategy and international positioning. In late 2013, seven years after having benefited from the HIPC initiative, Cameroon's external debt was sustainable at around 18% of its GDP. China also cancelled part of Cameroon's bilateral debt on several occasions. However, the International Monetary Fund (IMF) estimates that Cameroon's debt will increase to 34% of GDP in 2018, although this debt level is still seen as sustainable because many of the projects financed by China, such as the Kribi deepwater port, should

**Table 9.3** Current strengths and weaknesses of the Cameroonian economy

| Strengths | Weaknesses |
|---|---|
| Agricultural, oil and mining resources | External and public accounts still dependent on oil revenues |
| Diversified economy compared with that of other exporters | Rapid rise in debt due to ambitious public investment programme |
| Ongoing infrastructure modernisation | Lack of inclusive growth and problematic business climate |
| Debt reduction in 2006 as part of the HIPC initiative | Increased political risk: insecurity with Boko Haram threat in the north of the country and increasing tension between anglophone minority and francophone regime |

Coface Economic Study and Country Risk Analyses (2017)

increase development and improve tax revenue for the government (Cabestan 2015).

Cameroon has distinct cultural, religious and political traditions as well as a broad ethnic variety that influences the behaviour and attitudes of its people. There is a high degree of social inequality based on indigenous stratification, level of education and access to political power.

*The Creation of Growth Channels to Produce Wealth and Capital (Trunk of the Tree)*

A tree's roots absorb water and nutrients from the soil, store sugar and anchor the tree upright in the ground. Applying the tree analogy to the natural growth of a country means that the trunk of the tree will provide the growth channels for the creation of wealth upwards, as well as the distribution of capital (sugar) downwards, thus stimulating a new cycle of growth for the tree. An evaluation of the growth channels of Cameroon is given in Table 9.4.

### Governance and Regulatory

The Cameroonian government started with an extensive privatisation programme in 1995, first with the sugar, rubber and palm oil industries, followed by the railway and electricity-generating companies. In 1999 a new wave of privatisation targeted the major public services of telecommunications, water and port infrastructure. The restructuring of the banking sector followed, resulting in significant improvements in the sector (African Economic Outlook 2013).

**Table 9.4** The 'Trunk' of the African Tree of Organic Growth in Cameroon

| 'Trunk element' | Country evaluation | China's impact |
|---|---|---|
| Governance and regulatory | Evolution of government policies and legislation, especially since 1995, to enhance the enabling environment for growth<br>Privatisation of state institutions, industries and banks<br>Structural reforms in forestry boosted the sector's contribution to the economy<br>High levels of corruption are still considered the biggest stumbling block for growth from a government perspective | China has a policy of non-interference<br>China provided debt relief to Cameroon |
| Infrastructure | Cameroon engaged in major infrastructure projects to address massive backlogs in the country<br>Infrastructure development boosted transport effectiveness, production and export capacity | Chinese companies involved in the majority of infrastructure projects including about 90% of road building and rehabilitation |
| Economic growth and diversification | Cameroon achieved a remarkable 5% average economic growth in the last decade<br>Economy is still commodity-driven and dependent on export of oil, timber and agricultural products<br>Although more diversified than other oil exporters, diversification into manufacturing unsuccessful because of corruption and an unfriendly business environment | Chinese investment in industries in Cameroon has a comparative advantage such as timber production, rubber and telecommunications |
| Education and skills | Relatively high percentage of primary school enrolments<br>Better education indicators than the rest of sub-Saharan Africa<br>Disparity between rich and poor, boys and girls, rural and urban areas, and between regions, still reasons for concern | Building of schools<br>Establishment of the Confucius Institute for cultural and language training<br>Employed local workers in primarily unskilled labour positions |

(*continued*)

Table 9.4 (continued)

| 'Trunk element' | Country evaluation | China's impact |
|---|---|---|
| Markets | Primary sector dominates trade, with oil (40% of GDP) and agriculture (20% of GDP) the main export categories | China is one of Cameroon's top trading partners |
| Social and cultural investment | Cameroon is susceptible to disease, such as malaria, due to which thousands of Cameroonians die each year, many of whom are children under the age of five<br>Cameroon has a shortage of hospitals and doctors<br>Stringent labour policies to ensure employment of locals in Chinese projects | China contributed with malaria medicine, expatriate doctors and a malarial research centre |

Significant structural reforms have taken place in forestry. These have been aimed at increasing the sector's contribution to the country's economic and social development, while safeguarding stocks by reducing felling. In order to facilitate the shift away from pure exploitation, a law was introduced in 1994 banning unprocessed log exports, resulting in 70% of timber now being processed locally (African Economic Outlook 2013). This was followed by a ban on the export of some endangered hardwoods.

Weak governance and high levels of corruption continue to hamper the inclusive growth and development of Cameroon, which still has one of the highest corruption levels in the world. Private businesses still face numerous impediments, mostly related to regulatory inefficiency, corruption and non-transparency.

**Infrastructure**

Infrastructure development became a top priority of the Cameroon government—an area where Chinese companies have added much value over many years. Their spectacular ability to bid for, and win, large construction contracts has been well reported, with most of these projects having been financed by the Chinese Exim Bank. The interest rate is usually around 2%, and while the grace period can vary, it is normally about five years in duration. Chinese companies have also been able to secure funding from the

African Development Bank and the World Bank, especially for road projects (Cabestan 2015). The Cameroonian government, from their side, introduced more stringent labour regulations and compulsory company-based work agreements for foreign companies, including Chinese companies (Cabestan 2015). As a safeguard, the Cameroonian government has also appointed external companies to oversee Chinese infrastructure projects, for instance for the Yaoundé–Nsimalen highway, the project is being supervised by a Tunisian–Portuguese–French consortium (Cabestan 2015). It is likely that China will continue to dominate the infrastructure and construction sectors in Cameroon in the near future.

**Economic Growth, Diversification and Trade**
Cameroon's economy has averaged an annual growth rate of between 5% and 6% in the last decade. Although the economy is still primarily dependent on the export of commodities, it has become relatively diversified compared to other oil producers. This diversification is dominated by public sector spending. In the secondary sector, public investment and consumption resulted in robust growth of the construction and manufacturing industries since 2000. The economy grew by a brisk 5.7% in 2015, led mainly by the secondary sector (Coface 2017). The service sector has also grown during this time and become a driving force in the economy. The increase in household incomes has boosted commerce, the hospitality and entertainment sectors, transportation and facilitated the privatisation of mobile networks (African Development Bank 2009). The economy is still constrained by inefficient parastatal companies in key industries. Electricity provision also remains a problem, although this has improved with increased electricity generation capacity (African Economic Outlook 2013). The Agriculture Competitiveness Project that was launched in 2010 to boost the country's agricultural productivity, develop infrastructure and broaden value chains for rice and maize cultivation has achieved remarkable improvements in production and crop yields between 2010 and 2016 (World Bank 2016).

Cameroon is not an attractive industrial investment destination because of rampant corruption. Since the late 1990s, President Biya has tried to convince Chinese companies to invest more in Cameroon, especially in diversified industries such as manufacturing, but has not been very successful in his efforts. China, for example, had a plan to assemble motorcars in Cameroon, but abandoned it in 2013 because of delays in reaching an agreement with the government (Cabestan 2015). Although China bought a significant amount of Cameroonian oil in the mid-2000s, it only became a major actor in the oil industry in 2011 with two large investments in the sector. In the mining industry, the only noticeable investment has been made by Sinosteelcam for exploring iron in the Lobe concession, close to Kribi in the south region (Cabestan 2015). China is also seen as a potential shareholder of the Mbalam–Nabela iron ore project—located on the border of the DRC and 510 km from the sea, this mine will only become operational once the railway and mining terminal in Kribi are completed in 2017.

In the timber industry, the biggest investment by China was made in 1997 when Vicwood acquired the French group Thanry, becoming the largest timber company in Cameroon, controlling 10–12% of the total area of concession (570,000 ha). The Chinese government has approved a total of eight investments in the Cameroonian agricultural sector, including three farming, three cash crops and two livestock companies (Bräutigam and Zhang 2013). One of the larger investments was when Chinese state-owned enterprise Sinochems purchased 51% of a Singaporean Rubber company, GMG Global, in 2008—this company had long-term leases on rubber plantations in Cameroon. Most Chinese FDI remains in small-scale private ventures such as restaurants, shops and small farms (Cabestan 2015).

Since the late 2000s, China has become one of Cameroon's top trading partners. In 2012 China represented 18.9% of Cameroon's imports (US$1186 million) and 15.2% of its exports (US$819 million) or 17.2% of its trade. This is ahead of Nigeria (7.4%) and nearly half of the European Union's exchanges (39.9%) (Cabestan 2015). China mainly imports oil from Cameroon (62%), while exporting electrical appliances, textiles, footwear, vehicles, mechanical and electrical products, and cement to Cameroon.

**Education and Skills**
According to the World Bank (2012) Cameroon has made significant progress in education but still has a long road to go, especially in terms of primary education completion, gender disparity in enrolment, retention of pupils in schools and regional disparities of access to schooling—although there has been an increase in the enrolment rate at primary level and an increase in the literacy rate between 2001 and 2007. At the same time, less than half of the school-age population completed primary school in 2009, resulting in a large proportion of youth leaving school without mastering

skills such as literacy and numeracy. According to the World Bank report (2012) the significant differences in education outcomes amongst regions and the overall poor performance of the education system in Cameroon can partly be attributed to the inefficient management of the education system and the lack of accountability in resource allocation.

Since the 1970s, China has contributed towards education by building schools and offering scholarships. From 2000, China became even more visible as an education donor, including the opening of Cameroon's Confucius Institute in 2007, two years after the inauguration of the first Confucius Institute on the African continent in Nairobi, Kenya. The creation of the Yaoundé Confucius Institute has stimulated Cameroonians' interest in the Chinese language, and in 2013, 6500 Cameroonians were learning Chinese, up from 2500 just two years earlier (Cabestan 2015). The French government is still providing most of the support for tertiary education, and Japan remains the biggest builder of schools in Cameroon. In 2013, there were 6000 Cameroonian students studying both in France and Germany, 1500 in the United States and just over 100 in China.

**Social and Cultural Investment**
Cameroon has better health indicators than the rest of sub-Saharan Africa, with an infant mortality of 79 per 1000, and a life expectancy of 50 years (African Economic Outlook 2013). Diseases, especially malaria, are one of the biggest causes of death in Cameroon—thousands die each year of the disease, most of whom are under the age of five. Cameroon has a massive shortage of hospitals and doctors, and the health sector has been identified as one of the most fruitful areas of cooperation between China and Cameroon. China has constructed several hospitals and made a valuable contribution in medicine provision, especially efficient and cheap anti-malarial medicine and the introduction of traditional Chinese medicine. China also donated a malaria research centre housed at one of the hospitals in Cameroon. China has trained Cameroonian doctors and brought in expatriate doctors from China to assist with healthcare. In 2011, it was estimated that there were 10–30 Chinese doctors per hospital in Cameroon (Cabestan 2015).

*Creating Prosperity and Wealth for the People of Cameroon (Leaves and Fruit)*
The citizens of a country will constantly seek to find balance in their lives in a complex, organic country environment that is contradictory and complex. Working towards a paradigm of organic growth means that

communities must enjoy the fruits of this process, benefit from the wealth generated, and see an improvement in their lives year after year. A country must first produce wealth products that will better their lives, and second, produce capital, the 'sugar' that can be reinvested in the country. We categorise wealth as social wealth, cultural wealth and economic wealth. Capital, on the other hand, can be divided into tangible and intangible capital: tangible capital is the natural and produced capital, while intangible capital refers to human and institutional capital. An evaluation of the effect of the internal growth on the wealth and capital of Cameroon is given in Table 9.5.

**Table 9.5** The 'Leaves and Fruit' of the African Tree of Organic Growth

| 'Leaves and fruit' | Country evaluation | China's impact |
|---|---|---|
| Social wealth | High levels of poverty | Employment tensions on Chinese projects |
|  | The country is self-sufficient in food |  |
|  | Unemployment, especially amongst the youth, still very high |  |
| Cultural wealth | Cameroon has distinct regional cultural, religious and political traditions as well as ethnic variety | Confucius centre promoting internationalism, teaching the Chinese language and culture |
|  | A sentiment of common national identity is strong in major institutions of socialisation, such as schools and universities |  |
| Natural capital | Negative impacts of deforestation on natural capital | Foreign investors such as China sometimes, unsustainably, log their concessions without much concern over prosecution by corrupt forestry officials |
|  | Oil production is well managed and has had a minimum impact on the environment |  |
| Human capital | Human capital development not successful because of a theoretical educational focus and skills mismatch | Confucius centre and technical training eased transfer of knowledge and skills from Chinese companies to Cameroonians |
|  | Limited youth participation |  |
|  | Social discrimination and corruption |  |
| Institutional capital | Weak governance and poor resource management | Chinese assistance on a military level |
|  | Increased security risk due to the Boko Haram threat |  |
|  | Rising tensions with the anglophone minority |  |

*(continued)*

**Table 9.5** (continued)

| 'Leaves and fruit' | Country evaluation | China's impact |
|---|---|---|
| Produced capital | Cameroon still faces high cost factors of production particularly in energy supply, poor densification of the road network and inefficient port services The increase in infrastructure contributed hugely to produced capital in the country—the latest construction of three dams and the Kribi deepwater port will boost energy availability and export capacity | Contribution of China to infrastructure, production and trade capacity |
| Financial capital | The relationship with China provided financial capital for development The country recently received a Standard and Poor's B-credit rating | Loans and financial aid from China are making a direct contribution to financial capital |
| Economic wealth | Lack of inclusive growth and a difficult climate for business and entrepreneurs The primary sector continues to play an important role and generates significant earnings from oil and agriculture | China contributes indirectly to economic wealth of the country |

**Social and Cultural Wealth**

Although the country's poverty index is above the African average, poverty is still ravaging the country, holding it back from its potential. About 40% of the population is living below the poverty line, and because population growth outpaces the reduction in poverty, the number of poor increased between 2007 and 2014 to 8.1 million people. Poverty is increasingly concentrated in Cameroon's northern regions with an estimated 56% of the poor living in the North (World Bank 2016). Cameroon fortunately has sufficient agricultural production capacity to feed its people (World Bank 2016).

Cameroon has distinct regional cultural, religious and political traditions as well as ethnic variety. A sentiment of common national identity is strong in major institutions of socialisation, such as schools and universities, and during international soccer matches. Despite this common national identity, a high degree of social inequality is prevalent. Rising tensions between Cameroonian workers and Chinese companies have led to conflict including strikes at road projects over working conditions and pay.

## Natural Capital

Cameroon has extremely diverse ecosystems and the country is a signatory to several environmental conventions including the Convention on Biological Diversity (African Development Bank 2009). These ecosystems or natural capital of the country are negatively impacted by aggressive and unsustainable logging, which is damaging the delicate rainforests. Besides logging, deforestation is also a result of fuel-wood collection and subsistence farming. Cameroon has lost, according to estimates, about 13% of its forest cover between the years 1990 and 2005 (Butler 2015). Deforestation is beginning to have a significant environmental impact on parts of the country and has been blamed for increasing soil erosion, desertification and reduced quality of pastureland. Conserving Cameroon's forests should be a top priority given their high level of biodiversity, including 600 tree species of which 50 are critically endangered (Butler 2015). Although petroleum is a key export product for Cameroon, the production and transport, mostly by pipeline, is well managed and has had a limited impact on the country's environment (Butler 2015).

## Human Capital

Addressing the challenge of youth unemployment as a precondition to poverty reduction is recognised as a priority by the government, as thousands of young Cameroonians have few opportunities once they complete school—the unemployment rate in Cameroon was estimated at 30% in 2013 (Ekuh 2014). Ekuh identified the following factors negatively impacting employment in Cameroon:

- The educational system in Cameroon focuses mainly on theory and abstract concepts with little or no training in technology and entrepreneurship.
- Skills mismatch and inadequate job matching.
- Little or no entrepreneurship and business training.
- Limited youth participation.
- Social discrimination and corruption.

## Institutional Capital

President Paul Biya has ruled since 1982 and was re-elected in 2011 for his last seven-year term which will end in 2018. Although the long rule of President Paul Biya has brought some political stability in the country, corruption and poor resource management are major causes of poverty

(African Economic Outlook 2013). Cameroon ranks 130th out of 168 countries in the 2015 Transparency International Corruption Perception Index and ranks 172nd out of 189 economies in the 2016 Doing Business Report (World Bank 2016). According to the World Bank Report (2016), weak governance continues to hamper Cameroon's development. In a Master's research study that was conducted in 2012 on the consequences of corruption on economic development in Cameroon, respondents indicated that out of five factors listed, corruption had the biggest impact on poverty and underdevelopment, while the lowest impact was from political stability (Fombe 2012). Private enterprises also still face numerous impediments related to regulatory inefficiency and non-transparency, which restrict business development.

The main challenge facing the future Cameroonian government is the deterioration of its security situation since 2013, with incursions by the Nigerian Islamic terrorist group Boko Haram in the far north of the country (Coface 2017). Security and political stability are also threatened on a second front—in 2016 the anglophone minority in the north-west and south-west of the country started protesting to express their dissatisfaction with perceived political and economic marginalisation of their communities, to the benefit of the francophone majority (Coface 2017).

Despite the reports of corruption in Cameroon, the government in the 2000s embarked on many initiatives that had a positive impact on the economic growth of the country. Examples include the following:

- Embarking on a series of economic reform programmes supported by the World Bank and the IMF
- Initiation of a massive privatisation drive including the privatisation of electricity generation, water supply and the banking system
- Addressing the massive infrastructure backlog with the help of China
- Supporting the diversification drive of major industries such as the timber industry with supporting legislation and policies

**Produced Capital, Financial Capital and Economic Wealth**
Cameroon's economy, although relatively diversified with services accounting for around 40% of GDP, is still dominated by the public sector, and therefore lacks private sector development and capital. The increase in infrastructure investment described previously contributed significantly to the produced capital in the country, especially with the numerous projects made possible through the cooperation with China. The latest construction

of three dams and the Kribi deepwater port will boost energy availability and export capacity. Diversification into manufacturing is slow, a result of Cameroon's struggle to promote technical capacities, efficiencies and knowledge. In addition, transaction costs are still high due to factors like transport costs, unreliable infrastructure facilities like harbours and problems with electricity supply.

Political stability and the longevity of President Paul Biya's rule have facilitated the growing contribution of China to Cameroon's development capital and economic wealth. In spite of the fact that China's debt reliefs were much smaller than the relief offered by Western donors, they contributed significantly to the release of much needed financial capital for Cameroon. Further good news for Cameroon is that in 2017 one of the main credit agencies, Standard & Poor, affirmed their B-rating for the country (Coface 2017). In addition to judging the outlook to be stable, the agency emphasised promising economic indicators despite increases in government deficits. Amongst the positive points Standard & Poor highlighted was the increase in agricultural production and the positive influence of public infrastructure projects, especially investments for improving the road network and the construction of the deepwater port in Kribi.

The Cameroon government for the first time also embarked upon the formulation of a long-term Vision for Cameroon (African Development Bank 2009). The vision which projects a desired image of the country up to 2035 is portrayed in Table 9.6.

Cameroon's growth performance has strengthened in recent years but has relied largely on public investment. This public investment was mostly aimed at bettering the infrastructure for the country, in order to increase the productive and institutional capacity and capital of Cameroon. This economic growth, however, did not translate into broad social and economic wealth mostly due to spatial and social inequities, and an unfavourable business environment. Yet Cameroon has strong potential to develop and build on its vast potential, including its people and natural resources, to enable them to achieve optimum organic growth, which will include poverty reduction and improve the well-being of the populace.

## 9.2 THE CASE OF MAURITIUS

Located off the south-east coast of Africa, neighbouring the French Island of La Réunion, Mauritius is an island state of 1.3 million people spanning 1965 square kilometres (Maps 9.2 and 9.3). The people of Mauritius are

**Table 9.6** Cameroon's Vision 2035

The Vision aspires to make Cameroon "a democratic emerging country, united in its diversity". The Vision identified the following medium-term objectives:
- Reducing poverty to a socially acceptable level
- Reaching middle-income country status
- Becoming a newly industrialised country
- Consolidating the democratic process and strengthening national unity

African Development Bank (2009)

**Map 9.2** Mauritius. (Google Maps)

descendants of European (mostly French) settlers, the Franco-Mauritians; African slaves and creoles, the Afro-Mauritians; Chinese traders, the Sino-Mauritians; and Indian labourers, the Indo-Mauritians. The cultural diversity and geographic isolation of Mauritius have led to a national sense of pride despite the fact that they do not have a common culture, language or historical background (Matusky 2001).

The island of Mauritius was apparently uninhabited until 1638. It was then that the Dutch, under the name of the Dutch East India Company, made their first attempt to colonise the land, named after the prince of

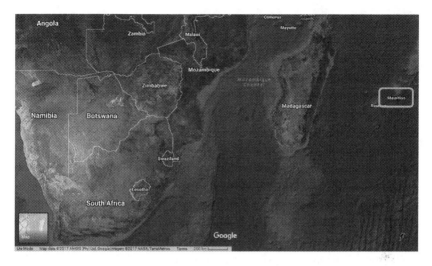

Map 9.3 Geographic location of Mauritius in the Indian Ocean off the African coast. (Google Maps)

Denmark, Maurice of Nassau. They brought small numbers of African slaves for labour and introduced sugarcane to the island. Trouble maintaining the settlements led to the Dutch abandoning the island in 1710, after which the French claimed it for France. The French already had the nearby island of Réunion and considered Mauritius of strategic importance, especially for providing a base for attacks on British possessions in wartime. Under French rule Mauritius developed colonial plantation patterns (Matusky 2001).

The British attacked and captured the island in 1810. In 1825 the preferential West Indian sugar tariff was repealed, and the island transformed itself into a sugar-based economy. With the abolition of slavery in 1835, the plantation slaves fled the plantations to live in shantytowns on unoccupied land. To make up for the loss of the workforce, plantation owners imported labourers from India, resulting in an increase of the Indian population on the island.

Mauritius initiated self-governance in the 1950s, which eventually led to the country's full independence from Great Britain on 12 March 1968. Sir Ramgoolam was the leader of this movement, and subsequently became the prime minister. He served in this post from 1968 to 1982.

In 1962 and 1972, Nobel Prize winners Meade and Naipaul, respectively, predicted a bleak future for Mauritius (Darga 2011). In 1972, Naipaul famously labelled Mauritius "The Overcrowded Bar Racoon", saying its "problems defy solution". He suggested that Mauritius was overpopulated with starving people, idled by unemployment and plagued by despair. The economist James Meade concluded that the outlook for peaceful development in Mauritius was limited as 'population pressure' would inevitably reduce real income and increase poverty. He predicted that this scenario would probably lead either to unemployment (exacerbating the scramble for jobs between the Indians and Creoles) or to even greater inequalities (especially between the Indian and Creole 'underdogs' and the Franco-Mauritian 'top dogs' who owned and controlled most of the sugar industry) (Darga 2011).

Defying the predictions of these two respected scholars, the small island nation has transformed itself from a poor sugar economy into a country with one of the highest per capita incomes amongst African countries. Mauritius managed to combine political stability, a strong institutional framework, low levels of corruption and favourable regulatory environment, to lay the foundation for their sustainable growth and development. Real GDP growth has averaged more than 5% since 1970 and real annual growth per capita has increased more than tenfold between 1970 and 2010, from less than US$500 per capita to more than US$6000 (Zafar 2011). At the same time, efforts to diversify the economy have been successful, allowing the country to move from sugar to textiles to a broader service economy. The country has also begun to position itself as a platform for investment linking East Africa with India and China. The well-being of Mauritians has also improved substantially. Despite being a small island economy vulnerable to exogenous shocks, they have been able to craft a strong development path of successful organic growth that has benefitted most of the population.

### 9.2.1 The Historical Relationship Between Mauritius and China

The Mauritius–China relationship goes back as far as 1972 when diplomatic relations between the two countries were established. The Mauritian government has supported the 'One China Policy' in defiance of most of the international community. The presence of a local Chinese community, while small in size but economically significant, has also helped maintain cultural ties with China (Ancharaz 2009). Cooperation between the two countries has spanned the cultural, scientific, technical and economic domains, and is presented in Table 9.7.

It is evident from the overview in Table 9.7 that cooperation between Mauritius and China has been particularly active in the cultural domain. Such cooperation was started by the signing of an agreement for cultural cooperation in 1980, followed by the setting up of a Chinese Cultural Center in Bell Village in 1988. In 1996, the two countries signed an investment and protection agreement. Cooperation has received added momentum since the first FOCAC Ministerial Conference in 2000 with an increase in the number and scope of agreements and investment (Ancharaz 2009).

### 9.2.2 *The Impact of China on the Integrated Growth and Development of Mauritius*

The significant success of Mauritius as it embraced an internal growth process will be evaluated against the African Tree of Organic Growth paradigm proposed in this book, while reflecting on the influence China has had on this organic growth process.

*The 'Root System' of Mauritius*

An evaluation of the root system forming the base of the African Tree of Organic Growth in Mauritius is presented in Table 9.8.

**People Resources, Natural Resources and Other Assets**

Mauritius is a small island economy with a small population that was constrained at inception by limited natural resources, a mono-crop sugar economy and low amounts of arable land. With high population growth, high levels of poverty and a small domestic market, the country's leadership realised that development for them will be a matter of survival against all odds (Darga 2011).

Mauritius started off with three important country assets, namely an established sugar industry, beautiful natural beaches and warm weather, and friendly people who were willing to stand together and make a difference.

**Location and Geopolitical Importance**

Mauritius Island has long been seen as a small and insignificant island in the Indian Ocean, somewhat difficult to access and not quite a significant player in regional politics and the world economy. Mauritius has, however, succeeded in the last three decades to position itself as an important tourism

**Table 9.7** Historical overview of the relationship between China and Mauritius

| Period | Years and leadership | Relationship detail |
|---|---|---|
| 1. | 1972–1982<br>Prime Minister: Sir Seewoosagur Ramgoolam<br>1982–1999<br>Prime Minister: Sir Aneerood Jugnauth | Diplomatic cooperation between Mauritius and China:<br>1972: Establishment of diplomatic relations<br>1972: Agreement on economic and technical cooperation<br>1980: Agreement for cultural cooperation<br>1986: Agreement on training for the personnel of the Ministry of Health<br>1987: Construction of a stadium at Belle Vue Mauricia<br>1988: Setting up of a Chinese Cultural Center funded by China in Bell Village<br>1989: Agreement on agricultural technical cooperation<br>1992: Agreement on education<br>1993: Construction contract for Beau Vallon Housing Project<br>1994: Agreement on the development of the Chinese language<br>1996: Investment promotion and protection agreements<br>1998: Executive Programme on the Cultural Agreement<br>China further provided loan assistance and FDI for the following projects:<br>1972: Construction of the Terminal Building at Plaisance Airport and technical assistance for agricultural projects<br>1985: Construction of the Sport Complex Anjalay; construction of two bridges; and construction of a police workshop<br>1990: Upgrading of Flacq Hospital<br>1991: Beu-Vallon Housing Project<br>1993: Atlee Housing Project<br>1997: Joint-venture projects; ship for Mauritius Shipping Corporation |

(*continued*)

**Table 9.7** (continued)

| Period | Years and leadership | Relationship detail |
|---|---|---|
| 2. | **2000–2016**<br>**Prime Minister: Sir Aneerood Jugnauth** | Diplomatic cooperation between Mauritius and China:<br>2004: Agreement on technical education cooperation<br>2005: Establishment of a political consultation mechanism; agreement on economic and technical cooperation; and an agreement on bilateral labour service cooperation<br>2006: Memorandum of understanding on air services<br>2007: The year represented a turning point in cooperation with the tripling of Chinese aid over the following three years, most of which were for infrastructural projects. The Mauritian Prime Minister led a 30-man delegation to China to discuss bilateral cooperation. The delegation finalised an accord with the Tian Li Group for setting up an economic cooperation zone in Mauritius with investments totalling US$500 million. Establishment of Friendship City Relationship between Grand Port Savanne District Council and City of Qingdao. Agreement of cooperation between the Mauritius Chamber of Commerce and Industry and the China Council for the Promotion of International Trade. Agreement for scientific and educational cooperation on oceanology. Total trade between the countries grew by 35% in 2007<br>2009: President Hu Jintao visited Mauritius to mark the first visit of a Chinese President to Mauritius, announcing measures to boost people-to-people exchanges<br>2013: Signed a visa waiver agreement between the two countries. Signed an agreement to strengthen trade ties and the quality of exchanges between the two countries<br>2014: Agreement between the Mauritius Promotion Agency and China Southern Airlines on Tourism<br>2016: 10th Sino–Mauritius Joint Economic Commission held in Beijing. Signing of memorandum of understanding on free trade. Technical expertise in bio-farming. Signing of an agreement for a Confucius Institute at the University of Mauritius |

(continued)

**Table 9.7** (continued)

| Period | Years and leadership | Relationship detail |
|---|---|---|
| | | China further provided loan assistance and FDI for the following projects:<br>2000: New market at Quatre Bornes<br>2001: Loan for a construction project<br>2002: Economic assistance loan; loan for low-cost housing; provision of X-ray scanning machines and equipment for the airport<br>2003: Economic assistance loan; sewerage project<br>2004: Major FDI project aimed at producing 18,000 tonnes of yarn per year for the clothing and textile industry<br>2005: Human resources training in textiles<br>2006: Human resources development<br>2007: Construction of the new Mauritian Broadcasting Corporation headquarters; investment agreement with Tianli Group for setting up an economic and trade zone in Mauritius for manufacturing diversification to the value of US$500 million over five years<br>2008: Mauritius' Police Force signed an agreement with the Chinese Institute of Research to install 300 surveillance cameras in the busy tourism areas of the island<br>2009: Chinese President Hu Jintao visits Mauritius, agreeing on new deals worth more than US$270 million including two agricultural schools and scholarships for Mauritian students to study in China<br>2013: China's investment in Mauritius: US$190 million in hospital construction<br>2015: Signing of agreement for JinFei Economic Trade and Cooperation Zone Ltd, which included the development of Smart City Riche-Terre; interest-free loan and grant of US$14 million for development projects<br>2016: 10th Sino–Mauritius Economic Commission in Beijing with the following outcomes: China wrote off Mauritius' debts to the amount of US$13 million; financing of a multipurpose sport complex of Olympic standard in the form of grants and interest-free loan; donation of a fleet of 30 semi-floor buses; setting up of a fishing port; and a desalination of seawater project |

Adapted from Ancharaz (2009)

**Table 9.8** The 'Root System' of the African Tree of Organic Growth in Mauritius

| 'Root system' | Country evaluation: Mauritius |
|---|---|
| People resources | Small diverse population forming a very small domestic market |
| Natural resources | Few natural resources including agricultural land and beautiful beaches |
| Other critical assets | An established sugar industry, popular beaches and a small but growing population were the only assets at independence |
| | Developed important public, tourism, manufacturing and export infrastructure after independence |
| Location and geopolitical importance | A tiny speck in the ocean, far away from developed markets and politically not important |
| Political structure | A multiparty parliamentary democracy |
| | Good governance and political stability |
| Economic structure | Good macroeconomic structure |
| | Diversified economy |
| | Attractive investment and business environment |
| Cultural and social structure | Multi-ethnic society |
| | Diverse cultures |

destination, and an important manufacturing and export hub, especially in clothing and financial services. Mauritius also enjoys a strategic location between Asia and Africa and has begun marketing itself as an excellent launch point for Asian business into the African market (Raine 2009).

**Political Structure**

The country's political situation has been stable since its independence from Great Britain in 1968. The political structure is that of a multiparty parliamentary democracy. The president is the head of state and the prime minister has full executive powers and heads the government. The search for consensus is one of the remarkable features of the Mauritian political economy, similar to that of the British system based on the principle of separation of power between the legislature, the executive and the judiciary (Zafar 2011).

Gulhati and Nallari (1990) argued that since no single political party has ever succeeded in securing a majority in the assembly, there has always been a need to work together across party lines. Sir Anerood Jugnauth, who recently announced his retirement at the end of this term, has filled the position of prime minister since his first appointment in 1982, spanning multiple non-consecutive terms and shifting coalitions. Despite being based on loose agglomerations of ethnic and economic interests, political parties in Mauritius have not been vehicles for ethnic separation. To the contrary, political parties have recognised that building consensus is necessary to avoid adverse growth and development effects in such a small and sensitive economy (Zafar 2011).

## Economic and Business Structure

A hallmark of economic management in Mauritius in recent decades has been prudent fiscal policy, which has helped to maintain macroeconomic stability while contributing to growth. Fiscal policy in Mauritius has focused on ensuring that spending remains linked to the resource availability (Zafar 2011). In tandem with fiscal policy, monetary policy in Mauritius has helped anchor economic growth and ensured competitiveness. Since its creation in 1967, the Bank of Mauritius has been concerned with ensuring the competitiveness of the country's export sectors, and second, with price stability (Zafar 2011).

Mauritius has transformed itself from a poor sugar-dependent economy into one of the most successful economies in Africa, largely through economic diversification and reliance on trade-led development. According to Zafar (2011) the following key factors were central in helping Mauritius achieve its remarkable economic success:

- Good macroeconomic policies
- Strong public sector and private sector institutions
- Strong pro-trade orientation and liberal trade regime
- Use of its ethnic diversity and strength to forge a consensus between the different groups

Mauritius is now essentially a service-orientated economy with a well-developed manufacturing sector. Although Mauritian-manufactured exports are still dominated by textiles and apparel, they are more diversified than those of the typical sub-Saharan African economy (Ancharaz 2009). Mauritius creatively used export processing zones (EPZs) to advance the export of key manufactured goods such as apparel and textiles.

Aggressive economic diversification resulted in a profound change in the sectorial composition of the Mauritian economy. Between 1976 and 2010, the share of primary sector production declined from 23% to 6%, while the secondary sector, including manufacturing, electricity, water and some construction, increased from 23% to 28%. The tertiary sector, which includes tourism and financial services, grew from just over 50% to nearly 70% of GDP (Zafar 2011).

Alongside trade policies and a healthy economic structure, another reason for Mauritius' economic success has been its business climate, and the incentives it has introduced to encourage foreign companies to locate there. Mauritius is a country with good infrastructure, a literate and bilingual labour force and a business-friendly environment. Mauritius is currently amongst the top-performing developing countries in starting a business, paying taxes and protecting investors. Mauritius has no capital controls, a relatively stable currency, a low flat corporate tax rate of 15% and a large number of double taxation avoidance agreements, making the country very attractive for financial sector investment (Zafar 2011).

**Cultural and Social Structure**
Mauritius is a multi-ethnic society comprising people of Indian (Hindu and Muslim), African, French, Chinese and mixed descent. English is the official language, but French and Creole remain the dominant languages, despite 150 years of British rule. No single ethnic group has a majority in Mauritius. People from Indian ancestry are the biggest group but are divided based on faith and along caste lines. The second largest group are the Creoles who comprise about a third of the population, followed by the Franco-Mauritians and the Sino-Mauritians, from Chinese descent, who comprise only 3% of the population (Matusky 2001).

Official Mauritian policy depicts Mauritian culture as a mosaic of Hindu, Muslim, European, African and Chinese influences, and it is highly unpopular to encourage the dissolution of cultural boundaries. Mauritians of different cultural backgrounds remain very distinct and most Mauritians of Indian ancestry have Indian first names and are able to communicate in Bhojpuri and write in Hindi. The small Chinese community, on its part, publishes two daily newspapers in Mandarin and frequently visits Hong Kong, while the Franco-Mauritians retain 'old-world' French in their language and lifestyle (Eriksen 2000).

In some areas of Mauritian social life, the forces working towards national integration are the strongest. This is surely the case in sports and in the growth sectors of the economy such as manufacturing and tourism. In other fields, cultural differences are acknowledged and respected (Eriksen 2000).

*The 'Trunk of the Tree' Growth Channels to Produce Wealth and Capital*
An evaluation of the growth channels of Mauritius is provided in Table 9.9.

**Governance and Regulatory**
Although the growth and development success of Mauritius has been a subject of considerable debate, the role of a supportive governance and

**Table 9.9** The 'Trunk' of the African Tree of Organic Growth in Mauritius

| 'Trunk element' | Country evaluation: Mauritius | China's impact |
|---|---|---|
| Governance and regulatory | Pragmatic approach to inclusive development<br>Strong support for export-led strategies<br>Strong and ethical government and institutional support for growth | Good diplomatic arrangements resulting in various supporting agreements |
| Infrastructure | Active investment in public, information and communication, and production infrastructure<br>Information communication infrastructure compares to the best in the world<br>Backlog on road and energy infrastructure impacts negatively on growth | Tripling in aid from China in 2007: most for public sector infrastructure projects<br>China to take part in road infrastructure upgrades |
| Economic growth and diversification | Successful export-driven economic growth<br>Successful vertical integration of the textile industry<br>Successful economic diversification from a monocrop economy to a service economy | Chinese investment in clothing manufacturing and spinning<br>Chinese investment in the economic zones<br>China to invest in diversification towards high-end products and 'smart cities' |
| Education and skills | Good and free education system serving the majority of the population<br>Skills mismatch in new productive sectors | Several agreements on educational cooperation<br>Chinese scholarships offered to Mauritian students<br>Greater aid and technical assistance in the area of human resource development<br>Imported Chinese labour and skills controversial in Mauritius |
| Markets and trading | International trade success based on preferential trade deals from the United States and the European Union<br>Repositioning of clothing industry as reliable supplier of quality clothing | Growing bilateral trade deficit with China as imports from China increase<br>Import substitution of yarn and textiles from China with China investing in spinning mill<br>Chinese cost advantage in clothing impacts international export markets |

(*continued*)

**Table 9.9** (continued)

| 'Trunk element' | Country evaluation: Mauritius | China's impact |
|---|---|---|
| Cultural and social investment | Accommodation of all ethnic groups utilising diversity as a strength rather than a weakness<br>Strong social support from government<br>Effective investment in education and health | Agreement for cultural cooperation signed in 1980 |

**Table 9.10** Pragmatic political approach to development taken by the Mauritian government

All political leaders take a pragmatic approach to development, first deciding on the objectives then determining the means to achieve the objectives
Objectives include the following:
- Ensure employment for all
- Broaden and sustain welfare state
- Ensure sustainable and inclusive national economic growth and wealth
- Ensure more equitable distribution of wealth

Summarised from Darga (2011)

policy framework were central in bringing about the Mauritius miracle: good macroeconomic policies, particularly fiscal prudence; a competitive exchange rate policy; strong public and private sector institutions; and a strong pro-trade and liberal trade regime have all provided an environment favourable for growth (Zafar 2011). Mauritius is not the only African country to have inherited a democratic political system, but is one of the rare ones to have maintained, developed and domesticated it to serve its development imperatives. According to Darga (2011), the creation of this favourable environment for growth can mainly be attributed to the Mauritian government's pragmatic political approach to development depicted in Table 9.10.

The Mauritian government did everything in its power to enhance and support the export-led growth strategy of the country, especially in the 1990s. This included the development of export zones, tariff-free access for productive inputs, tax incentive subsidies and relaxed labour market relations for the export sector. Mauritius' overall trade and investment policy has been based on enhancing competitive advantage and the cultivation of access to profitable markets (Zafar 2011).

The Mauritian government's response to the end of apparel quotas and the decline of the US market has been critical to the survival of the textile and clothing industry. Government and key stakeholders gathered to reflect on the challenges facing the industry and formulated and implemented a restructuring strategy to address competitiveness factors of the industry (Ancharaz 2009). In the 2006/07 budget, the government also proposed several measures to encourage vertical integration of the textile sector, which include aspects such as tax credits on equity investment in spinning and weaving, to an empowerment fund to support entrepreneurship and the employment of women (Ancharaz 2009).

Political decision-making is mostly based on the outcome of consultative processes and negotiations between the state and various formal and informal stakeholders, such as the private sector, trade unions, civil society, ethnic lobbies and interest groups of the entrepreneurial class (Darga 2011).

**Infrastructure**

There were, based on various media reports, more than 40 official Chinese development finance projects launched between 2000 and 2012 in Mauritius. These projects included projects such as low-cost housing, sewerage projects, an airport terminal building, a television broadcast building, schools and investment in information technology infrastructure. The latest and biggest envisaged project is the Tianli/Jinfei development zone of US$750 million, which includes industrial, business and residential development and construction. Most of the construction and infrastructure projects in Mauritius have been on a turnkey basis, and have primarily used Chinese materials and labour inputs (Ancharaz 2009).

Although very little evidence could be found in the literature on China's involvement in transport infrastructure, there seems to be an increased focus since 2009 on the development of road infrastructure. A Governmental Infrastructure Programme to the value of US$10 billion, which included public, transport, energy and communication infrastructure, was announced in 2012 (African Development Bank 2014). The programme that will run from 2013 to 2018 will partly be financed by the Mauritian government with a 38% contribution, while the rest will come from public and private enterprises, as well as foreign borrowing from The World Bank, India and China (African Development Bank 2014). The project includes the construction and upgrading of roads as well as the development of a Light Rail Mass Transit System. This became a priority after various reports showed that the congestion of the roads in Mauritius has become a handicap for further economic growth and investment.

Mauritian information communication infrastructure is the best on the African continent and ranked 55th out of 144 countries on the 2013 Global Information and Communications Technology (ICT) Network Readiness Index (African Development Bank 2014). ICT is also an important part of the Mauritian vision to become a high-income country in the future. Water and energy infrastructure is not sufficient, and are both priority areas for investment and development in the near future. About 83% of the electricity is still generated from imported fuel, while water security and infrastructure are also affected by frequent droughts and a high proportion of unaccounted water loss due to insufficient and aeging pipe infrastructure (African Development Bank 2014).

**Economic Growth and Diversification**

Mauritius went through a remarkable economic transformation since independence with economic growth rates at 5% between 1970 and 2000 and 4% between 2001 and 2015. Mauritius has transformed itself from a poor sugar-based economy into one of the most successful economies in Africa, largely through economic diversification and trade-led development.

The economic diversification trajectory of Mauritius is summarised in Table 9.11.

In the 1970s, the sugar sector in Mauritius accounted for close to one-third of employment, one-third of export earnings and one-quarter of GDP. Mauritius succeeded in obtaining preferential treatment from the European Economic Community (EEC) through the Sugar Protocol, under which it received more or less free access for its sugar exports to the EEC. The collapse in international sugar prices in the mid-1970s impacted Mauritius' sugar industry severely, leading to balance of payment difficulties. This was followed by an end to the preferential deals in 2005 (Zafar 2011).

Having studied the success of EPZs in East Asia, a group of visionary policymakers in Mauritius put forth the idea that the country's small economic size and distance from large developed markets presented an opportunity to develop an export-orientated textile and clothing industry. By the 1980s, EPZs had exceeded expectations and accounted for more than 60% of Mauritius' gross export earnings, and employed one-third of

**Table 9.11** The economic diversification trajectory of Mauritius

| Timeline | Diversification phase | Sector focus |
| --- | --- | --- |
| 1970–1975 | Mono-crop economy | Sugar |
| 1975–1990 | First phase of diversification | Sugar<br>Textiles (vertical integration)<br>Tourism |
| 1990–2005 | Development of 'Four-Pillar' economy | Sugar<br>Textile<br>Tourism<br>Financial services |
| 2005–2011 | Growth in services | Financial services<br>Real estate development<br>Business services<br>ICT services<br>Tourism and hospitality |
| 2011–2018 | Development of a 'knowledge economy'<br>Ocean economy<br>Higher-end products<br>'Smart cities' | Sustainable business centres, combining real estate and business activities in 'smart cities'<br>Financial and IT hub<br>Knowledge hubs<br>Ocean economy<br>Fashion products<br>Film producing<br>Bioenergy from sugarcane<br>Light manufacturing<br>Pharmaceuticals |

Authors' summary

the Mauritian labour force (Zafar 2011). A wave of FDI from Hong Kong–based companies into the clothing industry during this time period helped Mauritius to create thousands of jobs, and generate a high rate of export-led growth over a long period. Local investors also benefitted by themselves investing in this sector.

In the 1990–2005 time period, the sugar and textile industries had to deal with serious market and trade challenges, such as the phasing out of the Multi Fibre Arrangement (MFA) with the United States, and the reduction of sugar prices by more than 50% in the European Union in 2004 and 2005. As these two sectors struggled, the government's emphasis shifted to the expansion and growth of the tourism sector.

Mauritius is an attractive tourism destination because of its paradise-like beaches, luxurious hotels, rich culture, entertainment and warm weather. The public sector's master plan to expand tourism has been aggressively supported by private businesses including hotels, restaurants and Air Mauritius, resulting in a doubling of visitors from 400,000 in 2000 to more than 800,000 in 2005 (Zafar 2011). Tourism has consequently become an important pillar of the economy employing 26,000 people and representing 13% of the GDP (Ancharaz 2009). France produces the leading source of visitors accounting for 34.4% of tourists in 2006, followed by the United Kingdom, South Africa and India. Tourists from China represent a mere 0.6% of total arrivals but it is expected to increase in line with the exponential growth rate of the Chinese tourism market (Ancharaz 2009). The tourism industry became a vital economic pillar for the island and a key driver in advancing Mauritius towards a stronger economy in the future.

In addition to tourism, the government of Mauritius promoted the diversification of the economy into business process outsourcing (BPO), financial services and ICT. According to government figures, BPO has been growing at 70% per year and is currently worth US$1.6 billion, employing more than 100,000 people in 2011 (Zafar 2011). Offshore banking was introduced in 1988 as a first step towards developing Mauritius into an international financial centre. The development of the ICT sector intended to transform Mauritius into a 'cyber island' by creating a high-tech facility with strong technological capabilities that would be able to serve companies from all over the world (Zafar 2011).

The current diversification strategy aims to transform the traditional sectors towards the higher end of the market (Alves 2011). The sugar cane industry has been encouraged to diversify into processing by-products such as ethanol, spirits, electricity and speciality sugars, while the textile sector, to a more vertically integrated industry. Growth in new sectors such as financial services and information technology services have also been encouraged (Alves 2011).

In recent years the government and the private sector have solicited Chinese investors to invest in emerging industries such as light manufacturing, pharmaceuticals and the ocean economy. It was based on these efforts that an agreement was reached with the Tanli group in China for the setting up of an economic and trade cooperation zone (ETCZ) to boost the manufacturing of diversified products (Ancharaz 2009). After experiencing some initial delays due to environmental concerns and operational constraints, the project was restructured in 2009 and the name changed to Jinfei ETCZ. The pledged investment was increased from US$500 million to US$750 million and targeted the following sectors: residential developments, hospitality centres, knowledge hubs, and logistical and manufacturing sites. According to a news report (AfricaMoney 2016), the main vision for this urban renewal project is to make Mauritius a centre of excellence for international business and knowledge development that will create a sustainable circular economy and high quality of life through the development of so-called smart cities. The Highlands City Project was the first such project to materialise in July 2016, with an expected completion date in April 2018.

**Education and Skills**
Mauritius has always placed major emphasis on the development of its human resources and has a relatively good and functional education system compared to the rest of Africa. Primary school enrolment figures are above 90%, and the school system has become more universally distributed over the last two decades, achieving greater accessibility for secondary education, which was provided free of charge from 1975 (Duclos and Verdier-Chouchane 2011). Despite the positive enrolment figures, about a third of primary school students fail the Certificate of Primary Education, which makes it hard for them to benefit from the current transformation in the Mauritian economy (African Development Bank 2014). There is also evidence that the failure rate is concentrated in poor households, perpetuating the poverty trap.

The gross tertiary enrolment rate was at 32.4% in 2011, which is also lower than the average for middle-income countries (African Development Bank 2014). Authorities have articulated an Education and Human Resources Strategic Plan for the period 2008–2020 to address these challenges. Efforts also remain to improve relevance of Technical and Vocational Education and Training (TVET) and access, since 50% of the current demand for skills is not met, while employability is low (African Development Bank 2014). It was found that the skills mismatch also worsened in the context of structural economic changes, causing the demand for labour to drop in the traditionally low-skilled sectors such as sugar and textiles.

The Chinese government has regularly offered scholarships to Mauritian students to pursue university studies in China. Mauritius has benefitted from Chinese educational cooperation, as well as receiving technical assistance, for agricultural projects, customs upgrading and human resource development (Ancharaz 2009). There is some controversy about the motives surrounding the need for imported labour, especially in the EPZ. Officially employers blame it on local labour shortages; however, the true reasons suggested by Bunwaree could be the high levels of absenteeism amongst Mauritian EPZ workers, their refusal to work overtime, rising wages and dwindling productivity (Ancharaz 2009).

## Markets and Trading

Though a variety of explanations have been provided to explain Mauritius' growth performance, there is no doubt that the country's focus on international trade has been a critical element that contributed to this performance (Zafar 2011). Mauritius' preferential trading deals with partners such as the European Union and the United States in the sugar, textile and clothing sectors, resulted in significant growth of Mauritius' total exports, especially from the 1970s to the 1990s (Zafar 2011).

Europe and the United States are Mauritius' traditional export markets, with more than two-thirds of their exports going to these markets. The exports to China are insignificant, and represent less than 1% of Mauritian exports (Ancharaz 2009). The increase of imports from China, especially since the 2000 FOCAC Ministerial Conference agreement, propelled China into third position following France and India, ahead of South Africa—a traditional source of imports for Mauritius. Imports of textiles, machinery and equipment, and manufactured consumer goods, comprise the bulk of imports from China (Ancharaz 2009). In the textile sector, however, Mauritius has reduced its dependence on Chinese yarn and textiles through significant investment in local spinning capacity. Consequently, textile imports from China have fallen. The consequence of low exports and high imports between Mauritius and China is the widening of the trade deficit between the two countries.

Wearing apparel exports destined for the European and US markets represent nearly 90% of the total manufactured exports of Mauritius (Ancharaz 2009). Mauritius benefitted from the MFA quota system, which limited Asian exports into the US market, as well as the Lomé agreement, which granted duty-free access for manufactured goods from the African, Caribbean and Pacific Group of countries into the European Union market. These opportunities opened the door for Chinese and other foreign companies to invest in this sector, resulting in sustained export-led growth lasting nearly two decades. Since the expiry of the MFA in 2002, the US market has been flooded with cheap Chinese clothing with a direct negative effect on exporters of clothing, such as Mauritius (Ancharaz 2009). A number of enterprises began to withdraw from this sector and the export of apparel declined for the period 2001–2005. This trend was reversed in 2006 as apparel makers diversified their markets by exporting more to the European Union. Exports to South Africa also increased due to the duty-free treatment under the Southern African Development Community (SADC) trade protocol (Ancharaz 2009).

It was found that the unit labour cost of producing a garment is amongst the highest in Mauritius, leaving manufacturers little chance to compete with China on cost. Clothing is, however, a differentiated product that does not only compete on price, but has also other non-price competitive advantages such as quality, lead times, reliability, flexibility, knowledge of specific markets and cultures, and compliance with social and environmental standards. The Mauritian EPZ has used its 35 years of experience to strategically position itself as a reliable supplier of quality clothing, and therefore chooses to compete in a niche market—a less ruthless market than the generic low-cost market (Ancharaz 2009). Other companies have moved their low-end production to Madagascar to take advantage of its cheaper labour dispensation, while locally the focus is shifting towards more sophisticated and higher value-added activities. Adapting to the market and trade environment has resulted in more than 200 textile and clothing companies, of which the majority are locally owned, surviving the termination of quota advantages and the rise of Chinese competition.

**Cultural and Social Investment**
Ethnicity is a double-edged sword. On the one hand, ethnic groups will tend to promote the forces of development and growth and, on the other hand, ethnic groups will organise politically if they cannot find the space to advance the self-interest of their members. Mauritius became independent in the worst of political conditions. The campaign for and against independence was extremely bitter in rhetoric and pitched along ethnic division. In the months preceding and post their day of independence, ethnic violence claimed a number of lives (Darga 2011). The new ruling political elite quickly realised that such conflict would result in a 'lose-lose' situation for all, and that a strategy of accommodation would facilitate a better outcome for the future. This important realisation was supported by other important community groups, including the media, academia and church leaders. The power sharing and collaboration that followed became a solid base for the development of a stable governance system—a healthy and ethical democracy that Mauritius became known for (Darga 2011).

The Mauritian poverty reduction strategy has focused on expanding employment opportunities by developing and modernising its economy, while maintaining an elaborate social safety net (Duclos and Verdier-Chouchane 2011). Mauritius also allocated significant public resources to education and health. Adult literacy and life expectancy are now well above the sub-Saharan average. Healthcare is free and health facilities are of reasonably good quality and accessible throughout the country (Duclos and Verdier-Chouchane 2011).

## The 'Leaves and Fruit' Creating Prosperity and Wealth for the People of Mauritius

An evaluation of the effect of internal organic growth on the wealth and capital of Mauritius is provided in Table 9.12.

**Table 9.12** The 'Leaves and Fruit' of the African Tree of Organic Growth for Mauritius

| 'Leaves and Fruit' | Country evaluation: Mauritius | China's impact |
|---|---|---|
| Social and cultural wealth | Effective and generous welfare state<br>Free education and health<br>Low level of national poverty<br>Effective housing system | Aid and investment in health and education sectors<br>Low-cost housing projects |
| Natural capital | Natural environment negatively affected by development, especially agriculture and infrastructure<br>Deforestation and degrading of coral reef due to environmental damage | No evidence found of direct impact by China |
| Human capital | Skills mismatch—a need to refocus skills training to provide for future needs<br>Low productivity levels<br>Unemployment for low-skilled workers still a problem | Various programmes to boost human resource development through Chinese aid |
| Institutional capital | Strong and effective institutional framework<br>Low levels of corruption<br>Good cooperation between the public and private sector | Formal trade associations formed with China |
| Produced capital and financial capital | Attractive and friendly business environment is attractive for investment<br>Production capacity improved with EPZ development<br>Rents generated within the system during the 1970s and 1980s were used to finance capital accumulation rather than consumption | Most of the FDI from China was in textiles, followed later by financial services<br>Interest-free or low-interest loans provided by China for infrastructure and other projects |
| Economic wealth | Equal distribution of economic wealth<br>Textile sector boosts employment of women<br>Low-skilled workers are still excluded | China contributes indirectly through investments in growth sectors |

## Social and Cultural Wealth

Mauritius' generous social welfare system provides safety nets to vulnerable sectors of the population in terms of free access to education, health services, subsidised housing and subsidies in rice and flour (African Development Bank 2014). Economic growth has translated into improvements in the quality of life for Mauritians in terms of access to water and electricity, better public infrastructure like schools and hospitals, and access to housing and education (Darga 2011).

Mauritius has a relatively low level of national poverty in comparison to other African countries (Duclos and Verdier-Chouchane 2011). The percentage of people living below the poverty line has decreased from 40% in 1975 to 11% in 2010 (Zafar 2011). According to a World Bank report, the poverty rate of Mauritius, based on the US$3 a day poverty line, is projected to fall by a further 1.5% between 2012 and 2018, while unemployment is expected to remain at around 8%. Life expectancy at birth increased from 62 years in 1970 to 73 years in 2008, while infant mortality has dropped from 64 deaths per 1000 in 1970 to 15 deaths per 1000 in 2008 (Zafar 2011).

Following substantial investments in education in the 1980s and 1990s, primary school enrolments now average more than 90% (Zafar 2011). With a national Gini coefficient of around 0.36, Mauritius' level of inequality is also relatively low in comparison to other African countries (Duclos and Verdier-Chouchane 2011). All households are provided with safe drinking water and access to free essential drugs. The Mauritian citizen has free medical treatment of the highest technology, such as open-heart surgery and laser eye treatment (Darga 2011).

## Natural Capital

The competitiveness and sustainable growth potential of Mauritius is intrinsically linked to how it manages its natural and ecological capital. Being a small island, Mauritius is highly vulnerable to environment and climate change shocks. There is evidence that the natural environment has been affected by the development imperative of Mauritius. While initially, the clearing of natural forests was to make way for sugar cane and agriculture, the high population density and pace of growth in infrastructure development are also putting pressure on land resources and biodiversity (African Development Bank 2014). The African Development Bank Country Strategy Paper 2014–2018 (2014) found that carbon dioxide emissions have risen, 17 species are under threat of extinction and less than 2% of native forests are left. Estimates show that the country has seen a degradation of nearly 60–70% of corals, which could lead to rapid degradation of lagoons and erosion of beaches (African Development Bank 2014).

Environmental concerns were evidenced when environmental activists went on hunger strike to protest against government plans to develop a coal power plant. The government took steps to address the activist's concerns. They disclosed the contracts under the coal power project and set up the National Energy Commission (NEC) as an advisory body on power investments (African Development Bank 2014).

**Human Capital**
Mauritius has done well to increase the employability of its people through the diversification of their economy, especially the diversification into manufacturing in the early 2000s. Employment started to decline in 2006 because the textile and clothing sector consolidated and invested in capital-intensive spinning and weaving activities, aimed at increasing capacities and integration of the value chain. Productivity levels are still low in Mauritius, resulting in strategies to mechanise, which in turn negatively impacts employment levels (Ancharaz 2009). Poor education attainment at primary and secondary school levels is also a source of exclusion, with most unskilled and semi-skilled youth likely to be either in vulnerable employment or in unemployment. While the ICT and the financial service sectors are creating jobs, women have lost jobs in the textile and sugar sectors, and unskilled youth are unemployed due to the lack of relevant skills. A concern, though, is the low labour productivity levels which have only been growing marginally, necessitating a reorientation towards skills and productivity improvements.

**Institutional Capital**
Mauritius is fortunate to have a combination of political stability, strong institutional frameworks, low levels of corruption and a favourable regulatory environment. This has laid the foundation for economic growth, while its open-trade policy framework has been key in sustaining its competitive trade advantage and growth trajectory. In surveys of institutional quality, Mauritius repeatedly ranks high against comparable countries, particularly in terms of governance, rule of law and the control of corruption (Zafar 2011). The Ibrahim Index for African Governance captures this progress, with Mauritius ranking first in Africa for six successive years in 2012 (African Development Bank 2014).

A set of informal and formal mechanisms guide the interaction between the public and the private sectors, with the result that the private sector plays a seminal role in the policy formulation process. Mauritius has also been quite effective in establishing trade links on an international level. Mauritius serves as a trade hub for Chinese and Indian traders as an entrepôt for shipping across the Indian Ocean. These trade links developed over time into formal trade associations and entities, of which some achieved representation at a political level (Zafar 2011).

**Produced Capital and Financial Capital**
Mauritius offers an attractive investment climate. The EPZ boom years between 1983 and 1988 coincided with a significant increase in both domestic and foreign investment in the zone. The attractive and friendly business environment, as well as liberal investment regime, led to a rapid increase in FDI over the past several years (Zafar 2011). According to Zafar (2011), most of the investment inflows have gone towards the tourism, real estate, banking and finance, information technology, and health and educational sectors.

Chinese direct investment in Mauritius has been relatively low in comparison with other investors, but has increased especially since 2007. The biggest investor in Mauritius has historically been the United Kingdom, followed by South Africa, France and India. The banking and tourism sectors have been the main beneficiaries of foreign investment. Much of the Chinese investment since 2002 has flowed into the textile industry. In 2004, for example, a major investment project by the Chinese aimed at producing 18,000 tonnes of yarn a year, thus contributing to building a vertically integrated supply chain for the clothing and textile industry (Ancharaz 2009). Chinese aid, mostly in the form of interest-free or low-interest loans, was channelled principally into infrastructure projects such as health and sport facilities, an airport terminal, low-cost housing and sewage projects.

In the 2000s the government built up reserves that allowed Mauritius the freedom to expand fiscal policy even in the aftermath of the 2008–2009 global financial crisis, keeping their stock of domestic and international debt below an unsustainable threshold (Zafar 2011). Government expenditures have never much exceeded 20% of GDP and capital expenditures have been used productively to invest in infrastructure such as roads and operational infrastructure for the EPZs (Zafar 2011).

**Economic Wealth**

Mauritius' GDP per capita increased more than tenfold between 1970 and 2010, from less than US$500 per person to more than US$6000 per person (Zafar 2011). Mauritius has provided one of the best environments for the accumulation of economic wealth in Africa. The 2012 Index of Economic Freedom, which evaluates countries in terms of economic freedom, ranked Mauritius' economy as the eighth in the world and the first in Africa (African Development Bank 2014).

Ancharaz (2009) argued that the development of the textile export sector can be hailed as a catalyst of women's emancipation in the formal labour market, contributing to the growth of the country while at the same time achieving their own economic independence. While the expansion of textile manufacturing had been particularly beneficial to woman, its contraction and the resulting layoffs since 2001 have particularly hit female workers, leading to the 'feminisation of poverty' in Mauritius.

To improve the quality of life of all Mauritians, economic growth should uplift and upgrade low-wage workers as well. In this regard, the government should consider developing a structured programme to train and place low-wage workers in better jobs. To improve organic growth and inclusiveness in economic wealth, Mauritius needs to improve its labour force skills set, address the low-skilled unemployment problem and gender gap, and increase overall productivity and innovation.

## 9.3 Closing Remarks on the Integration of Organic Growth in Both Countries and the Impact of China on This Process

The mostly positive impact of China on the organic growth of Mauritius, as illustrated in this chapter, defies the opinions of many authors who suggest that Chinese interests in Africa are solely focused on the exploitation of the continent's energy and mineral resources. Mauritius has no such resources to offer. For the Mauritian government, China is not seen as a potential competitor for their textile and clothing sector but as a cash-rich investor and business partner who can provide much needed financial capital and support for the development of the social and production capacity of the country. It is further expected that Chinese aid flows to Mauritius will rise as China's presence in the local economy grows, backed by over three decades of friendly, diplomatic and cultural ties with China. In addition, Mauritius stands a chance to gain even more from Chinese FDI as

China considers Mauritius a strategic geographical location to penetrate the large market of the continent of Africa.

The Sino–Cameroonian relationship has grown rapidly since the first FOCAC Ministerial Conference in 2000, and China has played a key role in Cameroon's economic development, particularly with regard to the development of infrastructure. Weak and corrupt governance, however, continues to hamper Cameroon's development and obstructs the effective distribution of wealth to the population. Cameroon's economy, although relatively diversified with services, is still dominated by the public sector and structural reforms have done little to improve the overall business environment. Although government has been able to maintain a degree of balance between the country's various ethnic and linguistic communities, it appears that the anglophone minority is increasingly becoming dissatisfied with its perceived economic marginalisation to the benefit of the francophone majority. Sautman and Hairong (2009) did an empirical study on the perceptions of the Cameroon people on the impact of China in Cameroon. It is clear from the study that although the people of Cameroon have some negative feelings about the influence of China in the country, the overwhelming majority believed that China is making a positive contribution to the growth and development of the country.

## References

African Development Bank. 2009. Country Strategy Paper 2010–2014 Cameroon. [Online]. Available from: https://www.afdb.org/fileadmin/uploads/afdb/Documents/Project-and-Operations/CAMEROON_2010-2014%20COUNTRY%20STRATEGY%20PAPER.pdf (accessed: 14 May 2017).

African Development Bank. 2014. Country Strategy Paper 2014–2018 Mauritius. [Online]. Available from: https://www.afdb.org/fileadmin/uploads/afdb/Documents/Project-and-Operations/2014-2018_-_Mauritius_Country_Strategy_Paper.pdf (accessed: 24 May 2017).

African Economic Outlook. 2013. African Economic Outlook: Cameroon. [Online]. Available from: https://www.oecd-ilibrary.org/development/african-economic-outlook-2013_aeo-2013-en (accessed: 5 May 2017). © African Development Bank, Organisation for Economic Co-operation and Development, United Nations Development Programme, Economic Commission for Africa (2013). Republished with Permission Conveyed Through Copyright Clearance Center, Inc.: License ID 4215260667106.

AfricaMoney. 2016. Smart City Project Bring New Opportunities to the Doorstep of Every Mauritian. [Online]. Available from: http://africamoney.info/smart-city-project-to-bring-new-opportunities-to-the-doorstep-of-every-mauritian/ (accessed: 22 May 2017).

Alves, A. 2011. Chinese Economic and Trade Co-operation Zones in Africa: The Case of Mauritius. Occasional Paper No 74 China in Africa Project. [Online]. Available from: https://www.saiia.org.za/occasional-papers/71-chinese-economic-and-trade-co-operation-zones-in-africa-the-case-of-mauritius (accessed: 21 May 2017).

Ancharaz, V. 2009. 'David V. Goliath: Mauritius Facing Up to China', *The European Journal of Development Research*, 21 (4): 622–643.

Bräutigam, D. and Zhang, H. 2013. 'Green Dreams: Myth and Reality in China's Agricultural Investment in Africa', *Third World Quarterly*, 34 (9): 1682.

Butler R. 2015 Cameroon: Environmental Profile. [Online]. Available at http://www.rainforests.mongabay.com/20cameroon.htm (accessed: 13 May 2017).

Cabestan, J. 2015. 'China-Cameroon Relations: Fortunes and Limits of an Old Political Complicity', *South African Journal of International Affairs*, 22 (1). Copyright © The South African Institute of International Affairs, Reprinted by Permission of Taylor & Francis Ltd, www.tanffonline.com on Behalf of The South African Institute of International Affairs.

Coface. 2017. Economic Study and Country Risk Assessment: Cameroon. [Online]. Available from: www.coface.com/Economic-Studies-and-Country-Risks/Cameroon (accessed: 7 May 2017).

Darga, A. 2011. The Mauritius Success Story. Why is this Island Nation an African Political and Economic Success? Chapter in 'Advocates for Change: How to Overcome Africa's Challenges'. Edited by M. Mbeki. Johannesburg: Picador Africa.

Duclos, J. and Verdier-Chouchane, A. 2011. Growth, Poverty and Inequality in Mauritius and South Africa. African Development Bank. Africa Economic Brief Volume 2 Issue 3. [Online]. Available from: https://www.afdb.org/fileadmin/uploads/afdb/Documents/Publications/AEB%20VOL%202%20Issue%203%20April%202011_AEB%20VOL%202%20Issue%203%20April%202011.pdf (accessed: 21 May 2017).

Ekuh, E. 2014. Youth Unemployment Challenge in Cameroon. Eddyhopefoundation. [Online]. Available from: https://www.linkedin.com/pulse/20140718112132-138644527-youth-unemployment-challenge-in-cameroon (accessed: 12 May 2017).

Eriksen, T. 2000. Ethnic Relations in Mauritius. Equality (Port of Spain). [Online]. Available from: http://hyllanderiksen.net/Equality.html (accessed: 24 May 2017).

Fombe, N. 2012. Corruption and Economic Development in Cameroon. Master Thesis Aalborg University. [Online]. Available from: https://www.projekter.

aau.dk/projekter/files/68760145/Final_thesis_Nyemkuna_2012.doc (accessed: 26 May 2017).

Gulhati, R. and Nallari, R. 1990. *Successful Stabilization and Recovery in Mauritius.* EDI Development Policy Case Series. Analytical Case Studies; No. 5*World Bank Institute (WBI) Case Studies. Washington, DC: The World Bank. ©The World Bank. http://documents.worldbank.org/curated/en/604951468757475877/Successful-stabilization-and-recovery-in-Mauritius License: Creative Commons Attribution License (CC BY 3.0 IGO) (http://creativecommons.org/licenses/by/3.0/igo/).

Matusky, D. 2001. Everyculture.com: Mauritian Culture. [Online]. Available from: http://www.everyculture.com/Ma-Ni/Mauritius.html (accessed: 19 May 2017).

Raine, S. 2009. Sino-Mauritian Relations: The Geopolitical Perspective. The China Monitor Issue 39 China & Mauritius-Perspectives on a Trans-Indian Ocean Partnership April 2009. Centre for Chinese Studies, University of Stellenbosch. [Online]. Available from: http://www.ccs.org.za/wp-content/uploads/2009/04/china-monitor-april-2009.pdf (accessed: 20 May 2017).

Sautman, B. and Hairong, Y. 2009. 'African Perspectives on China-Africa Links', *The China Quarterly*, 199: 728–759.

World Bank. 2012. *Better Governance Improving Education Outcomes Through Better Governance in Cameroon: Integrating Supply and Demand-Side Approaches.* © World Bank. [Online]. Available from: http://www.worldbank.org/en/news/feature/2012/04/11/better-governance-improving-education-outcomes-through-better-governance-in-cameroon-integrating-supply-and-demand-side-approaches (accessed: 14 May 2017). License: Creative Commons Attribution License (CC BY 3.0 IGO) (http://creativecommons.org/licenses/by/3.0/igo/).

World Bank. 2016. *The World Bank in Cameroon: Overview.* © World Bank. [Online]. Available from: https://www.worldbank.org/en/country/cameroon/overview (accessed: 4 May 2017). License: Creative Commons Attribution License (CC BY 3.0 IGO) (http://creativecommons.org/licenses/by/3.0/igo/).

Zafar, Ali. 2007. *The Growing Relationship Between China and Sub-Saharan Africa.* World Bank. © World Bank. https://openknowledge.worldbank.org/handle/10986/4406 License: CC BY-NC-ND 3.0 IGO.

Zafar, Ali. 2011. *Mauritius: An Economic Success Story. Africa Success Stories Project.* © World Bank. [Online]. Available from: http://siteresources.worldbank.org/AFRICAEXT/Resources/Mauritius_success.pdf (accessed: 20 May 2017). License: Creative Commons Attribution License (CC BY 3.0 IGO) (http://creativecommons.org/licenses/by/3.0/igo/).

CHAPTER 10

# The Impact of China on the African Renaissance: Let the Baobab Grow...

Seven African countries are among the 13 fastest-growing economies in the world (World Bank 2015)—this growth lies at the heart of what some authors describe as 'Africa Rising'. Further analysis, however, shows that Africa remains behind in almost every other human development indicator including the Human Development Index. There is limited improvement in key areas such as health, education and inequality (Gumede 2009). It is further reported that many African states still have low levels of social protection, high unemployment, poverty and pervasive food insecurity (Mabasa and Mqolomba 2016).

According to Mabasa and Mqolomba (2016), Africa's development paradox can mainly be attributed to the dominance of economic liberalism in global economic development discourses. These discourses emphasise free trade, privatisation, market-led development, deregulation and financial liberalisation, as the magic solutions to development and growth for any country. There is, however, overwhelming evidence to show that the dominant Western principle of 'grow first and distribute later' has failed in Africa.

## 10.1 Growth in Africa: The Evolving Paradigm

The thinking about growth and development in Africa has evolved over time from a pure economic growth model towards an inclusive growth orientation, especially in the last decade. We demonstrate in this book that this thinking should be further refined to include organic growth. Organic growth not only includes the pace and pattern of growth but also the integrated development and multiplier process that is unique to each country.

### 10.1.1 Moving from 'Economic Growth' to 'Inclusive Growth' in Africa

Most African countries who experienced a positive, and even progressive, pace of economic growth in the last two decades, failed to deliver sustained improvements in the social and economic well-being of all their citizens. In fact, in some countries such as Nigeria and others, poverty and inequality levels increased even further despite the increase in economic growth. The United Nations Sustainable Development Goals (SDGs) discussed in Chap. 1 recognised these challenges, notably in Goal 8, which advocated "sustained, inclusive and sustainable economic growth, full and productive employment and decent work for all"; and Goal 10, which called for a reduction in "inequality within and among countries". Many of the issues pertaining to inclusive growth were addressed by the other goals, including wider access to healthcare; better quality education; access to basic services such as sanitation, clean water and energy; infrastructure that promotes industry; and innovation—these are all important factors that will ensure that economic growth is inclusive and sustainable. Ianchovichina and Lundstrom (2009) did a detailed analysis of the definition of inclusive growth, and proposed that inclusive growth incorporates the aspects described in Table 10.1.

Table 10.1 Definition of inclusive growth

| Inclusive growth is |
| --- |
| **Broad-based** across sectors, and **structural transformation for economic diversification** is therefore a priority |
| **Inclusive of a large part of the country's labour force**, providing equal opportunities to all in terms of access to markets and resources |
| Focused on **both the pace and pattern of growth**—the question of **how** growth is generated is critical for poverty reduction |
| Focused on **productive employment,** rather than income redistribution |
| Focused not only on the **firm, but also on the individual** |
| **Not defined in terms of specific targets** such as employment generation or income distribution |
| **Fuelled by market-driven sources** of growth with Government playing a facilitating role |

Ianchovichina and Lundstrom (2009)

Ianchovichina and Lundstrom (2009) argue that inclusive growth has a distinct character that focuses on both the pace and the pattern of growth, while the traditional economic growth paradigm deals with the pace of growth and the patterns of growth, such as inequality and poverty, separately. Growth is inclusive when it creates economic opportunities along with ensuring equal access to those opportunities. Apart from addressing the issue of inequality, the inclusive growth paradigm should also reduce overall poverty by creating productive economic opportunities for the poor and vulnerable sections of society (Ianchovichina and Lundstrom 2009).

In other words, inclusive economic growth is not only about growing national economies, but also about ensuring that the most vulnerable people benefit from this growth. The extent to which growth reduces poverty and inequality will therefore depend on the degree to which the poor participate in the growth process and share in its proceeds. For growth to be inclusive, the pace and the pattern of growth matter in reducing poverty.

### 10.1.2 Moving Towards the Paradigm of 'Organic Growth'

Although the organic growth paradigm acknowledges the principles of inclusive economic growth as being important, it further postulates that the unique developmental, historical, social, cultural and economic context will, in most cases, have the greatest impact on the overall growth trajectory of the country—similar to that of the organic growth of a tree. The overall objective is therefore to first build an effective developmental state, a state based on its own peculiar contextual historical and sociopolitical factors, and second, to stimulate and multiply the growth process through pro-poor, sustainable and inclusive growth.

*The Development Context*
Most, if not all, African countries can be classified as so-called development states. The term 'developmental state' gained prominence in policy discourses following the rapid rise of the East Asian Tigers in the 1980s. Gumede (2009: 4) describes this as "one of the greatest industrialisation transformations of the modern era". The development approach is based on channelling or guiding market activity through effective government policies such as incentives, controls and mechanisms. These policies enable the government to guide the growth process and allocate resources

towards supporting effective and inclusive growth and market development (Mabasa and Mqolomba 2016). According to Chang (2003), development states are viewed as coordinators and integrators of economic development, and should therefore be prominent actors in the process of inclusive growth.

According to Mabasa and Mqolomba (2016) the typical development state in Africa should

- Drive economic growth and development in the interest of the 'public good'
- Be viewed as coordinators of economic development
- Promote state-driven economic planning
- Enhance the dynamics between market and non-market institutions
- Play an important role in social restructuring and development required for industrialisation and market-led development

The African Tree of Organic Growth paradigm acknowledged the critical role of government, institutions and social society in shaping the development agenda of a country. It was, for example, clear from the Mauritian case study that the economic success and growth of the country was primarily based on the pragmatic approach of government towards development that included social development. This paradigm embraced the development concept further by acknowledging that growth will first be determined by the 'unique development status' of any country at a specific point in time.

*The Historical, Social and Cultural Context*
African countries are all experiencing their own particular historical, social and cultural context, the context of which forms the central fibre of their development process. Many African countries are ethnically diverse because of the historical context, including factors such as colonial borders and influences. In some countries, these ethnic differences were politicised, for example Rwanda and the Democratic Republic of the Congo (DRC), where ethnic conflicts were the major single stumbling block for development and growth. In Cameroon, the anglophone and francophone division of the country have had certain repercussions on development that would not have been applicable to a monoculture country. Countries that succeed in managing their diversity without discrimination, to the benefit of all, seem to achieve better results in development and growth.

Katy Wright in her paper published by OXFAM (Wright 2017) argued that to address poverty and inequality, African leaders need to think beyond 'inclusive growth', and rather consider a 'human economy' that will lead to economic prosperity for all. She argued that the shape of many of the continent's economies are characterised by an overreliance on the extraction of natural resources, and inadequate investment in agriculture and comparative advantage sectors, which has resulted in the consequences of inequality being mostly experienced by the youth and women. Despite being recognised as the future of Africa's economic success, it is the women and young people who work predominantly in the informal sector and agriculture, and while they should be first in line for opportunities of training, employment and investment, this does not always happen. It is furthermore young people and women who suffer the most when governments make questionable spending and investment decisions. The provision of a skilled and educated workforce to enable future growth, as discussed in Chap. 6, is therefore essential for future growth in an organic growth paradigm.

*The Economic Context*

Third, the organic growth paradigm is based on an economic framework that will encourage diversification in sectors in which the country enjoys a comparative advantage, or can develop a comparative advantage. The organic growth framework does not accommodate trade-offs between promoting social inclusion and promoting economic growth and development. It is impossible to improve everyone's living conditions without growing the economic pie. It is therefore possible to be pro-equity and pro-growth at the same time within this framework. The extent to which growth will reduce poverty and inequality will depend on the opportunities created and access provided for the poor to participate in a broader economic system.

This process will normally start with the evaluation of the country's current economic structure and industrial base. For many pre-transition economies in Africa, agriculture will be the centrepiece of their efforts to achieve growth, reduce poverty and secure enough food for the future. It will be crucial for these countries to raise their agricultural productivity and innovation, and release labour for more diversification into agro-processing and other sectors in which they have a comparative advantage. The case of Kenya discussed in Chap. 3 is a good example of how a country can move from pre-transition status towards a transition economy through agricultural diversification—Kenya did this with tea, flowers, vegetables and coffee, which have become their major export products. Nigeria, an oil exporter on the other hand, continued to depend mainly on oil for economic growth for many years. Although the Nigerian economy is diversified into primary, secondary and tertiary sectors, there is still very little progress in terms of value chain integration between these sectors. It seems further that these sectors were created almost independently, instead of being created within a broader framework of a natural organic process of diversification, as suggested in this book.

The development and diversification in both Kenya and Nigeria face the challenges of poor economic and social infrastructure. No country can sustain growth without investing in infrastructure, education and healthcare. Investors need an economic and social infrastructure framework that will facilitate access to labour and raw materials, as well as providing routes to markets.

*The Organic Growth Process*

Organic growth is a multidimensional process involving many, and sometimes major, changes to social and economic structures, infrastructure, education and training, economic growth and diversification, and governance. This is needed in order to generate enough capital for more growth cycles, while at the same time reducing inequality and eradicating poverty effectively, in an organic balance. The organic growth process described in this book was compared to the organic growth of a tree where the tree will be anchored in its roots (resources, assets and structures), enabling it to create growth through the trunk (growth channels and enablers), thus producing leaves and fruit (wealth) for consumption and reinvestment of sugar (capital) to the roots. From a similar perspective, organic growth is based on a physiological multiplier process: The more water and nutrients the tree can absorb through the roots, and transform through the trunk, the better the production of the leaves and fruit, which create a multiplier effect for the next growth cycle. Although the economic multiplier effect popularised by the Keynesian Model of Economics is not new, it can be applied to the context of an organic growth process—a process that is integrated and multidimensional, resulting in greater outcomes due to the multiplier effect. The multiplier effect is in this case not viewed as an economic bonus, but is rather considered as part of the integrated growth and development process which will either enhance the growth process or stifle it.

One pertinent example of this is the effectiveness of good governance and social development on this organic growth process, especially in a developing country, where government spending is a stimulus for economic growth. Ethiopia's economic growth and development have been driven by pro-poor public sector investment, with a boom in opportunities being experienced in private sector construction, transport, small and medium-sized business services, and education and skills. An investment in relevant education and skills will produce a labour force that can learn new tasks and skills more easily, and which can utilise a wider range of technologies and equipment, thus making them more creative and productive in the workplace. In an organic process, education and skills development will be aimed at providing for the future growth needs of a country. The provision of infrastructure can also have a number of important multiplier effects on the economy, one of which is the lowering of the cost of production, while another is the facilitation of access to markets. The vertical integration of sectors, and diversification into other relevant sectors in which the country has a comparative advantage, will also have downstream and upstream multiplier effects on the economy. The difference is that within an organic growth process, these multiplier effects are part of a natural integrated process, and can therefore have a significant impact if correctly planned and executed.

A comparison of the three approaches of economic growth, inclusive growth and organic growth is provided in Table 10.2.

Table 10.2 A comparison of economic growth, inclusive growth and organic growth paradigms

| Growth indicators | Economic growth | Inclusive growth | Organic growth |
|---|---|---|---|
| Pace of Growth | √ | √ | √ |
| Pattern of Growth | | √ | √ |
| Context of Growth | | | √ |
| Process of Growth | √ | √ | √ |

Authors' own analysis

## 10.2 Engagement and the Impact of China on the Organic Growth in Africa

A useful description of the elements that need to be considered in view of China's engagement on development in Africa was provided by Grimm (2011) and summarised in Table 10.3.

The engagement on behalf of Chinese state organs has been primarily facilitated by the Forum on China–African Cooperation (FOCAC) Ministerial Conferences that take place every three years, alternating between Chinese and African locations. These forums focus on the formation of bilateral and multilateral agreements between China and African states, and include foreign aid, loans and investments. These projects were, and continue to be planned and conducted with Chinese state funding, much of which is in some form of interest-free or low-interest loan granted bilaterally. The case studies analysed in this book clearly show how these agreements between state organs increased progressively since the first FOCAC Ministerial Conference of 2000. Chinese funding, for instance that of investments in manufacturing capacity, creates employment and can have a positive impact on the transfer of technology and skills. However, as Grimm (2011) suggested, the impact of this engagement can also have negative effects, for instance when environmental and social standards are not met in countries in which Chinese businesses invest. These considerations will have to be included in negotiations to ensure a 'win-win' outcome of sustainable growth and development.

Chinese entrepreneurs are innovative and highly agile people who are constantly searching for new international opportunities and markets for their products. The presence of Chinese entrepreneurs and traders is often presented as evidence of an official policy to engage with Africa, yet Grimm (2011) suggests that in most cases, their engagement is initiated by the individual business people who are searching for business and market

Table 10.3 The four elements of Chinese engagement and impact in Africa

Engagement on behalf of Chinese state organs in African states
Chinese business and entrepreneurial interactions with people in African states
Indirect impacts on African development
Political impact on the development discourse of Africa

Grimm (2011)

opportunities. This direct engagement of individuals has broad repercussions and can contribute to growth and development, but can also create challenges, for instance reactions to local competition created by Chinese entrepreneurs has led to cases of xenophobia in South Africa and Zambia. It is clear that both China and the host country will be equally responsible for managing these situations in a constructive way.

Chinese growth can also have an indirect impact on the development of Africa. A good example of this is the effect of China's penetration of textile markets on the textile industry in Mauritius. China and Mauritius were competing for the same market and, as a result, Mauritius had to change its competitive focus from low-cost to quality differentiation to remain competitive. Domestic policy changes in China (as with policies of other world powers) can also have significant repercussions for African countries. Timber is an example of this, where stricter forest protection legislation in China led to an increase of importation of timber from Ghana and Cameroon.

The last element identified by Grimm (2011) is the political effect on the international discourse around development in Africa. China's approach to development in Africa, and its success in this regard, has had a direct effect on the development discourse from the Western world, and resulted in a shift from purely conditional assistance to approaches better aligned to African development policies. Chinese engagement seems to deliberately mix trade, aid and investment and often blurs the line between the three. In many instances, China's engagement can be classified as a modern form of barter trade, such as when infrastructure investment is funded by China and constructed by Chinese companies in exchange for the delivery of raw material ('Angola-mode' framework agreements)—a more integrated approach that has significantly impacted development.

### 10.2.1 Does China's Own Experience as a Developmental State Offer Lessons for the Growth of Africa?

Remarkable similarities were found in the organic growth paradigm defined in this book and the growth trajectory experienced by China since its structural economic transformation in the 1970s. China's determination to pursue economic reforms in 1978 took place within the cultural and historical context in China. The state had always played a central role in China, in line with its Confucian culture supporting the respect for authority and social stability. Chinese society rejected this atomistic view of the state and embraced an organic paradigm, which conceptualises the state as the custodian of the general will of the people. The failure of the historical political and economic system, commonly referred to as Maoist socialism, also provided the impetus for a new development path under economic reformer Deng Xiaoping, who prioritised economic development and growth as the main objective going forward, without compromising on China's social focus (Mabasa and Mqolomba 2016).

The nature of the Chinese post-socialist state has largely been driven by market-orientated reforms such as state-driven industrial strategies, trade policies and macroeconomic controls, boosting economic diversification into manufacturing and exports. China has also experienced strategic institutional reforms, which have proven to be effective in promoting development and growth.

According to Maru (2016), a series of economic reforms that were introduced and directed by the state accelerated the increase in productivity and capital asset accumulation through domestic savings, providing the major source of 'fuel' for growth in China. The second reason for this growth is that it did not come from the forces of the free market as conventional theories of economic development dictate, but from state-led economic reform. Hence the role of the state in economic development was unprecedented in conventional economic theory as prescribed by international institutions such as the International Monetary Fund (IMF) and the World Bank. The successful economic diversification in the agricultural sector and the economic transformation towards manufacturing have moved many people out of the highly congested agricultural sector. To reduce poverty and inequality, both the pace and the pattern of growth were considered. By encouraging the growth of rural enterprises, China has successfully moved millions of workers off farms and into factories, without creating an urban crisis (Maru 2016).

To boost the rural reform programme, priority was given to infrastructure development in those areas, much of which was through food-for-work programmes, and which focused on a holistic approach of developing the village or town as a whole. Special Economic Zones (SEZs) were used to facilitate diversification from agriculture to manufacturing. As the rural economies and the SEZs took off, infrastructure became a growth bottleneck resulting in infrastructure development being prioritised in the 1990s. As part of this process, inter-regional infrastructure was planned with the main aim being to effectively integrate the Chinese economy. The focus on infrastructure development in China since the 1990s played a prominent role in reducing poverty, providing food security and generating export-orientated growth for China.

The lessons that China offered for the organic growth of African countries is summarised in Table 10.4.

Table 10.4 Lessons that China offered for the organic growth of African countries

| Main characteristics of China's growth | Lessons for organic growth in Africa |
|---|---|
| Determined by historical, cultural and economic context of China | Historical, cultural and economic context is an important base for economic growth and development in Africa |
| State-led economic reforms directed economic growth and social development | Government, institutional reforms and social development are key determinants of successful growth |
| Economic growth and development followed a natural process starting with the uplifting of the majority of people in the rural agricultural sector | Many African nations can follow a similar route in leveraging the agricultural sector |
| Economic growth and development focused on pace and pattern of development to ensure equal distribution of wealth, and reduction of poverty on a wider level | Generating growth in rural areas is also important for Africa as opposed to creation of growth in urban areas only |
| Increasing productivity through education and relevant training were one of the major contributors to growth | Low productivity levels are one of the major constraints of growth in Africa, and relevant education and training is urgently needed |
| The outstanding success of diversification, from a predominantly agriculturally dominated economy to manufacturing and services was through an organic process | Most African countries have struggled with this natural process of diversification |
| Important role of infrastructure development as an enabler for economic development and empowerment of rural communities | Infrastructure development is a critical enabler of economic development and empowerment |

Authors' own

### 10.2.2 The Fallacies and Facts About the Impact of China in Africa

China is often depicted by critics as the new colonialist in Africa, rapacious exploiter of resources who lack transparency and good corporate citizenship. Discussions in the popular press and policy institutions sometimes tend to focus on economic and security concerns from a global perspective, rather than implications for African growth and development. Doubts have also been raised in the international community over the nature of cooperation between China and Africa. In 2006, the then British foreign secretary, Jack Straw, remarked that what China was doing in Africa was much the same as what Britain had done 150 years earlier; in June 2011, Hillary Clinton, the then American Secretary of the State, insinuated in Zambia that China's presence in Africa was a new colonialism (Jianbo and Xiaomin 2014).

We found and present in this book a rather different reality, with China in most cases playing a constructive role in the development and growth of African countries. We identified the most prominent fallacies and facts about the involvement of China in Africa.

*Trade Deficits with China Impact Negatively on Africa*
Many authors argued that the impact by China on Africa is negative because of the large trade deficits that China has with most African countries. The case study on Kenya presented in this book illustrated that it is the overall trade balance that matters, and not the bilateral trade deficit. Kenya has no minerals to export to China and exports most of its agricultural products successfully to other international markets. Kenya further imports consumer and technical products that it needs at competitive prices from China, thus creating the deficit.

*China Has a Thirst for Africa's Natural Resources and Energy*
It is true that China is a large consumer of commodities and energy, and has a vital interest in developing Africa's natural resources, but it is not just a resource hunt. Africa's resource endowments are attractive for Chinese firms in the same way as they are attractive for the oil and mineral giants from the West, some examples being Shell, Exxon Mobil and Glencore.

Although China's attention was initially focused on a narrow subset of energy and commodity-rich countries, this has changed dramatically in the last decade as China's economic footprint on the continent grows. China is currently involved in a wide range of sectors in Africa including infrastructure, manufacturing, information technology and financial services. China's investment also reaches nearly all of the continent's countries.

Since 2003, resource-rich economies have received on average only 37% of Chinese FDI outflows into Africa. In non-resource-rich economies, for example Tanzania, Kenya and Mauritius, the Chinese have made significant investments in manufacturing and established industrial zones that produce manufactured goods for export (Jafrani 2012).

*China Is Using Its Infrastructure-for-Resources Loans (Angola-Mode Framework Agreements) Primarily to Get Easy and Cheap Access to Resources*

The well-known resources-for-infrastructure deals, or Angola-mode framework agreements as they are better known, are constantly used by authors to construct the argument that China's main motive is to develop the infrastructure of roads, rail and harbours to get access to natural resources. Another group of scholars perceive China as Africa's development partner, and argue that the benefits of obtaining infrastructure contracts accrue mostly to the developing country, and is not just about gaining access to natural resources. Most African countries are way behind in infrastructure development, which severely limits their ability to reach their development potential. Infrastructure programmes funded creatively by China have therefore reduced bottlenecks and allowed for the building of much needed roads, bridges, railways, harbours, schools and hospitals. China has further developed strong capabilities in the field of infrastructure construction, due to its own development trajectory, and therefore has the expertise and capacity to offer to African countries often lacking such a capacity.

A similar general accusation is made about China focusing its finance and aid on countries in order to buy their favour for securing benefits like oil concessions and mining rights in those countries. A group of researchers who actually tracked Chinese aid commitments reported that natural resource acquisition did not explain this pattern (Brautigam 2015). The Mauritius case study in this book also clearly demonstrates that although Mauritius has no resources to offer China, China has increased its cultural, financial and aid support over many years to the country.

*Chinese Companies Employ Mostly Their Own Nationals in Projects in Africa*

Research that was done on this phenomenon, including cases on Angola and the DRC discussed in this book, prove that this assumption is mostly a fallacy as Chinese companies employed on average between 70% and 80% of the nationals in the countries in which they operate. Sautman and Hairong (2009) surveyed 400 Chinese companies operating in over 40

African countries and found that although management and senior technical positions tended to remain Chinese, more than 80% of workers were local employees. The Chinese primarily employed Chinese managers and technical people like engineers because of the scarcity and price of people with these skills in African countries.

*China Wants to Grab Up Farmland in Africa to Deal with Its Own Food Insecurity*

Brautigam (2015) pointed out that several fake news stories about this allegation circulated in the last few years. One such widely circulated story alleged that China had purchased half the farmland in the DRC. Others claimed that the Chinese were establishing rural villages across Africa. Deborah Brautigam (2015) and her research team investigated a total of 60 stories about Chinese agricultural investments in Africa and found that out of the 15 million acres that Chinese companies allegedly acquired, evidence indicated that the actual figure was fewer than 700,000 acres. They also found that the largest existing Chinese farms are farming in rubber, sugar and sisal plantations, and that none was growing food for export to China, as alleged in the media reports.

*China's Manufactured Exports Are Crowding Out Opportunities for Africa's Economic Diversification into Manufacturing*

Many authors attribute the decline in Africa's manufacturing value added in the last two decades to the growing imports of Chinese-manufactured goods into Africa. China is a notable competitor for Africa's clothing and textile sector—a key employment-creating sector and an accepted springboard for diversification. The decline of the textile industry is also then used as a prominent example to show how cheap imports from China killed this industry. Examples of this were also found in country case studies analysed in this book, such as Kenya and Nigeria. In the case of Mauritius, the textile industry survived and prospered by shifting their competitive advantage to quality instead of cost, and by creating an enabling environment to support their export-led strategy. The export similarity index, a measure of the extent to which exports overlap, is only 7.3% between Africa (excluding South Africa) and China (Jafrani 2012) and proved that Chinese and African exports overlap only in a few industries such as clothing and footwear.

It seems that China's strategy to shift its production structure and move up the value chain is resulting in reforms of its industrial capacity, and ultimately will lead to a shift from 'Made in China' to 'Created in China' (Davies and Edinger 2013). The World Bank estimates that more than 80 million Chinese lower-end manufacturing job opportunities will in the near future move offshore to countries like those in Africa, because of rising labour and input costs in China. Chinese companies are increasingly seeking to expand their investment beyond resources towards manufacturing sectors, such as automobile assembly, electronic products, cement, steel, clothing and shoemaking. China is also playing an important role in the SEZs established in Africa to promote industrialisation and export-driven growth.

## China Has a Dubious Human Rights and Environment Legacy

Authors argued that China's close association with questionable African leaders like Robert Mugabe of Zimbabwe and Omar al-Bashir of Sudan is testimony to China's seeming indifference to human rights abuses. China does not have a clean record of human rights and environmental protection in their own country, and is often accused that its remarkable industrialisation at home has been accompanied by widespread environmental damage. The latest reports reflect a commitment by China to rectify the situation, evidenced by its strong support of the Paris Accord on climate change and anti-ivory initiative in Africa.

A summary of the fallacies and facts about the impact of China on Africa is given in Table 10.5.

**Table 10.5** Fallacies and facts about the impact of China on Africa

| Assumption | Fallacy | Fact | Comment |
|---|---|---|---|
| 1 Trade deficits with China impact negatively on Africa | √ | | It is the overall trade deficit that is important |
| 2 China has a thirst for Africa's natural resources and energy | | √ | China has a huge need for resources |
| 3 China is using its infrastructure-for-resources loans primarily to get easy and cheap access to resources | √ | | This is a by-product rather than the main aim |
| 4 Chinese companies employ mainly their own nationals in projects in Africa | √ | | This is only true for managers and technical staff who are scarce in most African countries |
| 5 China wants to 'grab' farmland in Africa to deal with its own food security concerns | √ | | Proved to be false propaganda with no substance |
| 6 China's manufactured exports are crowding out opportunities for Africa's diversification into manufacturing | √ | √ | This is true for products like textiles and footwear, but seems to be limited for other products |
| 7 China has a dubious human rights and environment legacy that impacts negatively on Africa | | √ | This is true although it seems that China is sensitive towards this and committed to change it |

Authors' own interpretation

## 10.3 Responsibility for the Future of Africa

The arguments in this book bring us time and again back to an attempt to answer the following question: How should African countries grow and develop, and who should take responsibility for this process? We believe that this responsibility should be based on the philosophy of the 'African Renaissance' discussed in Chap. 2. The African Renaissance is the concept that African people and nations shall take personal responsibility to overcome their current challenges confronting them, through an integrated process of cultural, scientific and economic renewal. We also believe that this cannot be done in isolation from the international world, and the challenge for Africa will be to make sure that each country first defines its role and responsibility in terms of the future it wants to pursue, and second, determines the role that international powers like the United States, the European Union, India and China can play in achieving this goal.

### 10.3.1 The 'African Responsibility'

Mqolomba (2016) describes 'The African Renaissance' of today as a new African identity of self-determination for Africa's destiny. The African Renaissance, therefore, is not merely a political philosophy based on political emotion, but is a call for action. According to Mqolomba (2016), the African Renaissance is about

- Social cohesion
- Democratic institutions
- Economic rebuilding and growth
- The establishment of Africa as a significant player in geopolitical affairs

We believe that most authors overemphasise the unity aspect of the African Renaissance and some argue that there will be no African Renaissance without 'African Unity'. Although we believe unity in Africa is an important goal, with pertinent benefits for all, we also believe that the growth in each African country is a unique organic process based on the historical and social context of that country, and should be guided by responsible indigenous leaders to create prosperity for all over the longer term, no matter where they reside.

Thabo Mbeki, the Past President of South Africa (Mbeki 2000), identified two moments in Africa's rebirth after years of colonialism and exploitation (Mbeki 2000). The first moment was the liberation struggle following the Second World War, which culminated in the continent's political liberation bringing independence to most African countries. The second moment was the collapse of the social community of states at the end of the Cold War in 1989, which manifested itself in campaigns for democratisation in independent African countries. According to Moletsi Mbeki (2000), the former president's brother (2000), the first and second moments served as 'dress rehearsals' for the African Renaissance, which has a far broader and deeper agenda than political liberation and democracy, namely to restore Africa as a contributor to, as well as a beneficiary of, the achievements of human civilisation (Moletsi Mbeki 2000).

For the African Renaissance to materialise, Thabo Mbeki identified preconditions and actions for this to happen, of which the following are the most prominent:

- The emergence of a new social class that will not be primarily concerned with traditional issues, such as working conditions and wages, a social class that will be involved in ownership and enterprise development.
- The emergence of a large professional and entrepreneurial middle class that is property-owning and active participants in the economy.
- The emancipation of women.
- The emergence of able political leadership that will deliver relevant education and effective healthcare services.
- The achievement of greater unity in Africa.

According to Moletsi Mbeki (2000), the African Renaissance is therefore not a policy, or a prescription, but a description of the 'coming epoch' in Africa's history, and of the emerging or organic socio-economic process that will bring this epoch about. It will therefore be the unique emerging socio-economic forces, guided by government, that will organically create the future of most African countries.

### 10.3.2 Responsibility of China in the Future Development of Africa

It is an internationally accepted principle that a nation's foreign policy will primarily serve the national interests of that country. This principle was also recently used by the current American President Donald Trump as one of his main election principles for the future. China, or any other country for that matter, will first protect and look after its own interests before judging its responsibility to the rest of the world.

We make two important observations about China in this regard. It is first in China's own interests to get access to Africa's resources and markets in order to satisfy the demands of its own economic growth. Second, it is expected that China would do this in a responsible way, without taking primary responsibility for the development of Africa. Africa, or each individual African country, is therefore responsible for its own growth and development. China's responsibility entails China acting in a responsible way towards Africa without using its power to exploit any other country. China is currently the second biggest economy in the world and its relationship with Africa is therefore unequal. The colonial experience of Africa is a good example of how such an unequal relationship can lead to exploitation if it is only to the benefit of the stronger global partner.

This stark inequality in economic and political power results in an obligation by China to make sure that their impact on African growth and development takes place in a responsible manner (Grimm 2011). One of the most outstanding features of China's African policy from the outset was the emphasis on the South–South cooperation aimed at achieving the bigger renaissance objectives of Asia and Africa (Jianbo and Xiaomin 2014). This process is not without its problems, and there are many examples of a lack of corporate social responsibility orientation, some intended, some not, as explained earlier in this chapter. The fact is that China's engagement in Africa is providing an integrated growth stimulus to African countries that would otherwise be very difficult to achieve under normal circumstances. The resources-for-infrastructure arrangement, or Angola-mode framework agreement, is a prime example of an approach that enables many African countries to directly trade resources for desperately needed infrastructure—in many cases this would have been almost impossible to achieve due to the crippling effects of corruption and the inability of many African nations to convert these resources and effectively reinvest the gains into infrastructure. China, as the largest developing nation in the world, has learnt great lessons about integrated growth, specifically on how to reduce poverty by increasing productivity—this is of great value to Africa when these lessons are shared. China's experience and competencies, specifically in the construction sector as well as its low-cost business models in comparison to the West, are of great value to Africa.

One concern often evoked in discussions by Western observers is the assumed negative Chinese effect on government standards (Grimm 2011). China does not actively promote 'good and ethical governance' as a goal in its Africa policy, but instead follows a route of non-political interference. The responsibility of China in this regard can be questioned, especially given the fact that good governance appears in the assessment of its own development successes, as well as the importance of ethical good governance in making a developmental state successful.

## 10.4 Concluding Remarks

Africa is not a country but a continent with 52 different countries, each with a unique cultural and historical context, resource and asset base, as well as economic and welfare structures. Achieving the goals of an African Renaissance, therefore, needs be specifically defined in terms of the individual context of the country, rather than in generic terms for the continent. In this sense, the African Renaissance for a diversified country such as South Africa, with its own particular cultural and historical history, will have a different meaning than, for example, a transitional economy such as Cameroon. Although unity and cooperation between nations in Africa are important for success, they all represent different 'trees of organic growth', and will experience organic growth based on their individual context and efforts.

China is overall contributing to the development and organic growth of African countries with which they actively engage, but sometimes finds it difficult to balance its direct engagements with the indirect effects and consequences on those countries. Chinese and African governments have a combined responsibility to ensure that the situation will be a 'win-win' and contribute to the African country in terms of what is needed most in its specific stage of organic growth. According to Grimm (2011), it sometimes remains unclear how the shares of gains of these 'win-win' situations are distributed—African countries will have to define and advocate their own interests in this regard. African policymakers have undoubtedly the

prime responsibility to make use of opportunities and to pre-empt challenges in dealing with global powers like China.
Now is the time for the Baobab to flourish and grow.

## REFERENCES

Brautigam, D. 4 December 2015. 5 Myths About Chinese Investment in Africa. Foreign Policy. [Online]. Available from: http://foreignpolicy.com/2015/12/04/5-myths-about-chinese-investment-in-africa/ (accessed: 8 June 2017).

Chang, H. 2003. Globalisation, Economic Development and the Role of the State. London: Zed Books Ltd. In Mabasa, K. and Mqolomba, Z. 2016. 'Revisiting China's Development State: Lessons for Africa', *Strategic Review for Southern Africa*, 38 (1): 69–84.

Davies, M. and Edinger, H. 2013. Structural Transformation: Is China Bad for Africa's Industrialisation? Deloitte: Bridges Africa, 2 (6).

Grimm, S. 2011. China as Africa's Ambiguous Ally—Why China Has a Responsibility for Africa's Development. Centre for Chinese Studies. University of Stellenbosch. Accessed from: https://scholar.sun.ac.za/handle/10019.1/21177 (accessed: 4 June 2017).

Gumede, W. 2009. Delivering the Democratic Development State in South Africa. Development Bank of Southern Africa. Development Planning Working Paper Series 9. In Mabasa, K. and Mqolomba, Z. 2016. 'Revisiting China's Development State: Lessons for Africa', *Strategic Review for Southern Africa*, 38 (1): 69–84.

Ianchovichina, E. and Lundstrom, S. 2009. What Is Inclusive Growth? Note Prepared for the Diagnostic Facility for Shared Growth. © World Bank. [Online]. Available from: http://siteresources.worldbank.org/INTDEBTDEPT/Resources/468980-1218567884549/WhatIsInclusiveGrowth20081230.pdf (accessed: 3 June 2017). License: Creative Commons Attribution License (CC BY 3.0 IGO). (http://creativecommons.org/licenses/by/3.0/igo/).

Jafrani, N. 9 February 2012. China's Growing Role in Africa: Myths and Facts. Carnegie Endowment for International Peace. [Online]. Available from: http://carnegieendowment.org/2012/02/09/china-s-growing-role-in-africa-myths-and-facts-pub-47140 (accessed: 7 June 2017).

Jianbo, L. and Xiaomin, Z. 2014. China in Africa: Devil or Angel? [Online]. Available from: http://www.focac.org/eng/xsjl/xzzs/t1131873.htm (accessed: 10 June 2017).

Mabasa, K. and Mqolomba, Z. 2016. 'Revisiting China's Development State: Lessons for Africa'. *Strategic Review for Southern Africa*, 38 (1): 69–84.

Maru, M. 7 March 2016. Lessons for Africa from the Economic Development of China and India. [Online]. Available from: http://hornaffairs.com/2016/03/07/lessons-africa-development-china-india/ (accessed: 11 June 2017).

Mbeki, M. 2000. Issues in South African Foreign Policy. The African Renaissance. Souls. [Online]. Available from: http://www.tandfonline.com/doi/abs/10.1080/10999940009362215 (accessed: 6 June 2017).

Mqolomba, Z. 16 February 2016. A Return to the African Renaissance. Mail and Guardian Thought Leader. [Online]. Available from: http://thoughtleader.co.za/mandelarhodesscholars/2016/02/16/a-return-to-the-african-renaissance/ (accessed: 5 June 2017).

Sautman, B. and Hairong, Y. September 2009. 2009 African Perspectives on China-Africa Links. The China Quarterly No 199, China and Africa: Emerging Patterns in Globalisation and Development.

World Bank. 2015. Global Economic Prospects. The Global Political Economy in Transition. © World Bank. [Online]. Available from: https://openknowledge.worldbank.org/handle/10986/21999 (accessed: 8 June 2017). License: Creative Commons Attribution License (CC BY 3.0 IGO). (http://creativecommons.org/licenses/by/3.0/igo/).

Wright, K. 2 May 2017. Starting with People: A Human Economy Approach to Inclusive Growth in Africa. Oxfam Briefing Paper. [Online]. Available from: http://www.oxfam.org.za/wp-content/uploads/2016/06/bp-inclusive-growth-africa-020517-en.pdf (accessed: 2 June 2017).

# Index

**NUMBERS AND SYMBOLS**
13th Five-Year Plan for Economic and Social Development of the People's Republic of China, 85
20+20 cooperation programme, 145

**A**
Abuses, 117
Academic institutions, 185
Accountability, 114
Action plan, 9
Action Plan for the Accelerated Industrial Development of Africa, 44
Addis Ababa Light Rail Transit (AA-LRT), 93
Africa Infrastructure Development Index (AIDI), 39
African Development Bank (AfDB), 39, 147, 182, 228, 233
African Development Bank Group, 8
African Economic Outlook, 141
African Economic Outlook Report, 42
African Gender Equality Index, 200
African Growth and Opportunity Act (AGOA), 59, 65, 100
African Human Resource Development Fund, 144
African Peace and Security Architecture, 203
African renaissance, 158, 217, 263–282
African Tree of Organic Growth, 22, 36, 51, 78, 108, 129, 137, 138, 140, 167, 187, 191, 213, 217, 231–232, 266
African Union (AU), 10, 17, 41, 116, 121, 122, 141, 203, 210
African Union 2063, 12
African Union Disease Control Centre, 202
African Union's Agenda, 45
African Union's Agenda 2063, 9, 10
African unity, 11
Africa's renaissance, 11, 193
Agri-business, 141, 184, 187

Agricultural, 16, 48, 50, 63, 67, 73, 85, 115, 142, 147, 171, 183, 225, 226, 240, 242, 252
  activities, 200
  and commodity exports, 55
  development, 79, 82, 168
  diversification, 55
  exports, 71, 115
  investments, 276
  land, 243
  policies, 126, 127
  policy, 126
  potential, 21
  processing, 48
  production, 169, 172, 177, 232, 235
  productivity, 228
  products, 218, 222, 223, 274
  reforms, 43
  sector, 42, 50, 52, 74, 126, 127, 187, 197, 229, 272
  technologies, 185
  transformation, 26, 39, 42
Agriculture, 26, 36, 38–39, 42, 50, 57, 62–64, 89, 100, 141, 145, 151, 154, 159, 167, 169, 202, 219, 221, 224, 227, 255, 256, 267
Agriculture and resource sectors, 32
Agro-industry, 43
Agro-processing, 41, 50, 267
Aid, 160, 246, 255, 271
  dependency, 30
  programme, 7
  support, 275
  workers, 203
Air and water, 168
Airport, 67, 72, 83, 85, 88, 153, 184, 240, 248, 258
Algeria, 3, 7, 31, 40, 41, 84, 147–150, 160, 192
American, 154, 155, 203

Amnesty International, 211
Angola, 3, 20, 21, 31, 48, 88, 90, 152–157, 161, 275
Angola-mode, 86, 93, 108, 133, 148, 209, 271, 275, 280
Asia, 37
Asia Pacific, 4
Asset, 22–28, 36, 46, 222, 268
  structures and resources, 46
Asset base, 281
Autocratic leadership, 115

B
Balance of payments, 39, 68
Bandung Conference, 6
Banking, 32, 64
Barriers, 73, 82, 129
Barriers to production, 60
Belgium, 53
Belt and road initiative, 87
Beneficiation, 8, 32, 38, 41
Benin, 60, 128
Bilateral, 270
  agreements, 14, 65
  cooperation, 159, 241
  debt, 224
  economic, 148
  efforts, 121
  mediation, 122
  trade, 4, 16, 246, 274
Bilharzia, 184
Botswana, 21, 38, 113, 132, 204
Bottleneck, 108, 272, 275
Bottlenecks in infrastructural, 86
Brazil, 26, 155
British, 222
Broad-based economic growth and diversification, 193
Bureaucracy, 129, 133
Bureaucratic, 70, 156
Burkina Faso, 128, 139

# INDEX

Burundi, 52, 57, 111, 122, 130, 139
Business efficiently, 132
Business environment, 33, 226, 243
Business services, 48

## C
Cameroon, 3, 32, 60, 88, 199, 217–260, 266, 271, 281
Canadian, 92
Cancer and cardiovascular disease, 128
Capabilities, 23, 45, 46, 142, 158, 275
Capacity, 255, 257
Capacity building, 8, 56, 121, 141, 145
Capital, 33, 36, 39, 191, 192, 225–231, 268
Capital asset, 272
Central African Economic and Monetary Community (CEMAC), 223
Central African Republic, 139, 204, 218
Central bank, 26
Chad, 31, 60, 218
Cheap imports, 55
Children, 11, 210
China, 1–18, 26, 37, 53, 65, 248
China Africa Development Fund, 16
China Africa Joint Business Council, 8
China Africa Products Exhibition Centre, 8
China–Africa Research and Exchange Programme, The, 145
China–Africa Think Tank Forum, 145
China Chamber of Commerce for Minerals, Metals, and Chemical Importers and Exporters, 178
China Development bank, 87
China financing, 128
China is a significant investor, 100
China is providing critical funding, 71–72
China is still in mining, 48
China on Growth and Diversification, 48–49
China's African policy, 280
China's African Policy 2016, 45
China's commitment to peaceful development, 122
China's development path and growth experience, 43
China's direct investment in Africa, 48
China's economic and social conditions, 43
China's environmental policies, 180
China's first overseas military outpost, 97
China's foreign policy towards Africa, 5
China's GDP, 41
China's Green Credit Policy, 178
China's investment in the manufacturing sector, 48
China's investments, 179–180
China's large investment, 86
China's major import source, 41
China's Ministry of Foreign Affairs, 209
China's model, 39
China's non-interference policy, 14, 17, 122
China's Social Harmony Policy, 212
China's Two Centenary Goals, 9
China successfully introduced SEZs, 44–45
Chinese aid, 13–15, 241, 255
Chinese-built, 94
Chinese business and entrepreneurial, 270
Chinese businesses and financial institutions, 89
Chinese businesses do localise their workforce, 55

Chinese Communist Party, 124, 146
Chinese companies, 67, 68, 96, 148, 150, 275
Chinese construction, 182
Chinese Cultural Research Centre, 69
Chinese culture, 69
Chinese culture and language, 160
Chinese-driven projects, 108
Chinese employees, 154, 162
Chinese enterprises, 48, 163, 176
Chinese entrepreneurs, 270
Chinese firms, 73, 90
Chinese foreign direct investment, 259
Chinese foreign policy, 11
Chinese funds and investment, 70
Chinese government, 43
Chinese Government's Five-Year Plan, 177
Chinese investment, 69, 92, 146, 151, 152, 162, 246
Chinese language and Chinese culture, 145
Chinese language institutes, 4
Chinese migrants, 148
Chinese mining companies, 209
Chinese multinational corporations, 73
Chinese nationals, 72
Chinese products imported, 151
Chinese researchers, 185
Chinese skills and technological transfer, 187
Chinese society, 271
Chinese state funding, 270
Chinese state organs, 270
Chinese teachers, 144
Chinese tourism, 221
Chinese workers, 162, 207
Civil society, 185
Civil wars, 17, 152, 161
Climate change, 81, 169–172, 177, 187, 197, 202, 256

Colonial, 20, 113, 114, 117, 126, 217, 266
Colonialism, 148, 279
Colonialist, 186, 274
Colonisation, 20, 192
Colonise, 236
Colonists, 1–18
Colony, 219
Communal, 197
Communications, 50, 54
Community, 124, 179, 187, 192, 204, 209–212
 engagement, 212–214
 members, 203
 participation, 79
 self-help, 196
Comparative advantage, 37, 42, 46, 59, 64, 74, 141, 159, 226, 267, 269
Comparative advantage sectors, 267
Competencies, 156
Competencies required, 149
Competition, 55, 155, 254, 259, 271
 advantage, 46, 142, 248, 254, 276
 countries, 74
 exchange, 247
 industries, 60
 markets, 130
 trade advantage, 257
Competitiveness, 30, 97, 244, 248, 256
Complementary development, 5–10
Conditional, 13
Conditions, 13
Conflict, 17, 30, 38, 120, 122, 130, 139, 140, 198, 207
 areas, 213
 situations, 121
 zones, 197, 198
Confucian culture, 271
Confucius Institute, 69, 145, 159, 226, 230

Confucius Institutes and Cultural Centres, 145
Congo, 31
Constraints, 77, 161
Construction, 41, 50, 63, 65, 108, 153, 155, 157, 202, 227, 228, 240, 244, 248, 275
  projects, 162
  sector, 147, 281
Consumer goods, 153
Consumer growth, 23
Consumer industries, 41
Context of Growth, 269
Cooperation, 8
Cooperative engagement, 10
Core competencies, 78
Core institutions, 124
Core resources, 22–28, 222
Corporate citizenship, 212, 274
Corporate Social Investment (CSI), 211
Corporate Social Responsibility (CSR), 280
Corrupt, 114, 122, 231
  governance, 260
  governments, 14, 152
Corruption, 13, 14, 21, 38, 48, 55, 60, 62, 64, 73, 111, 117, 130, 132–134, 139, 193, 195, 196, 203, 204, 211, 224, 226–228, 233, 234, 238, 255, 257, 280
Corruption Perception Index, 56, 132, 234
Corrupt leadership, 17
Cost of doing business, 55
Côte d'Ivoire, 87
Country assets, 222
Create jobs, 74
Creation of wealth, 29
Crime, 196, 198
Crime levels, 198
Critical assets, 24–25, 79

Cuba, 113
Cultural, 8, 11, 21, 28, 62, 68, 69, 140, 213, 217, 218, 223, 225, 227, 232, 236, 238, 240, 243, 245, 247, 254–255, 265, 271, 273, 275, 281
  capital, 192
  cooperation, 10
  differences, 245
  diversity, 236
  heritages, 28
  identity, 192
  investment, 230
  practices, 200
  renewal, 278
  and social structure, 27–28
  ties, 259
  wealth, 191, 231, 232, 255, 256
Cultural Revolution, 7
Curve, 180
Cyber economy, 85
Cyber security, 203

D
Dam, 77, 87, 183, 221, 223, 232, 235
Debt, 128, 225
  burden, 108, 183, 187
  cancellation, 8, 128
  financing and debt cancellation, 16
  levels, 4
  reduction, 223, 225
  relief, 128, 226, 235
  repayment, 128
Deforestation, 171, 172, 177, 183, 187, 197, 233, 255
Democracy, 11, 13, 21, 113–122, 195, 219, 243, 254
Democratic, 52, 236, 247
  institutions, 33, 278
  processes, 117

Democratic Republic of Congo
    (DRC), 16, 17, 32, 52, 111, 140,
    152–157, 161, 167, 172, 182,
    201, 207, 211, 266, 275, 276
Democratisation, 279
Dependence, 63, 219, 253
Dependence on a few export
    commodities, 36
Dependent, 226, 228
Desertification, 171, 172, 177, 197,
    233
Development, 35–74, 84, 122, 158
    assistance, 8
    context, 265–266
    objectives, 172
    policy, 128, 134
    states, 265
Developmental state, 265
Dictatorships, 21, 113–122
Different phases of growth and
    development, 13–14
Diplomacy efforts, 121
Diplomatic, 7, 147, 209, 213, 259
    arrangements, 246
    corporation, 220
    interventions, 210
    relations, 65, 238
    relationship, 220
Direct investment, 187
Discrimination, 28, 231, 233, 266
Discriminatory legislation, 200
Disease, 183, 199, 202, 227
Disease control, 168
Disruptive solutions, 138
Distribution network, 78
Distribution of capital, 29
Diverse, 64
Diversification, 23, 31, 32, 35–74, 77,
    141, 152, 160, 226, 228–229,
    234, 235, 242, 246, 249–252,
    257, 267, 268, 272, 273,
    276–277

of the economy, 64
strategy, 251
Diversified, 31, 42, 46, 48, 50, 74,
    219, 228, 234, 243, 244, 260,
    268
    country, 281
    economies, 31, 48, 225
    production, 42
    products, 251
Diversify, 64, 67–69, 74, 86, 238
Diversifying, 30
Diversity, 28, 192, 247, 266
Djibouti, 97, 210
Domestic, 258
    African and international markets,
        43
    consumption, 31
    economy, 46
    and global market, 46
    industries, 60
    market, 30, 36, 46, 55, 59, 69, 71,
        74, 239
    policy, 271
Donation, 210, 242
Driver of growth, 42
Drought, 186, 195, 197, 207, 213,
    249
    relief, 210
Drought-affected, 204
Drought-hit, 204

E
Ebola, 127, 201–207, 213
Ebola Virus Disease, 201
Economic, 63, 217, 255
    cooperation, 9
    development, 17, 96, 172, 178,
        183, 260
    diversification, 21, 30, 31, 42, 47,
        108, 160, 163, 244, 264
    fundamentals, 33

investment, 213
opportunities, 191, 200
participation, 71
prosperity, 143
reform programmes, 234
reforms, 31
relations, 147
renewal, 278
sectors, 45
and social development, 129
and social infrastructure, 71
transformation, 24, 31, 41–46, 71, 138, 158
transformation and growth, 39
wealth, 33, 78, 231, 234–235, 255, 259
Economic Community of West African States (ECOWAS), 116
Economic growth, 16, 29, 35–74, 77, 78, 84, 85, 97, 108, 111, 126, 127, 129, 153, 167, 168, 187, 199, 224, 226, 228–229, 235, 244, 246, 249–252, 256, 257, 265, 268, 269
and development, 117
and diversification, 36, 57
sector, 197
Ecosystem, 19
Educated, 92, 137–163, 267
Education, 24, 30, 31, 33, 46, 65, 71, 79, 104, 115, 127, 128, 130, 137, 138, 140, 150, 152, 153, 156, 158, 159, 161, 187, 191–193, 197, 202, 209, 221–223, 225, 226, 229–230, 240, 246, 247, 252, 254–257, 263, 264, 268, 269, 273, 279
programmes, 202
and skills, 31, 36, 71
system, 252
Educational, 64, 70, 252, 258

cooperation, 241
development, 159
facilities, 196
sector, 156
system, 72, 139, 140, 161, 163, 222
Effective governance, 111, 113
Effective governance and leadership, 134
Efficiencies of scale, 41, 42, 127
Efficiency, 141
Efficiency of public spending, 132
Efforts in Africa, 120–122
Egypt, 3, 20, 26, 31, 40, 41, 45, 48, 147, 150–152, 192
Egyptian government, 160
Electrical, 221
Electricity, 25, 39, 78, 161, 187, 198, 209, 213, 228, 234, 256
Electricity generating, 225
Employ, 68, 71, 149
Employability, 252, 257
Employed, 161, 226, 275
Employer, 71
Employing local, 68
Employment, 42, 44, 46, 60, 67–69, 73, 74, 79, 104, 126, 137–140, 142, 143, 151, 152, 154, 155, 157, 158, 160–162, 195, 196, 207, 209, 231, 247, 255, 257, 264, 267, 270
creation, 39, 147–152
growth, 65
opportunities, 254
Employs, 171
Enable, 126, 129, 280
Enable people, 192
Enabler, 77–108, 273
of development, 48
of economic development and diversification, 72
Enabling, 268

Enabling environment, 47, 78, 158, 162, 226, 276
Energy, 24, 46, 151, 167, 169, 202, 248, 249, 259, 264, 274–275, 277
  availability, 232
  conservation, 178
  generation, 53
  infrastructure, 246
  needs, 74
  resources, 147
Engineering, 159
Engineering skills, 187
Engineers, 155, 157, 158, 161
England, 222
Entrepreneurial, 26, 74
Entrepreneurial middle class, 279
Entrepreneurs, 270
Entrepreneurship, 27, 33, 233, 248
Environment, 145, 167, 178, 209, 231, 255, 256, 277
Environmental, 8, 63, 94, 176–179, 185, 233, 270
  concerns, 17, 251
  damage, 184
  externalities, 180
  impact, 179–180, 187
  issues, 212
  management, 187
  policies, 180
  protection, 96, 167, 178–180, 183, 187, 202, 277
  protection and tackling climate change, 10
  requirements, 178
  standards, 254
  sustainability, 167, 168, 171, 178, 180, 187
  threats, 183
Environmentally friendly, 177
Environmentally sensitive, 179
Equality, 196, 200

Equal opportunities, 264
Equatorial Guinea, 31, 117, 172, 218
Eritrea, 97
Ethical conduct, 72
Ethical governance, 281
Ethical government, 111, 246
Ethiopia, 20, 21, 32, 43, 45, 48, 49, 52, 83, 86–89, 92–97, 128, 139, 141, 179, 204, 207, 269
Ethiopia-Djibouti, 90
Ethiopians, 96
Ethnic, 21, 222, 231, 243, 245, 248, 260
  conflict, 111
  diversity, 244
  groups, 218, 223, 247
Ethnical, 28
Ethnically diverse, 266
Ethnicity, 254
Ethnic minorities, 63
Ethnic variety, 225, 232
Europe, 37, 65, 71, 72, 82, 142
European, 4, 154, 155, 203
European Investment Bank, 182
European Parliament Research Service (EPRS), 35
European Union (EU), 24, 53, 65, 229, 253, 278
Exchange rate policy, 247
Exim bank, 57, 87, 93, 133, 178, 209, 221, 227
EXIM Bank of China, 150
Export, 32, 41, 44, 59, 68, 147, 151, 171, 172, 222, 226–228, 233, 243, 244, 253, 272
  capacity, 232, 235
  commodities, 27
  competition, 217
  competitiveness, 42
  costs, 40
  earnings, 249
  growth, 187

opportunities, 65
products, 68, 268
sector, 244, 259
Export-driven growth, 246, 277
Exporter, 63, 71
Export-led growth, 44, 250, 253
　strategy, 246, 247, 276
Export similarity index, 276


**F**
Facilitating environment for business, 77
Facilitators, 111
Famine, 197, 205, 210, 213
Famine relief, 125
Favourable loans, 8
Film industry, 64
Finance, 48, 108, 115, 197
Financial aid, 232
Financial capital, 71, 78, 234–235, 255, 258, 259
Financial policies, 47
Financial services, 40, 50, 59, 65
Financing, 126
Fiscal and monetary policies, 128, 129
Fiscal policy, 128, 244, 258
Five Principles of Mutual Coexistence, 5, 6
Five Principles of Peaceful Coexistence, 14, 122
FOCAC Action Plan, 144
FOCAC Johannesburg Action Plan (2016–2018), 10–19, 178
FOCAC Ministerial Conference, 253, 260
Food, 167–169, 196
　imports, 63
　insecure, 186
　insecurity, 126, 172, 177, 179, 185–187, 197, 205, 263, 276
　production, 172
　provision, 209
　security, 185, 187, 197, 202, 213
Foreign aid, 21, 270
Foreign debts, 152
Foreign direct investment (FDI), 24, 25, 44, 48, 53, 60, 65, 73, 74, 78, 126, 150, 160, 178, 180, 223, 229, 242, 250, 255, 258
Foreign exchange earnings, 171
Foreign investment, 44, 258
Foreign policy, 121, 122, 280
Formal, 123
　and informal institutions, 111, 123
　institutional, 124
　institutions, 134
　sector employment, 143
　sectors, 27
Forum on China–Africa Cooperation (FOCAC), 5, 7, 128, 218, 221
Forum on China–Africa Cooperation 6th Ministerial Conference, 89
Forum on China–Africa Cooperation (FOCAC) Summit in Johannesburg in 2015, 45
Forum on China–Africa Cooperation's (FOCAC) Johannesburg Action Plan, 89, 201
Forum on China–African Cooperation (FOCAC) Ministerial Conferences, 270
France, 40, 121, 251, 253, 258
Freedom, 193
Free trade area, 41
French, 222, 228, 230


**G**
G20, 16
Gabon, 31, 88, 172, 218
Gambia, The, 114–120
Gambian, 200
Gender disparity, 229

Gender equality, 196, 199
Gender gap, 259
Gender inequality, 200
Genocide, 25
Geographic, 50
Geographical location, 140
Geo-political, 278
Geo-political importance, 24–25
Germany, 84
Ghana, 32, 43, 114–120, 131, 139, 179, 204, 271
Global climate change, 169–171
Global community, 114
Global competitiveness, 127
Global Fund, 16
Global Information and Communications Technology (ICT) Network Readiness Index, 249
Globalisation, 10, 28, 48
Globally competitive, 44
Globally more competitive, 32
Global markets, 108
Global peace and stability, 122
Global power, 122
Good governance, 134
Govern, 77
Governance, 11, 30, 33, 46, 47, 60, 123, 130, 183, 192, 204, 225–227, 231, 234, 243, 245–248, 257, 268, 269
   efficiency, 125
   structures, 48
Government, 46, 72, 111–134, 158, 186, 195, 213, 264, 266
   capabilities, 70
   effectiveness, 111
   efficiency, 72
   inefficiencies, 73, 130
   institutions, 64
   leadership, 193
   policies, 226, 265
   revenue, 97, 126
Governmental, 71
*Government Policies Fail: Corruption*, 132–134
Grand Inga Dam, 182
Grants, 8
Green growth, 10, 167–187
Green technology, 187
Gross domestic product (GDP), 63, 64, 224
   annual growth rate, 50
   growth, 100, 124, 125, 143, 238
   per capita, 33, 193, 259
Gross National Income per capita, 198
Growth and development, 17, 121, 124, 222–235, 260, 263
Growth channels, 29–33, 225–230, 245–255, 268
Growth constraints, 14
Growth drivers, 41–46
Growth process, 31
Growth sectors, 36–41, 137
Guinea, 139, 200–207
Guinea Equatorial, 141

**H**
Happiness, 194
Harbour, 71, 85
Health, 24, 33, 70, 115, 127, 128, 168, 191–193, 197, 202, 205, 223, 230, 247, 254–256, 258, 263
Health and welfare, 16, 104
Health care, 71, 79, 104, 126–128, 145, 198, 209, 210, 264, 268, 279
   facilities, 130
   services, 201
   systems, 152, 161
Health services, 130
Health systems and policies, 202

Heavily Indebted Poor Countries (HIPC) initiative, 224, 225
Higher education, 159
Higher wages, 143
HIV, 16
HIV levels, 115
HIV/AIDS, 117, 127
Hospitals, 128
Household economy, 200
Household rights, 200
Housing, 130, 148, 150, 209, 248, 255, 256, 258
Human capability, 199–200
Human capital, 64, 72, 127, 233, 255, 257
Human capital development, 44, 52, 156
Human development, 192, 193, 198, 200
Human Development Index, 192, 193, 263
Human economy, 267
Human growth and development, 192
Humanitarian, 10
  crises, 193
  efforts, 213
  support, 210
Humanity, 29
Human progress, 30
Human resource development, 202
Human resources, 74, 163, 252
Human rights, 11, 15, 17, 114, 117, 179, 191, 196, 198–200, 214, 277
  abuses, 115, 211
  violations, 14
Human trafficking, 203
Hydroelectric, 220
  dams, 182
  power, 21, 181
Hydropower, 87

## I

Ibrahim Index for African Governance, 257
Illegal trade, 203
Immigration, 10, 203
Import, 149, 276
Importation of labour, 17
import duties, 65
imported, 55
importer, 68, 71, 253
importing, 55
import of sub-standard Chinese products, 68
Import substitution, 27, 64
Inadequate governance, 14
Inclusive, 127, 247
  development, 246
  economic growth, 265
  growth, 137, 141, 225, 227, 232, 263–265
  growth and development, 143
  sustainable growth, 152
Income distribution, 42
Independent judiciary, 26
Index of Economic Freedom, 259
India, 26, 37, 71, 72, 248, 251, 253, 258, 278
Industrial, 228, 248
  capacity, 276
  development, 86
  development policies, 45
  diversification, 43–45
  growth, 26
  and other policies, 74
  parks, 45
  policies, 44, 46, 73, 127
  production, 40
  sector, 21
  strategies, 46, 272
  vision, 46–47
Industrialisation, 27, 44–47, 64, 108, 127, 182, 266, 277

Industrialise, 44, 86
Industrialised, 236
industrialised middle-income, 52
Industry, 69, 264
Ineffective, 14
Inefficiency, 38, 81, 193, 227, 234
Inefficient, 228, 230
Inequality, 5, 35, 48, 139, 140, 143, 192, 195, 197, 199, 223, 225, 232, 238, 256, 263–265, 267, 268, 272
Inequity, 131, 235
Infant indigenous industries, 71, 74
Infant industries, 59
Informal, 123
    employment, 161
    institutions, 124, 134
    sector, 27, 33, 139, 267
Information, 40
Information and communication, 89
Information and Communication Technology (ICT), 2, 39, 81–82, 151, 209, 257
    sector, 251
Information communication infrastructure, 249
Information flow, 28
Information technology, 50, 159, 248, 258, 274
Infrastructural development, 14, 16, 83
Infrastructural investment, 85, 91, 162
Infrastructural projects, 126, 133, 134
Infrastructure, 8, 21, 24, 25, 31, 36, 39–41, 44, 46, 49, 55, 57, 64, 65, 67, 71, 74, 77–108, 115, 126, 127, 143, 144, 150, 153, 156, 159–161, 180, 183, 193, 195, 196, 202, 209, 213, 223–228, 232, 234, 235, 246, 248–249, 255, 260, 264, 268, 269, 274, 275, 280
    construction, 157
    development, 148, 272, 273
    investment, 196, 234
    and market development, 31
    is properly maintained and managed, 78
    projects, 53, 93, 220, 248, 258
    and regulatory systems, 32
Innovation, 31, 33, 137, 259, 264, 267
Insecurity, 198, 225
Insecurity and fear, 196
Institutional, 43, 71, 143
    arrangements, 111
    capacity, 235
    capital, 231, 233–234, 255, 257–258
    framework, 123, 238, 257
    process, 31
    reforms, 272, 273
    support, 246
Institutions, 64, 111–134, 156, 183, 231, 232, 247, 266
Intangible capital, 33
Integrated development, 264
Integrated growth, 222
Integrated growth and development, 268
Integrated growth stimulus, 280
Integrated process, 278
Interest-free loan, 16, 221, 255, 270
Intergovernmental Panel on Climate Change (IPCC), 170
Intermodal transport, 83
International aid agencies, 104
International assistance, 203
International business, 252
International communities Malaria, 210
International community, 197, 274
International cooperation, 10, 203
International efforts, 120
International Labour Office (ILO), 137

International Labour Organisation (ILO), 68
International markets, 24, 46, 97
International Monetary Fund (IMF), 16, 142, 224, 234, 272
International Organization for Migration, 207
International partnerships, 78
International trade, 25, 30, 141, 253
Intra-African trade, 32, 41
Intra-regional, 41
Invest, 132
Invested, 220
Investment, 13–15, 67, 71, 72, 90, 139, 147, 149, 151, 154, 162, 186, 207, 226, 243, 247, 253, 267, 270, 271
  climate, 258
  destination, 41, 228
  partner, 207
  policy, 247–248
  in science and technology, 163

**J**
Japan, 60, 230
Japanese, 203
Jobs, 108, 156
  creation, 56, 94, 108, 125, 126, 152, 160, 162
  market, 104
  opportunities, 156
Judicial system, 124
Judiciary, 10, 198, 203
Justice system, 132

**K**
Kenya, 3, 27, 32, 41, 43, 45, 48–60, 65, 71, 72, 74, 83, 87, 88, 90, 97, 139, 146, 179, 184, 204, 207, 267, 276

Kenyan, 70–74
Kenya Vision 2030, 51
Knowledge, 30, 40, 45, 57, 78, 142, 145, 156, 187, 252
  creation, 150
  economy, 250
  sharing, 56
Knowledge-based, 141
Knowledge-based economy, 137
Kuznets, 180

**L**
Labour, 86, 108, 126
  conditions and ill-treatment, 211
  force, 40
  market, 158
  needs, 161
  policies, 227
  regulations, 228
Labour from China, 68
Lack of competition, 82
Lake Victoria, 167
Land acquisition, 16
Land locked, 24, 40, 71, 97, 102
Land ownership, 39, 124, 197
Land reform, 115, 126, 197
Language, 21, 28, 60, 146, 226, 230, 236, 240
Language barrier, 55, 155
Latin Americans, 4
Law, 123, 257
  enforcement, 10, 121, 203
  and institutions, 200
  and order, 26, 114, 191, 196, 198
Leaders, 200
Leadership role, 163
League of Nations, 222
Leather industry, 179
Leather products, 41
Legal framework, 118
Legal institutions, 196

Legal practices, 222
Legal systems, 123
Legislation, 198, 234
Lesbian, gay, bisexual, transgender and intersexed (LGBTI), 200
Lesotho, 97–108, 140
Liberia, 88, 201–207
Liberty and freedom, 192
Libya, 31, 147, 192, 200
Life expectancy, 35, 192, 193, 198, 230, 254, 256
Literacy, 70, 156, 254
Literacy rate, 31, 35, 50, 52, 72, 229
Living conditions, 131
Living standards, 195, 196
Loan assistance, 242
Loans, 88, 90, 232, 270
Local economy, 259
Local employees, 157, 276
Local employment, 152–157, 160–162
Local fishing industry, 184
Local government, 185
Localisation, 155, 157, 162
Local labour, 108, 126
Local market, 69
Local suppliers, 155
Local workers, 155, 156, 161
Location, 24–25, 49, 243
Location and geopolitical, 223
Logistics, 141, 186
Low interest loan, 16, 67, 255, 270
Low productivity, 63
Low-skilled workers, 154
Low technology, 63

**M**
Machinery and equipment, 68
Macro-economic, 47, 115, 243, 272
  instability, 64
  performance, 26
  policies, 247
  stability, 244
Madagascar, 39, 88, 128, 211
Maintained, 108
Maintenance, 96, 155
Maintenance and management, 79, 126
Malaria, 127, 171, 184, 202, 204, 205, 220, 227, 230
Malawi, 3, 84, 88, 144, 171, 173, 200
Mali, 20, 32, 48, 128, 200, 201, 204
Malnourishment, 127
Malnutrition, 35, 127
Manage and maintain, 86
Management, 68, 157
Managers, 155, 276
Manufactured, 147
Manufactured exports, 253
Manufactured-led growth, 44
Manufacturers, 56, 254
Manufacturing, 23, 40–42, 44, 48, 50, 54, 63, 64, 69, 141, 184, 226, 228, 235, 243, 245, 251, 252, 257, 272–274, 276–277
  capacity, 270
  investment, 74
  machinery and equipment, 68
  sector, 55, 92, 244, 277
Market, 196, 197, 253–254, 264, 266, 268–270, 280
  activity, 265
  expansion, 78
  institutions, 130
  size, 44
  system, 129
Market-driven, 264
Maternal mortality, 130
Mauritania, 128
Mauritian, 266
Mauritius, 44, 45, 192, 200, 217–260, 271, 275, 276
Micro and small enterprises, 27
Microfinance, 197

Middle class, 40, 41
Middle-class population, 186
Middle Eastern, 4
Middle-income, 44
Migrant, 209
Migration, 8, 186, 195
Military support, 147
Millennium Development Goals (MDGs), 11, 39, 81
Mineral resources, 259
Minerals, 62, 147, 153, 211, 218, 223
Mining, 63, 114, 115, 141, 157, 179, 225
  industry, 229
  operations, 79, 209–212
  rights, 275
Minority ethnic groups, 199
Mobile operators, 82
Modernising farming, 197
Mombasa–Nairobi corridor, 52
Monetary policy, 128
Morocco, 7, 31, 40, 41, 48, 147, 204
Mortality, 177
Mozambique, 3, 7, 20, 32, 88, 139, 140, 167, 172, 186
Multiplier, 269
  effect, 42, 268
  process, 264, 268

**N**
Namibia, 7, 20, 88, 113, 200, 204
Natural, 23–24
  beauty, 21
  capital, 78, 233, 255–257
  disasters, 186
  and ecological capital, 256
  environment, 256
  resource, 8, 13, 20, 33, 37, 42, 49, 52, 57, 62–64, 78, 187, 218, 222, 223, 239, 243, 267, 274–275, 277

Netherlands, 53
New jobs, 137
New Partnership for African Development (NEPAD), 17, 141, 178
Niger, 60, 128, 139
Nigeria, 3, 20, 21, 26, 27, 31, 38, 41, 45, 48, 61–65, 69–71, 74, 88–90, 117, 139, 200, 201, 218, 229, 234, 264, 268, 276
Nigeria Industrial Revolution Plan, 64
Nigerian, 68, 70–74
Non-governmental organisations (NGOs), 26
Non-interference, 5, 114, 122, 226
Non-interference policy, 114, 121–123
Non-political interference, 281
Non-sustainable economic structures, 26
Norway, 84
Numeracy, 156, 230

**O**
Ocean piracy, 203
Oil, 16, 21, 63, 68, 148, 151, 225, 226, 229, 275
  exporter, 31–32, 268
  and gas, 57, 63, 65, 71, 218, 222, 223
  and gas exporters, 31, 48
  industry, 229
  and mineral extraction, 36
  and mining resources, 219
  producers, 228
  production, 63, 64, 231
  revenue, 74
Oil-exporting, 217
One Belt One Road, 90
One-China Policy, 4

Organic, 279
  country environment, 230
  development, 42
Organically, 124
Organically develop, 31
Organic growth, 21, 29, 33, 46,
    48–49, 64–71, 74, 77–108, 113,
    138, 142, 158, 162, 163, 191,
    192, 196, 217–260, 263–269,
    281
  and development, 134
  paradigm, 265, 267, 271
  process, 72, 268–269
Organic process, 63, 269, 273, 278
Organic Tree of Organic Growth, The, 222
Organisation for Economic
    Co-operation and Development
    (OECD), 139

P
Pace of growth, 269, 272
Partnerships, 30
Pattern of Growth, 269, 272
Peace, 11, 33
  and development, 121
  and security, 16, 122
  and stability, 204, 210
Peace-building, 207
Peaceful, 11
  coexistence, 122
  development, 238
Peacekeeping efforts, 121, 213
Peacekeeping forces, 204
Peacekeeping mission, 205
People, 222
People Liberation Army (PLA), 121
People resources, 23–24, 222, 223, 243
People's Liberation Army, 203
People-to-people exchanges, 10

Per capita incomes, 42
Personal Freedom, Security and Social
    Capital, 33
Pew Global Attitude Survey, 4
Pew Research Centre's Global Attitude
    Project, 178
Pirate attacks, 210
Plagues, 186
Police sector, 198
Policy, 51, 53, 114, 148, 158, 187,
    196, 234
  development and implementation,
    79, 130
  environment, 43
  failures, 115
  framework, 46, 247
  implementation, 130, 193
  options, 197
  planning, 132
Political, 53, 140, 157, 158, 160, 187,
    199, 270
  cooperation, 9
  decision-making, 248
  and economic structures, 25–27
  economy, 243
  elite, 199
  and governance framework, 125
  instability, 120
  institutions, 120, 130
  opportunism, 25, 111, 224
  power, 123, 199, 225
  stability, 117, 224, 234, 235, 238,
    243, 257
  support, 2, 16
  traditions, 225, 232
  violence, 25, 35, 111
  will, 73, 186, 220
  willpower, 125
Politically stable, 49, 223
Polluting industries, 179
Pollution, 168, 169, 171–178, 180,
    185, 187

Pollution control, 185
Poor, 36, 97–108, 123, 125, 196, 199, 252, 265
  people, 196
  working conditions, 4
Poorer communities, 127, 183
Populated, 60
Population, 60, 100, 125, 147, 150, 223, 238
Population growth, 23, 35, 63, 196, 232, 239
Port, 83, 88, 89, 97, 129, 150, 218, 223, 225, 232, 235
Portugal, 155
Portuguese, 228
Positive impact on Africa, 15
Poverty, 26, 33, 35, 36, 42, 43, 48, 89, 100, 111, 125, 129, 140, 142, 143, 186, 195, 196, 207, 224, 231–233, 236, 238, 239, 255, 256, 263–265, 267, 268, 272, 273, 281
  alleviation, 10, 17, 125, 196
  eradication, 202
  rates, 192
  reduction, 39, 69, 74, 145, 162, 233, 235, 254, 264
  reduction exchanges, 10
  trap, 196, 252
Power, 71, 77, 80–81, 93, 130, 150
  distribution, 53
  generation, 154
  provision, 108
Precious minerals, 16
Premature deaths, 128
Pre-transition economies, 32–33, 48, 268
Primary, 137, 140, 197, 268
  education, 158, 229
  factors, 37
  healthcare, 128
  resources, 74

resource transformation, 43
school, 139, 156, 226, 252, 256, 257
sector, 26, 36, 63, 127, 227, 232, 244
Private Chinese companies, 133
Private investment, 42, 78
Private sector, 27, 46, 154, 248, 251, 255, 258
  construction, 269
  institutions, 244
Privatisation, 25, 226, 234
Privatisation programme, 225
Pro-business, 49
Process of Growth, 269
Produced capital, 78, 234–235, 255, 258
Production capacity, 78, 81, 259
Production efficiency, 24
Productive, 137, 141, 146, 154, 163, 192, 198, 235, 269
Productivity, 36, 39, 44, 46, 67, 78, 137, 138, 141, 143, 155, 160, 161, 177, 252, 255, 259, 272, 273, 281
Productivity levels, 257
Pro-poor, 196, 265, 269
Pro-poor policies, 125, 196
Prospering, 115
Prosperity, 11, 33, 70, 138–144, 158, 230–235, 267, 278
Prosperity Index, 33, 56
Public administration, 132, 134
Public administration infrastructure, 111
Public goods, 26, 33, 114
Public infrastructure, 256
Public investment, 228, 235
Public investment programme, 225
Public policy design, 111
Public–private cooperation, 52
Public resources, 254

## 302  INDEX

Public sector, 27, 234, 244, 246, 260
Public-sector investment, 269
Public sector spending, 228
Public services, 225
Public spending, 132

## Q
Quality and relevant education, 138–142
Quality of life, 33, 70
Quota advantages, 254
Quotas, 156

## R
Races, 28
Rail, 71, 85, 93, 97, 150, 162, 223, 275
Railroad, 89, 153
Rail transport, 96
Railway, 57, 87, 88, 91, 92, 97, 225
Railway network, 83, 209
Rain forests, 20
Refugee camps, 209
Refugees, 207, 208, 210
Regional conflicts, 10, 203
Regional development, 79
Regional economies, 71, 147
Regional integration, 50
Regional trade, 42
Regional trade and integration, 97
Regional trading partner, 223
Regulated, 222
Regulations, 64
Regulatory, 225–227, 245–248
  controls, 187
  environment, 114, 238, 257
  frameworks, 51
  process, 31, 192
  structures, 30
Relevant and quality education, 163

Religion, 50, 62
Religious, 21
Religious views, 200
Renewable energy, 16, 85, 145, 178
Renewable energy provision, 16
Renewable water, 145
Renewal energy, 151
Reproductive health, 202
Reproductive health services, 200
Republic of the Congo, 229
Research, 127
Research and development, 52
Resource, 24, 31, 36–38, 46, 71, 264, 268, 280, 281
  acquisition, 17
  allocation, 124
  curse, 17, 32, 38
  deprivation, 17
  diversification, 42–43
  management, 233
  market, 209
  use, 187
  wealth, 31, 38
Resource-poor, 217
Resource-rich, 217, 275
Retail, 63
Retailing, 32
Retail sector, 157, 161
Rights and freedoms, 52
Road, 25, 40, 57, 71, 88, 93, 97–108, 126, 195, 196, 198, 207, 209, 221, 223, 226, 228, 232, 235, 246, 248, 258, 275
  construction, 100
  infrastructure, 53, 100, 108, 132, 162
  network, 82
  and transport, 132
Rule of law, 33, 52
Rural, 81, 97–108, 140, 152, 202, 226, 272
  agricultural reforms, 196

agricultural sector, 273
areas, 42
communities, 78, 104, 127, 205, 209
enterprises, 272
health, 131
populations, 32
road infrastructure, 82
Russia, 113, 121
Rwanda, 21, 43, 52, 57, 87, 88, 128, 172, 199, 200, 204, 207, 266

**S**

Safe and stable, 121
Safety, 60, 196
and security, 73, 132
and security services, 130
Sanitation, 39, 77, 81, 89, 130
Saudi Arabia, 208
Scholarships, 205
School, 104, 105, 126, 127, 153, 159, 222
School education, 163
Schooling, 200
Science and technology, 48, 145, 160
Science and technology cooperation and knowledge sharing, 10
Scientific, 8, 217, 239, 241
Scientific renewal, 278
Secondary, 197, 268
education, 137, 140, 161, 252
school, 139, 158, 257
sector, 26, 44, 63, 127, 228, 244
Sector development, 69
Security, 122, 192, 196, 203, 210, 234, 274
cooperation, 10
risk, 231
Self-reliance and self-determination, 10

Senegal, 32, 117, 128, 139
Senegalese, 117
Service delivery, 79, 108, 126, 130, 156
Service economy, 238, 246
Service industry, 97
Service-orientated economy, 244
Services, 40, 64, 196, 273
Service sectors, 48, 50, 65
Settlements, 172
Sewage, 258
Sewerage, 184, 195, 209, 213, 242, 248
facilities, 81
works, 77
Sierra Leone, 32, 172, 199, 201–207
Skill development programmes, 152
Skilled, 137–163, 267
positions, 154
workers, 255
workforce, 137, 162, 163
Skills, 41, 43, 46, 55, 65, 71, 72, 115, 137, 140, 143, 155, 158, 160, 161, 226, 229–230, 246, 252, 257, 269, 270
base, 31
development, 42, 137, 138, 150, 157, 159
development and skills transfer, 16
development policies, 163
development programmes, 152
improvement, 156
level, 155, 163
mismatch, 150, 152, 233
needed, 141
set, 127
training, 68, 255
transfer, 17, 55, 68, 74, 78, 86, 94, 108, 160, 162, 196
Small and medium Chinese investors, 48
Small and medium enterprise, 108

Small and medium sized business, 269
Small to medium-sized enterprises (SME's), 45, 151
Social, 63, 191, 227, 230, 232, 255, 256, 259
   capital, 213
   concerns and expectations, 47
   development, 10, 167, 168, 202
   development cooperation, 9
   and economic, 264
   and environmental effects, 46
   engagement, 126
   investment, 247, 254–255
   justice, 192
   security, 196
   structure, 245
   unrest, 148
   wealth, 78, 192
Socio-economic, 92, 108, 221
   assumptions, 125
   development, 8, 111
   environmental, 114
   growth, 200
   factors, 265
   stability, 64
Somalia, 49, 97, 111, 132, 140, 186, 200, 204, 207
Somalian, 207–209
Somaliland, 20, 179
South Africa, 3, 7, 20, 21, 27, 31, 41, 45, 48, 63, 65, 82–84, 87, 97, 100, 132, 146, 156, 179, 182, 192, 200, 204, 251, 253, 258, 271, 281
South African, 154, 155
South Sudan, 16, 57, 111, 121, 122, 132, 186, 207
Southern Africa, 20
Soviet Union, 92
Special Economic Zones (SEZs), 8, 44–46, 55, 59, 127, 149, 272
Stages of development, 39

Standards of living, 198
State capture, 129
State-driven, 266
State-led economic reforms, 272, 273
State-owned, 153
   companies, 157
   enterprise, 129, 133, 134, 180, 229
Strategic process for the industrial transformation of a country, 47
Structural, 31, 264
   growth, 24
   reforms, 226, 227
   transformation, 30–31, 42, 46, 77
Structures, 22–28, 36, 222, 268
   resources and industrial base, 46
Student exchanges, 69
Subcontracting, 156
Subsidies, 73, 127, 197
Subsistence-based farming, 63
Subsistence economy, 140
Subsistence farmers, 197
Subsistence farming, 100, 233
Subsistence fishermen's, 179
Subsistence-orientated, 71
Sudan, 7, 17, 49, 88, 97, 151, 200, 205, 277
Supply chain, 127, 156, 179
Supply chain development, 162
Supporting institutions, 72
Supportive governance and policies, 30
Sustainability, 167–171
Sustainability reporting, 212
Sustainable, 33, 44, 48, 167–187, 213, 247, 250, 264, 265
   approach, 214
   development, 5, 89, 137, 141, 145, 167, 196, 202
   economic development, 120
   economic growth, 122
   energy provision, 182

growth, 30, 108, 138–144, 256
growth and development, 238, 270
and renewable energy, 81
Sustainable Development Goals (2015), 11

**T**
Tangible capital, 33, 231
Tanzania, 27, 32, 52, 88, 90, 92, 93, 174, 175, 184
Targeted transfer programmes, 125
Technical, 68, 70, 162, 221, 239
   assistance, 246, 252
   capacities, 235
   competencies, 143
   education, 163, 241
   institutes, 156
   institutions, 159
   people, 276
   positions, 157
   skills, 73, 163
   training, 153, 156, 185, 231
Technical and Vocational Education and Training (TVET), 252
Technicians, 144, 154, 158, 161
Technological, 8, 65, 151, 160, 180
   capabilities, 251
   transfer, 178
Technology, 31, 40–43, 46, 55, 65, 68, 71, 72, 85, 127, 137, 155, 185, 203, 233, 256, 269, 270
   and skills, 162, 163
   transfer, 57, 147–152, 157, 163
Technology Partnership Programme, The, 145
Telecom, 157
Telecommunication, 40, 63–65, 93, 153, 154, 225
Terrorism, 148, 198, 203, 204
Terrorist, 208
Tertiary, 268
   education, 127, 137, 139, 141, 163, 230
   enrolment, 252
   sector, 26, 63, 244
Textile, 41, 55, 60, 65, 68, 147, 151, 217, 229, 238, 242, 244, 246, 248, 252, 253, 255, 257, 259
   exports, 100
   industry, 71, 258
   markets, 271
   sector, 276
   trading, 157
Thabo Mbeki, 21
Think Tank Forums, 10
Three Gorges Dam, 181
Tourism, 8, 40, 50, 52, 59, 74, 96, 151, 242–245, 250, 258
   corridors, 96
   destination, 239–243
   potential, 187
   sector, 21, 173, 184, 250, 258
Tourist, 104, 174
Trade, 2, 39, 41, 42, 44, 65, 67, 92, 147, 159, 228–229, 241, 247, 258, 271
   agreement, 220
   balance, 54, 59
   barriers, 27, 127
   benefit, 104
   capacity, 232
   deficit, 4, 55, 71, 253, 274, 277
   imbalance, 68
   and investment, 67
   liberalisation, 43
   orientation, 244
   patterns, 41
   policies, 244, 272
   policy framework, 257
   regime, 247
Trade-led development, 244, 249
Trading, 154, 157, 161, 207, 246, 253–254

Trading partners, 79, 227, 229
Traditional, 41
  economy, 36
  sectors, 251
Train, 151
Training, 17, 153, 155, 157, 162, 197, 267, 268, 273
  institutes, 45
  programmes, 60, 155
  and support, 127
Transfer of knowledge and skills, 231
Transfer of technology, 155, 160
Transfer payments, 196
Transfer programmes, 128
Transformation, 264
Transit corridors, 102
Transitional economy, 219, 281
Transition Economies, 32, 48
Transparency, 133
Transparency International, 132, 234
Transparent, 114
Transport, 77, 91, 93, 127, 248, 269
Transportation, 152, 161, 228
  construction, 90
  infrastructure, 39–40
Transport corridor, 52
Transport costs, 24, 39, 82, 235
Transport effectiveness, 226
Transport infrastructural, 78
Transport infrastructure, 82–84, 93, 209
Transport link, 104
Transport network, 97
Tuberculosis, 127
Tunisia, 31, 40, 48, 84, 147, 192, 228

U
Uganda, 32, 49, 52, 57, 130, 140, 184, 200, 205
Underdevelopment, 26
Unemployed, 50, 142, 152, 196

Unemployment, 69, 125, 147–150, 160, 179, 231, 233, 238, 255–257, 259, 263
Unethical conduct, 14
Unethical governance, 30
United Kingdom (UK), 53, 84, 92, 121, 251, 258
United Nation's Security Council, 121
United Nation's 17 Sustainable Development Goals (SDGs), 12, 36, 167, 169, 193
United Nation's Sustainable Development Goals, 160
United Nations (UN), 7, 11, 92, 121, 170, 203, 210
United Nations 2030 Agenda, 193
United Nations Convention to Combat Desertification, 172
United Nations Educational, Scientific, and Cultural Organization (UNESCO), 139
United Nations Environment Programme, 171, 172
United Nations Framework Convention on Climate Change (COP 21), 170
United Nations Global Compact, 179
United Nations International Organization for Migration, 210
United Nations Migration agency, 204
United Nations Millennium Development Goals, 36
United Nations peacekeeping mission, 204
United Nations Security Council, 16, 116, 122
United Nations Security Council's Big Five, 121
United Nations Sustainable Development Goals, 138, 264
United States (US), 4, 24, 37, 40, 60, 65, 68, 71, 72, 92, 100, 121, 150, 253, 278

University, 45, 90, 141, 142, 145, 146, 159, 160, 162, 163, 232
  graduates, 149
  scholarships, 60
  sector, 72
UN peacekeeping, 121
Unproductive, 71
Unskilled, 161, 226, 257
Unskilled labour, 153
Unsustainable, 193
UN sustainable development goals, 10
Urban, 202, 272, 273
  areas, 130
  economic growth, 96
  greenery, 96
  land, 96
  policy, 131
  rail transport, 96
  road and railway infrastructure, 131
  road infrastructure, 82
  transport, 131
Urbanisation, 40, 42, 81, 85, 96, 172, 196

V
Value chain, 38, 45, 70, 73, 74, 228, 257
Value chain integration, 268, 276
Value systems, 28
Values and attitudes, 28
Vocational, 146
  education, 141, 162, 163
  education centres, 144
  training, 137
Vocation and education programmes, 163

W
War, 152, 162, 186, 197, 198
War and strife, 111
Waste, 169, 171–176, 179

Waste management, 126, 173
Water, 25, 39, 77, 78, 81, 89, 126, 130, 152, 153, 161, 167, 169, 172, 177, 183–185, 187, 195, 196, 198, 204, 205, 209, 211, 213, 221, 225, 234, 244, 249, 256, 264
  heating, 198
  projects, 53
  resources, 39, 153, 170
  security, 85
  services, 81
  supply, 89
Water-scarce regions, 171
Wealth, 24, 33, 192, 225–231, 268
Wealth creation, 69
Welfare, 26
  state, 255
  system, 256
Well-being, 19, 29, 30, 35, 36, 42, 77, 123, 125, 131, 183, 191–214, 217, 235, 238, 264
Well-educated, 115
West, 37
Western countries, 14
Western powers, 15
Western Sahara, 20
Wholesale and Retail, 40
Wholesale and retail sectors, 40
Wholesale and trade, 50
Wild-life, 180
Wild-life conservation, 204
Women, 11, 153, 199, 204, 248, 255, 257, 259, 267, 279
Women and children, 202
Workfare, 126
Workfare approach, 125, 126
Working conditions, 213
Work opportunities, 104
World Bank, 16, 30, 33, 39, 86, 142, 143, 147, 149, 152, 182, 228, 229, 232, 234, 248, 256, 272, 276

World Bank Report, 234
World Bank's Equator Principles, 179
World Food Programme, 204, 205
World happiness Report, 193
World Health Organisation, 201
World Trade Organization (WTO), 2, 16
World Wildlife Fund, 168

## X
Xenophobia, 271

## Y
Yemen, 208
Young, 140, 161, 163

Young people, 199
Youth, 11, 28, 127, 138, 141–144, 147, 148, 150, 152, 157, 158, 160, 195, 196, 229, 231, 267
Youth employment, 153
Youthful, 74
Youthful population, 138
Youth participation, 233
Youth unemployment, 156, 233

## Z
Zambia, 3, 21, 27, 32, 41, 43, 45, 48, 90, 114, 139, 176, 199, 205, 271, 274
Zimbabwe, 7, 17, 21, 27, 92, 114–120, 126, 200, 205, 277

Printed in the United States
By Bookmasters